AF478660

Mario La Torre and Gianfranco A. Vento
MICROFINANCE

Philip Molyneux and Munawar Iqbal
BANKING AND FINANCIAL SYSTEMS IN THE ARAB WORLD

Philip Molyneux and Eleuterio Vallelado (*editors*)
FRONTIERS OF BANKS IN A GLOBAL WORLD

Anastasia Nesvetailova
FRAGILE FINANCE
Debt, Speculation and Crisis in the Age of Global Credit

Dominique Rambure and Alec Nacamuli
PAYMENT SYSTEMS
From the Salt Mines to the Board Room

Andrea Schertler
THE VENTURE CAPITAL INDUSTRY IN EUROPE

Alfred Slager
THE INTERNATIONALIZATION OF BANKS

Noel K. Tshiani
BUILDING CREDIBLE CENTRAL BANKS
Policy Lessons for Emerging Economies

Palgrave Macmillan Studies in Banking and Financial Institutions
Series Standing Order ISBN 978- 1–4039–4872–4

You can receive future titles in this series as they are published by placing a standing order. Please contact your bookseller or, in case of difficulty, write to us at the address below with your name and address, the title of the series and the ISBN quoted above.

Customer Services Department, Macmillan Distribution Ltd, Houndmills, Basingstoke, Hampshire RG21 6XS, England

New Drivers of Performance in a Changing Financial World

Edited by

Alessandro Carretta, Franco Fiordelisi,
Gianluca Mattarocci

Contents

List of Tables

List of Figures

Preface

Over recent decades financial systems have been going through a historical phase of major change. This financial revolution concerns new products and markets, new configurations of players in the competitive arena, a growing symbiosis between markets and intermediaries, the role of regulation and control authorities, and the relationships with clients. New determinants of performance arise and the interest to the way performance is ensured and communicated to stakeholders grows.

This book is intended as a unique tool for policy makers, practitioners and scholars to enable them tounderstand and discuss the new drivers of performance in this changing financial world.

The book is the result of significant academic experience and strong theoretical and empirical works conducted by the authors, all engaged in research activities in their Universities, that actively participate to PhD Program in Banking and Finance at the University of Rome 'Tor Vergata'.

Ideas, preliminary assumptions and working papers concerning the research programmes upon which this book was built have been presented and discussed at many academic workshop and international conferences, and particularly at the 'FMA European Conference', Siena, Italy, 2005; the International Symposium of Forecasting, San Antonio, Texas, 2005; the International Tor Vergata Conference on Banking and Finance, Rome, 2005; the European Academy of Management (EURAM) Annual Conference, TUM Business School, Munich, 2005; ECRI European Credit Research Institute) Consumer financial capability workshop, Brussels, 2005; the International Symposium of Forecasting, Santander, Spain, 2006; the Rapporto sul Sistema Finanziario Italiano – Fondazione Rosselli, Bellagio, Italy, 2006; the Cattolica University of Milan and London School of Economics Conference on Coordination and Cooperation across Organizational Boundaries, Milan, 2006; the International Tor Vergata Conference on Banking and Finance, Rome, 2006; the European Real Estate Society (ERES) Conference, Cass Business School, London, 2007; Real Estate Investment World (REIW) Global Opportunities, Princeton Club, New York, 2007; Real Estate Investment World (REIW) Nordic, Stockholm, 2007; and the 'Financial Management Association annual meeting, Orlando, Florida, 2007'.

Alessandro Carretta
Franco Fiordelisi
Gianluca Mattarocci

Acknowledgements

We would like to thank the contributors Massimo Caratelli, Vincenzo Farina, Claudio Giannotti, Lucia Leonelli, Gianni Nicolini, Marcello Pallotta, Claudio Porzio, Gabriele Sampagnaro, Paola Schwizer: this book has only been possible because of their specific contributions and expertise. The contents of this book have also benefited substantially from the help and useful suggestions of many readers and anonymous referees.

Special thanks are given to Andrea Cipollini, Umberto Filotto, John Goddard, Phil Molyneux and Daniele Previati, for their comments, support and advice covering many areas covered in the text.

Finally, thanks to Aareal Bank, Experian, Fimit, Ktesios, Neos Banca, who give financial and organizational support to the activities of the PhD program in Banking and Finance at the University of Rome 'Tor Vergata'.

ALESSANDRO CARRETTA
FRANCO FIORDELISI
GIANLUCA MATTAROCCI

Notes on the Contributors

Editors

Alessandro Carretta is full professor in Financial Markets and Institutions and director of the PhD programme in Banking and Finance at the University of Rome 'Tor Vergata'. He has been teaching Banking and Finance for more than 25 years, being formerly at the Universities of Urbino, Lecce and Milan Bocconi. His main research interests relate to banking management, focussing on banking groups and diversification, regulation and control, corporate governance, and culture and organizational change in banks. He has published widely, having produced a number of books and articles in academic journals. He is a member of the committees and boards of several journals, research bodies and financial institutions.

Franco Fiordelisi (MA, PhD) is professor in Banking and Finance at the Faculty of Economics 'Federico Caffè' of the University of Rome III, Italy. He is also a member of the PhD in Banking and Finance academic board at the University of Rome Tor Vergata and Visiting Research Fellow at the University of Essex, UK. His main research interest relates to the economics of banking and other financial institutions, focussing on efficiency, productivity and shareholder value creation. His research has been published in the *Journal of Banking and Finance*, *Applied Economics*, *ABI* and other leading academic journals and he has recently published *Shareholder Value in European Banking* (Palgrave 2007). He has also acted as a consultant to many banks, leasing and factoring companies.

Gianluca Mattarocci (MA, PhD) is lecturer of Economics and Management of Financial Intermediaries at the Faculty of Economics of the University of Rome 'Tor Vergata', Italy. His main research interest relates to the asset management, real estate, rating and corporate finance. He has also acted as a consultant for banks and factoring companies.

Authors

Massimo Caratelli is lecturer of Financial Markets and Institutions at the Faculty of Economics 'Federico Caffè' at the University of Rome III. He holds a PhD degree in Banking and Finance from the University of Rome 'Tor Vergata'. His research Interests include financial marketing, the distribution of financial services and clients' needs, banking strategies and organization and consumer credit.

Vincenzo Farina is a PhD candidate in Banking and Finance at the University of Rome 'Tor Vergata'. His research interests include corporate governance, organization and corporate culture of banks.

Claudio Giannotti is Associate Professor in Banking at University LUM of Casamassima (Bari, Italy). He is the Director of the Real Estate Finance Center within the PhD program in Banking and Finance of the University of Rome 'Tor Vergata'. He holds a PhD in Banking and Finance from the same institution.

Lucia Leonelli is a graduate in Economics at the University of Rome 'Tor Vergata'. At present she is associate professor of Economics and Management of Financial Intermediaries in the Faculty of Economics at the University of Rome 'Tor Vergata'. Her main field of interest is in payment systems.

Gianni Nicolini is lecturer in the Economics and Management of Financial Intermediaries at the University of Rome 'Tor Vergata'. The main topics of his research activity are e-finance, leasing evaluation and the exchange-industry integration processes. Prior to becoming a researcher, Gianni Nicolini received a PhD. in Banking and Finance from the University of Rome 'Tor Vergata'. Recently he has been conducting a study of the financial capability problems in retail banking.

Marcello Pallotta graduated in Business Economics. He is currently attending the PhD in Banking and Finance at 'Tor Vergata' University, Rome and is working as an associate consultant for Bain & Company.

Claudio Porzio is full professor of Banking at the University of Naples 'Parthenope' and senior professor at SDA Bocconi Business School, Milan. His primary research areas include financial institutions and credit risk, the failures of markets and banks, bank loans and securitization, asset management, private equity and real estate.

Gabriele Sampagnaro is associate professor of Banking at the University of Naples 'Parthenope'. He received his doctorate in Banking and Finance from the University of Rome 'Tor Vergata' in 2004. He is currently researching into real estate finance, risk management, portfolio techniques and investment analysis.

Paola Schwizer is full professor of Banking at the University of Parma and Professor at the SDA Business School, Bocconi University, Milan.

She is the author of several publications in the fields of banking strategies and organization, the corporate governance and internal control systems of financial institutions, regulation and competition in the financial system, corporate banking and financial services for SMEs, and value creation in banks and other financial institutions.

Part I
New Financial Products and Approaches: Focus on Performance

1
European Exchanges, Investors' Behaviour and Asset Allocations Criteria: Country Approach vs Industry Approach

Alessandro Carretta and Gianni Nicolini[1]

1.1 Introduction

Several years have now passed since the first attempts at integration were made by European stock exchanges. The first stage of the process, from the end of the 1990s to the first years of 2000, led to a number of different solutions being tried and tested, and the outcome was not always encouraging. The iX (International Exchange) project between the London Stock Exchange and the Deutsche Börse and the 'Group of Eight' between the principal European bourses are just two examples of unsuccessful integration projects.

This experimental phase was followed by a stage in which the markets started the effective implementation of the projects and in which the integration of the national markets focused decidedly on strong partnerships or even M&A operations. They were the years in which the Euronext, Omx and EuroMTS projects, to mention but a few, were launched.

The evolution of these integration projects, which were extended gradually following the entry of new national markets, characterized stage three of the integration process. Today, the market has entered a new fourth phase, in which integration no longer consists in a dialogue between the ongoing projects and the single exchanges, but is based on agreements between a number of integration stakeholders.

The integration of the European exchange industry has now reached a mature stage, even though the process is still far from being concluded. However, it is possible to make some first assessments about the effects of integration on market trends.

The aim of this chapter is, first and foremost, to investigate the relationship between stock exchange integration and investor behaviour. The analysis is based on the assumption that the investors' asset allocation strategies are linked to the structure of the securities market. In particular, the gradual reduction of the market's (geographical) segmentation, by altering the operators' investment horizons and affecting portfolio composition, may have modified the diversification criteria, resulting in a shift of focus on industry- rather than country-based segmentation (that is, based on the industry sectors rather than the nationality of the issuer of the stocks).

By applying a cluster analysis and a principal component analysis of the weekly index yields of the principal European stock exchanges, we intend to show how the asset allocation behaviour of European investors has changed over the years, while at the same time assessing the effects of integration on the performance of the European stock markets.

1.2   Home bias, investor behaviour and exchange industry integration

Stock exchange performance is the overall result of the behaviour of the individual investors, which, in turn, is the result of complex decision-making processes that take into account a large number of variables. In addition to the characteristics of the single financial instruments, asset allocation by operators is also implicitly influenced by the structure of the securities market.

The European stock market of the 1990s was fragmented into a multiplicity of national bourses, in which trade focused primarily on domestic securities; this was highly inhibitive of cross-border transactions and fostered the phenomenon known in literature as home bias. The impossibility for investors to trade securities by foreign issuers, or even the mere existence of more restrictive regulations for this type of trade, naturally determined a distortion in the investors' selection criteria. The geographical segmentation of the European securities market, by isolating the single national stock exchanges, had inhibited the creation of links between the markets, while at the same time fostering a Country-based diversification.

The collapse of the currency, political, psychological and structural barriers has radically altered this state of affairs, and also paved the way for changes in asset allocation strategies. The change-over to the euro has significantly reduced currency exchange risks in international trade (Alemanni, 2003). At the same time, European integration and, generally speaking, market globalization, have broadened the operators' investment horizons. Last but not least, the launching of the integration projects has modified the structure of the market, removing the technical and operating obstacles (Alemanni, 2001).

The removal of the barriers hindering cross-border transactions has laid the foundations for integration in the field of stock trading (Cybo-Ottone, Di Noia and Murgua, 2000). By putting the trading of foreign securities substantially on an equal footing with the trading of domestic securities, the range of available stocks for investors has broadened considerably, which entails the likelihood of investments in foreign stocks being preferred to domestic ones (Coffee, 2002). Expectations are that the overcoming of geographical segmentation in stock trading will determine an increase in cross-border trade and, consequently, an increase in stock market correlation.

In many countries the removal of barriers to cross-border trade has occurred over a certain number of years (Lee, 2002). Therefore, it is now possible to assess the consequences of the exchange industry integration process on investor behaviour (asset allocation).

Before continuing with the analysis, however, a few observations should be made. First of all, it must be taken into account that changes in the decision-making processes of operators, in relation to asset allocation, require a cultural change and, therefore, a transition period, the length of which it is difficult to forecast. Therefore, it is possible that the changed market conditions have not yet translated into changed operator behaviour.

Secondly, account must also be taken of the fact that the relationship between home bias and the integration of stock market yields is not a univocal one. If, on the one hand, a market in which investors show an interest in cross-border trade is encouraged to integrate the single stock exchange structures, in order to create institutions that operate simultaneously in a number of countries, it is also true, on the other hand, that the availability of integrated structures permitting cross-border transactions are an incentive to cross-border trade (Domowits, 2002; Krantz, 1999). Rather than conducting an analysis aimed at measuring the extent to which home bias has been reduced as a result of the integration of the exchange structures, therefore, it would be expedient to assess how market behaviours (asset allocation) change in a more highly integrated market environment, in an attempt to examine the parallel trends of these two phenomena, which are related, but with respect to which it is difficult to establish a cause-effect connection.

1.3 An overview of the experiment

This transformation from a geographically segmented European securities market to an integrated market, and from a country to an industry approach, with respect to asset allocation criteria, should be reflected in the performance of the single markets.

Based on this assumption, our aim is to assess the behaviour of the principal European exchange markets in recent years, based on the stock market data. We use these data because we believe it to be the most suitable sector for understanding the changes in investor bias. In consideration of the fact that the integration process began between the end of the 1990s and the first years of 2000, we have examined the period from 1995 to 2006. The decision to start back in 1995 is aimed at creating a term of comparison, between the last few years, in which integration has affected most of the European stock exchanges, and the previous period, which will be considered as the benchmark against which to measure the differences resulting from integration. If the basic assumption is true that integration is capable of modifying the asset allocation behaviour of investors, then the performance of the market in recent years should feature changes compared to the initial period.

We are interested in examining two effects of change; in the first place, whether the launching of the integration projects (alliances, agreements, mergers and so on) has been followed by harmonization in market performance, because if integration is effectively capable of influencing investor behaviour then the possibility of trading foreign stocks, alongside domestic stocks, should lead to increased cross-border trade and, consequently, an increased correlation between the performance of the two markets (Lucarelli, 2001).

The second objective is more closely related to the operators' asset allocation behaviour. In a geographically segmented market, where the stock exchange of each single country offers investors the possibility of trading domestic securities alone and where contacts between investors from different countries are only marginally significant, it is understandable that a Country approach prevails. The scarce relevance of cross-border trade enhances geographical portfolio diversification, the greater the independence of the single markets.

Integration tends to question the benefits of geographical diversification, while alternative approaches become more credible – being based, for example, on industry diversification. If, therefore, integration has changed investor choices it would be interesting to assess the predominant asset allocation criteria in Europe and, above all, if these have changed over the years.

In order to answer these questions, we have applied two different methods – cluster analysis and principal component analysis (PCA) – to the time series of the stock market indexes of the EU-15 (except Greece and Luxembourg), the Czech Republic, Estonia, Hungary, Latvia, Lithuania, Norway and Switzerland.

Each index is representative of the performance of a specific industry in a certain country.[2] This has enabled a twofold interpretation of the data: one based on the country (for example, Italy-Oil&Gas, Italy-Basic materials, Italy-Consumer goods and so on) and the other based on the industry (for example, Oil&Gas-Italy, Oil&Gas-Austria, Oil&Gas-Belgium and so on).

We use weekly rather than daily data because of our conviction that weekly values are less subject to the short-term variations that are incorporated in daily data. Although this gives a smaller database, this has not impaired the reliability of the analysis in any way; the length of the observation period, in fact, has assured approx. 650 readings per index. Based on the performance of each index we have calculated the percentage yield on a weekly basis. These historical series have then been segmented on a year-by-year basis. We have applied both methods to each period from 1995 to 2006.

The methods considered here, even though they are based on different rationales, nevertheless share the capacity to highlight similarities within the data. This makes it possible to compare different results, using the indications from one analysis to confirm (or disprove) the results obtained from the other.

The use of the abovementioned statistical methods (cluster analysis and PCA) has been preceded by an analysis of the correlations, which was conducted in advance to assess the expediency of employing more sophisticated statistical methods. The assumed relationship between market performance and integration, therefore, is based on an indication of changes in market correlation. In particular, the study of correlations near to an integration event (such as mergers, use of similar technologies, and so on) has been used to assess interest for a detailed statistical analysis. If the correlation between the various markets concerned by an integration project featured no changes, in connection with certain significant events, there would be no reason to assume an influence of the integration process on investor behaviour.

The use of the cluster analysis method is based on the intention to assess the changes, occurring over the years, in the similarities of the single markets examined. The cluster analysis enables the grouping into uniform groups (or clusters) of different subjects of a population, which, in this case, consists of the stock indexes of the different countries. The inclusion within the same cluster of indexes/countries belonging to the same integration project, in conjunction with the tendency over the years to reduce the 'optimum' number of clusters, have been viewed as reactions by the market to certain integration phenomena. The expression 'optimum number of clusters' earns a number of clusters such as to optimize the reliability of the results.

A 'non-hierarchical' cluster analysis has been used here, because it has been deemed more suited to the survey objectives. For a year we used an iterative process, beginning with two clusters and increasing the number by one unit until the number of clusters equalled the number of samples (countries examined). The optimum number of clusters was determined discarding the extreme results (analysis with a number of clusters equal to 2 or number of clusters equal to n) and using as the stopping rule the marginal increase of the level of reliability of the results: among the solutions taken into account we have identified the one that maximizes the (positive) differential of reliability between the analysis with adjacent number of clusters. The decision to base the number of clusters on a standardized process made it possible to reduce the discretionary degrees in relation to the use of this method.

The principal component analysis (PCA) is a dimensional reduction method for summarizing the behaviour of a large number of variables in a population in a smaller number of 'new' variables (called principal components or PCs). Statistically, each principal component represents a linear combination of the variables observed. All the PCs are orthogonal to each other, in order to eliminate the risk of information redundancy. The PCA, therefore, enables the identification of the presence of base market trends, which influence its behaviour to a greater or lesser extent.

In order not to rule out the possibility that there are no factors capable of summarizing the behaviour of the single indexes taken into account, or not to rule out the possibility that each index is wholly independent of the others, we have considered a number of PCs equal to the larger of: (1) the number of countries; and (2) the number of segments corresponding to the different indexes. If each index were entirely independent of the others we would have 'n' PCs, each of which would be capable of explaining the behaviour of the single index with which it is associated. In this case the market segmentation would be perfect and, consequently, integration would be scarce.

1.4 The results[3]

The preliminary analysis of the correlation between the European exchanges has provided encouraging results. In particular, the analysis for the 1996–2005[4] period has highlighted significant variations in the correlation of the yields, in correspondence of significant integration-related events.

With regard to the Euronext project, we have assumed the following sensitive dates 2000 (project launch date), 2002 (extension to the Portuguese market) and 2004 (integration of the trading information systems). With regard to the Omx project, the sensitive dates are 2003 (project launch date), 2004 (extension to the Baltic States market) and 2005 (entry of the Danish market). With regard to the Bmex project, the sensitive date is 2003 (project launch date), while in the case of the other markets concerned the analysis has examined the historical development of correlation with the other European markets.

In this specific case, it may be observed how, for each integration process examined, the correlation of the stock market yields increases sizably in the periods after the event.

Moreover, observing correlations in the periods prior to the single events, we may notice that the markets involved in the integration process have heterogeneous values. This is significant because it does not seem to highlight a relationship between the degree of correlation of the markets and the launching of the integration projects.

The highest degree of correlation is observed with respect to the indexes of the leading markets in the various projects (Euronext-Paris, Omx-Stockhölmborsen, London Stock Exchange and Deutsche Börse). It is also interesting to note how geographically contiguous markets tend to feature a higher degree of correlation.

It may be noted how, between 1996 and 2005, the average annual correlation trends of markets have increased, painting a picture characterized by the absence of strong negative correlations and the nonsignificant nature of the correlations close to zero.

Comforted by the correlation analysis results, we then proceeded with the cluster analysis and PCA.

Table 1.1 features an overview of the results of the cluster analysis on the sectoral index yields of the European market. The figures shown are based on the average concentration of the analysed indexes. This summary indicator represents a measure of the trend of the representative indexes of a country (or industry) to concentrate in the same cluster. Expressed in percentage terms, it assumes the maximum value

Table 1.1   Concentration of the industrial sector indexes based on the cluster analysis results, 1995–2006

	Optimum number of clusters	Concentration					
		Industrial sector			Country		
		Avg (A) (%)	Std (B)	Correct concentration for the risk (A/B)	Avg (C) (%)	Std (D)	Correct concentration for the risk (C/D)
1995	12	45	13	3.46	76	17	4.47
1996	10	63	17	3.71	86	21	4.10
1997	10	39	15	2.60	72	22	3.27
1998	11	45	15	3.00	60	18	3.33
1999	9	54	20	2.70	53	19	2.79
2000	8	68	22	3.09	55	14	3.93
2001	11	57	17	3.35	54	14	3.86
2002	12	47	13	3.62	57	20	2.85
2003	9	45	12	3.75	59	19	3.11
2004	4	94	8	11.75	95	12	7.92
2005	6	80	8	10.00	78	19	4.11
2006	7	48	14	3.43	66	19	3.47

Source: Thomson-Financial (Datastream) data processed by the author.

(100 per cent) when all of the sectoral indexes of a country (or all the indexes of a country relating to a certain industry) are gathered in the same cluster. The concentration is at a minimum (0 per cent) when the indexes are distributed uniformly within the different clusters. The average concentration is the result of the arithmetic medium of the concentration of the single countries (or industries). In order to take account of the dispersion of the figures within the average value, the table also features the values of the correct indicators for a measure of dispersion (standard deviation).

The cluster analysis highlights a clear predominance of the country factor in the first stage of the integration process (1995–2001), followed by the increased influence of the industry factor in the second stage (2002–05). The latest figures, relating to 2006, show a substantial balance between country and industry, which is probably due to the relative scarcity of the data. Given that the analysis of the data has been made in Autumn 2006, there is a lower number of readings compared to the previous years.

Based on an analysis by industrial sector, we can see how the Telecommunication&Media industry exhibits different behaviour compared to the other sectors (especially in the initial period), thus manifesting a certain affinity with the Technology sector.

There are also situations that result from economic contingencies, such as, for example, the Oil&Gas industry, which, since 2005, is characterized by a high degree of independence.

The tendency of the industry indexes to concentrate in the same cluster increased over the years. At the same time, the representativeness of the cluster, with reference to a single sector, also increased – especially in the period from 1998 to 2002. During this period clusters composed of practically all the indexes in a certain industrial sector, and by these alone, were more frequent.

The data of the latest period are influenced by a reduction of the optimum number of clusters, which tends to reduce the discriminatory capacity of the results. From a general interpretation of the results there nevertheless emerges the gradual assertion, over the years, of an industry versus a country approach. Comparing the country figures with the industry figures, in relation to asset allocation, there seems to have been a gradual 'substitution' of the former by the latter, thus highlighting a change probably due to a more integrated market situation.

A last consideration on cluster composition concerns the tendency over the years towards the formation of maxi-clusters hosting the market indexes of what can be defined as 'core-Europe',[5] which is opposed by certain marginally significant clusters containing the sectoral indexes of the Eastern European countries (Poland, Hungary and the Czech Republic).

The results of the principal component analysis (PCA) are consistent with the cluster analysis. Even lacking PCs capable of highlighting an Industry-based behaviour, the country-related PCs tend to be downsized over the years, highlighting the gradual inability of the country approach to explain market behaviour. Compared with the cluster analysis, the PCA results are, therefore, more cautious in indicating a shift towards the Industry approach, identifying, instead, an ongoing transitional phase.

1.5 Conclusions

The analysis of the weekly yields of the European stock markets over the last 12 years has highlighted a relationship between the European exchange market integration process and market operator behaviour.

In the first period examined (1995–2001) – which featured integration only in the later part – and assuming that a shift in asset allocation criteria from a country to an industry approach should be accompanied by a change in the performance of the market indexes, the market interpretation based on geographical segmentation (country approach) is the one best suited to represent investor behaviour. On the contrary, in the second period (2002–05), an industry-based interpretation provides a more reliable picture of the market. The assumption that a change in the organizational structure of the markets and the launching of integration projects should necessarily be reflected in an adaptation of the operators' asset allocation criteria seems, therefore, to be confirmed.

The cluster analysis has also highlighted how the number of clusters capable of representing the market situation in an optimum manner tends to diminish in time, thus confirming the thesis of a gradual market integration, with respect to both the organizations responsible for managing market operations (management companies/stock exchanges) and trading. At the same time, the distance within the single clusters tends to diminish, indicating a further strengthening of relations among the exchanges.

The concept of the European securities market in which each country is a separate market, with its own securities, intermediaries and investors, is no longer a truthful picture of the situation. In fact, there seems to be a larger number of operators who prefer asset allocation based on industry, rather than country.

The integration of the European exchange industry, however, is still an ongoing process and, as such, it is difficult to give an accurate outline of its evolutionary trends. However, the assertion of an industry-based segmentation of the market seems set to become stronger and stronger with the development of the market integration process, and the integration trends will become a significant variable in the investors' asset allocation processes.

Notes

1. This chapter is the result of the authors' common efforts and continuous exchange of ideas. The individual parts of the chapter can be attributed as follows: introduction and conclusions to Alessandro Carretta and other paragraphs to Gianni Nicolini.
2. The Datastream classification includes the following ten industry sectors for each country: Oil&Gas, Basic materials, Industrials, Consumer goods, Health care, Consumer services, Telecommunications&Media, Utilities, Financials, Technology.
3. This paragraph sets out the summary results of the analyses carried out. More detailed results may be obtained directly from the authors.

4. The correlation data refer to a survey conducted in 2005, whose results are set out in the paper 'L'impatto dell'integrazione tra borse valori sui rendimenti azionari in Europa' (Nicolini, 2005) presented at the National Conference on the Economy of Financial Intermediaries, held in Parma on 4 November 2005. The analysis has been conducted on Reuters data with a weekly frequency of observations.
5. The expression 'core-Europe' is used to indicate the Countries that host the principal European exchanges, which are characterised by high levels of yield correlation and which, as a rule, tend to feature a strong mutual influence.

References

Alemanni, B. (2001) 'La concorrenza nella exchange industry' in I. Basile (ed.), *Nuove frontiere dei mercati finanziari e della securities industry*, Roma: Bancaria editrice.

Alemanni, B. (2003) *L'integrazione dei mercati finanziari nell'era dell'Euro*, Università commerciale Luigi Bocconi – Newfin working paper.

Coffee, J.C. (2002) *Competition Among Securities Markets: Path-Dependent Perspective*, Columbia University – Columbia Law School – The Center for Law and Economic Studies.

Cybo-Ottone, A., C. Di Noia, M. Murgia (2000) *Recent Development in the Structure of Securities Markets*, Brooking-Wharton Papers on Financial Services.

Domowitz, I. (2002) *Automation and the Structure of the Trading Services Industry*, Sugeval working paper.

IOSCO Technical Committee (2001) *Discussion Paper on Stock Exchange Demutualization*, IOSCO – International Organization of Securities Commissions.

Krantz, T. (1999) *The Danger of Price Fragmentation*, Westminster & City Conference, London, 10 November.

Lee, R. (2002) *The Future of Securities Exchanges*, The Wharton financial institution center – University of Pennsylvania.

Lucarelli, C. (2001) 'Gli accordi internazionali fra mercati', in L. Anderloni, I. Basile, P. Schwizer (eds), *Nuove frontiere dei mercati finanziari e della securities industry*, Roma: Bancaria editrice.

Nicolini, G. (2005) 'L'impatto dell'integrazione tra borse valori sui rendimenti azionari in Europa', Convegno nazionale di Economia degli intermediari finanziari Parma, Italy, 4 November.

2
The Performance Evaluation of Hedge Funds: a Comparison of Different Approaches

Alessandro Carretta and Gianluca Mattarocci[1]

2.1 Introduction

The term 'hedge fund' defines heterogeneous types of financial instruments that are characterized by lower restrictions being applied to the fund manager in the investment selection process (Pia, 2002). Hedge funds can also be defined as an investment partnership that could take either long or short positions (Agarwal and Naik, 2004) and is not subject to the information disclosure rules that are established for other investment funds (Liang, 2003).

One of the distinctive characteristics of hedge funds concerns the active strategy adopted by the fund manager who tries to take the best results from all investment opportunities using some instruments that are not available for other funds' managers (Agarwal and Naik, 2004).

The models outlined in the literature demonstrate that the performance of hedge funds cannot be explained by using only one benchmark – as for some other financial instruments – and it is necessary to decompose the performance into a group of heterogeneous factors (Capocci et al., 2003).

Differences in the determinants of hedge funds' performance make it evident that it is necessary to use evaluation measures that are designed specifically for this type of instrument. In fact, in the case of hedge funds the standard approaches used to analyse investment funds may be misleading and a reformulation of these methodologies is necessary to consider those characteristics that make hedge funds distinctive (Getmansky, Lo and Makarov, 2004).

This chapter presents a critical analysis of the Risk Adjusted Performance (RAP) approaches. Its aim is to present the new approaches that have been proposed for the study of these instruments and to verify if these measures are more useful in selecting hedge funds than are the standard approaches: the study points out differences in hedge funds classifications realized with different RAPs and tries to identify the best ones. The analysis of the European market demonstrates that standard approaches to evaluating hedge funds are unsatisfactory.

Section 2.2 analyses classical and new RAPs, explaining standard measures, their limits in evaluating hedge funds and new measures that are proposed for the examination of these particular instruments. The final section tries to verify if new measures that have been introduced are able to overcome the limits of the standard approach using a sample of European hedge funds.

2.2 Literature review

The selection of a particular fund must consider the possible gains related to the investment and the risk exposure that is necessary to achieve these results (Sharpe, 1966). The RAP approach represents one solution to summarize the risk–performance profile of the instrument in a unique number that is easy to understand for all investors.

The choice between investment opportunities is based on past performances achieved by instruments and results obtained with these approaches could be considered rational only if results are time persistent. Empirical analyses demonstrate that selections founded on RAP approaches are better than simpler funds' selections founded on past gains (Blake, Elton and Gruber, 1996) but results obtained with these approaches could be correct only if the analysis is released using a large database. In fact, only long time series allow to evaluate an historical trend in performances of the funds' managers and to discriminate between good and lucky managers (Abernathy and Weisman, 2000).

2.2.1 The Risk Adjusted Performance approach to fund evaluation

The RAP approach allows a summary of the risk and return profile of an investment that can then be used to compare different funds (Colombini et al., 2003). Generically, a RAP is defined as:

$$RAP = f(gains) - f(risk)$$

Normally, the higher the value of the measure the better the solution for the typically risk-averse investor.

The first type of measures, RAP utility based, allows the selection of the optimal fund for the investor analysing his utility function. The general formulation is:

$$RAP = U(gains) - U(risk)$$

The best funds are those that give the possibility of achieving the higher utility level for the investor, but the results obtained through the use of this approach are influenced highly by the hypotheses used to define the shape of the utility function. In fact, the type of utility function is defined arbitrarily by the evaluator and the results of funds' selection are highly influenced by this choice (Carluccio, 1999).

The second one, RAP scale independent, can be formulated in different ways and the literature features a number of different approaches that can be particularly useful in the evaluation of some types of funds or in considering a particular aspect of some funds. The main difference between these measures can be identified in the types of return and risk measures utilized.

The most famous RAP scale independent measures are:

- the Sharpe ratio (Sharpe, 1994);
- Modigliani's RAP (Modigliani and Modigliani, 1997);
- the Information ratio (Goodwin, 1998);
- the Treynor index (Treynor, 1985);
- the Sortino index (Sortino and Forsey, 1996);
- the Jensen alpha (Jensen, 1968).

All of these RAPs are based on the assumption of a normal return distribution. This assumption is useful in defining a theoretical model because it permits the description of the distribution using only the first two moments. The simplification assumed in the formulae presented means that standard RAP approaches are not appropriate for instruments characterized by not normal distribution because the results obtained for these funds tend to underestimate or overestimate the performance (Chen and Passow, 2003).

In addition to this approach, there are other hypotheses:

- investors' choices are realized using a mean-variance approach (Hubner, 1999);
- market risk is the only source of risk for the investment analysed (Klemkosky, 1973).

2.2.2   Limits of standard Risk Adjusted Performance on hedge funds

The analysis of the performances of hedge funds demonstrates that these instruments achieve different results in comparison with other funds traded in the same market (Ackermann et al., 1999). The analysis of the impact of the fund's characteristics and the manager's qualities on the fund's performance makes it clear that hedge funds have distinctive characteristics (Boyson, 2003). The different results achieved can be explained by an analysis of the constraints to which the fund manager is submitted. In fact, in the hedge fund scenario:

- it is possible to use leverage (Fung and Hsieh, 1999);
- there are no restrictions to invest in a particular type of assets (Bing, 1999);
- the manager can make long-term planning for investments without considering the possibility of withdrawals of investments that are limited by the regulation of funds (Tsatsaronis, 2000);
- fees corresponded to the manager are partially fixed, but substantially related to absolute performances achieved (Brown et al., 1998);
- fees computation is released considering past performance achieved and frequently higher fees are corresponded to managers that achieve higher results than those realized in the past (Boido and Riente, 2004);
- investors are potentially more financial skilled because the instrument is reserved to wealthy individuals (Das et. al., 2002);
- it is imposed a manager's participation to the investment (Kouwenberg and Ziemba, 2003).

These differences make hedge funds a unique instrument and it is likely that the nonnormality of return distribution could be considered to be a consequence of these characteristics (Moix and Schmidhuber, 2001). The typical return distribution for this instrument is negatively skewed and leptokurtic (Favre-Bulle and Pache, 2003) and, frequently, the performance that is achieved differs significantly from the expected value (Favre and Ranaldo, 2003).

Factor model regressions of hedge funds' performances make it clear that these instruments are more complex than other mutual funds (Fung and Hsieh, 2002) and it is unreasonable to assume that the only risk factor related to this investment can be identified in the market risk (Schneeweis and Spurgin, 1996).

The nonnormality means that the standard RAP approach is not useful for selecting hedge funds and highlights that it is necessary to offer a reformulation of measures proposed for the performance evaluation.

2.2.3 New Risk Adjusted Performance proposed

The new RAPs proposed for the evaluation of hedge funds are particular measures that do not assume the normality hypothesis for returns distribution.

The first contributions tempt us to modify classical measures to evaluate hedge funds by considering the autocorrelation of hedge funds returns (Gehin, 2004) or to replace the standard deviation with a risk measure founded on VAR (Gregoriou and Guevie, 2003).

The new RAPs proposed are not only a revision of the standard approach; they also analyse different aspects that can be evaluated only through the use of different information that is not considered in the standard approach. As is the case with the standard RAP approach, these RAPs could be either utility based or scale independent.

The new utility-based RAPs are:

- the Q-ratio;
- the AIRAP.

The Q-ratio analyses the impact of hedge funds' inclusion in a well-diversified portfolio and verifies the possible impact of this new instrument on the investor's utility function considering the possible correlation with a portfolio's assets (Gulko, 2003).

The AIRAP is a measure that considers the impact of the specific characteristics of hedge funds and their impact on the investor utility function. It considers the fund's leverage, investors' preferences and the nonnormality of the return distribution (Sharma, 2004).

A more objective approach is founded on new RAPs scale independent such as:

- the Stutzer index;
- the Omega function;
- the Sharpe Omega;
- the Kappa;
- the D-Ratio;
- ROAS;
- ROPS;
- the Hurst ratio;
- the Calmar ratio;
- the Sterling ratio.

The Stutzer index is a measure that also considers the skewness and the kurtosis of the return distribution and penalizes distributions characterized by negative skewness and high kurtosis (Bacmann and Scholz, 2003).

The Omega function considers all higher moments of return distributions and provides a full account of the risk reward characteristics of the distribution. It is calculated as a ratio of the total gains to the total losses related to the investments in a hedge fund for the time period under examination (Keating and Shadwick, 2002).

The Sharpe Omega uses the same approach as is utilized for the Sharpe ratio, but the risk measure is estimated analysing the Omega function (Kazemi et al., 2003).

The Kappa represents a modified Sortino Ratio that uses, as measure of the fund's gains, the excess return of the fund with respect to the minimum return that is acceptable for the investor. The RAP is computed as the ratio of this difference to the lower partial moment of the return distribution (Kaplan and Knowels, 2004).

The D-Ratio does not consider the moments of the returns' distribution and classifies funds only on the basis of the frequency of losses and gains. Hedge funds' rankings are calculated by taking into account the ratio of positive and negative performances achieved in the time period analysed (Koh et al., 2002).

The ROAS and the ROPS use the same approach proposed by Sharpe for the performance measure – the mean excess return of the hedge funds' performance on the risk-free rate – but use a different risk measure: the first one uses the absolute shortfall and the second one uses the probability of losses (Koh et al., 2002).

The Hurst ratio is a measure of the persistence of the time series that can be useful in evaluating the validity of a performance evaluation based on historical data. The Hurst ratio is useful in allowing an investor to distinguish between the good portfolio managers and the 'lucky' portfolio managers (Amenc et al., 2002).

The Calmar ratio and the Sterling ratio are computed using another risk measure, the potential maximum loss related to a specific investment (Braga, 2001). The Calmar ratio is calculated as the ratio of mean return over the maximum drawdown and the Sterling ratio is the same measure evaluated using a smoothed maximum drawdown (Pedersen and Rudholm-Alfvin, 2003).

These approaches are more complex than the standard RAP used to evaluate other funds and they therefore need more detailed information in selecting the best fund available. It is not easy to calculate the new measures and it is necessary to evaluate if the sophistication of the approach guarantees a return that justifies a more detailed analysis.

2.3   Research design

The study considers the performance achieved by hedge funds and evaluates their risk-performances profile using classical and new RAPs. The purpose of the analysis is to evaluate benefits related to new approaches and to verify if these new measures are effectively a useful instrument to select hedge funds.

Utility-based RAPs based are excluded from the empirical analysis because a generic utility function is not available and the results obtained using these measures are highly influenced by the type of function that is selected. In fact, the aim of the work is to verify the superiority of new RAPs to evaluate this type of funds and the unavailability of a standard utility function make these measures useless in defining a ranking of different RAPs.

The approach proposed in this study considers the classification based on each RAP scale independent and tries to identify the RAP that defines a better and more stationary classification of hedge funds. In order to verify the superiority of new measures we analyse the selection capability of these new measures and results obtained with different RAPs criteria. The study of results achieved is completed with a more detailed analysis of RAP performance that allow the verification of the usefulness of different measures in different market phases (bull and bear markets) and the persistence of rankings defined with each RAP.

2.3.1   Data

The characteristics of the instrument make it impossible to conduct an analysis of all available hedge funds: managers have the freedom to restrict the availability of data about funds managed (Brooks and Kat, 2001) and so all of the databases must be considered to be only partially representative (Posthuma and Van der Sluis, 2003) (Table 2.1).

A hedge fund is reported in no more than one or two databases offered by data vendors and so it is necessary to select the database that offers the highest level of coverage for the market analysed (Kat, 2003).

The analysis proposed does not consider the American market, the biggest market in the world. Rather, we focus on the major European markets that trade in hedge funds. The decision to concentrate on European hedge funds allows us to compile a more complete database of all of the instruments traded because, even though the market is growing, the number of funds offered today in the market is still lower than the number offered in the United States (Amin and Kat, 2003). Our

Table 2.1   Top data vendors for hedge funds on the basis of funds' coverage

Database	No. of hedge funds considered	Website
Van Hedge Funds Advisors International	>6,000	www.vanhedge.com
Tass/Tremont	>3,000	www.hedgeindex.com
Hennessee Group	>3,000	www.hennesseegroup.com
Hedgefund.net	>3,700	www.hedgefund.net
Zurich Capital Markets	>1,500	www.marhedge.com
Hedge Fund Research	>1,300	www.hfr.com
Investor Force	>1,000	www.altvest.com

Source: Author's elaboration on data vendors' information.

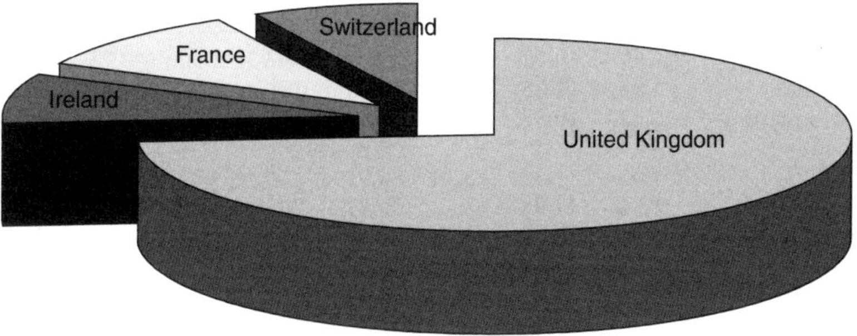

Figure 2.1   Sample description
Source: Author's elaboration on data vendors' information.

sample includes 556 hedge funds traded in at least one of the following countries: the United Kingdom, France, Ireland and Switzerland (Figure 2.1).

Data are collected using the two major data sources for the hedge funds' market – Hedge Index Tass/Tremont and Hedgefund.net. These databases are selected in preference to other data collections because they offer a more comprehensive dataset on the European market. The sample includes daily historical quotes of major funds traded in the four markets for the period 1993–2003 and considers all of the funds independently of the year of institution. The sample is not affected by survivorship bias indicated in the literature (Koh et al., 2003) because none of the funds selected expired before the end of the time period under consideration.

2.3.2 Comparison between Risk Adjusted Performance classifications of hedge funds

The analysis of the usefulness of the new RAPs is realized by considering the differential capabilities of standard RAPs and new RAPs to identify the best-performing hedge fund. The first aspect to be analysed is the capability of the different RAP to select funds that, in the future, will achieve best performances. To evaluate the selection capability, results achieved one year later by the funds recognized as the best using a particular RAP are compared with performances of other funds.

Table 2.2 RAP measures as instruments to forecast hedge funds' performance

	High performers t − 1				Low performers t − 1			
	Media (%)	Max (%)	Min (%)	%	Media (%)	Max (%)	Min (%)	%
Sharpe	0.99	10.72	−3.24	76.79	0.86	5.50	−2.25	26.58
Sortino	1.04	11.35	−3.14	30.53	0.97	4.92	−1.82	69.14
Information ratio	1.12	10.38	−2.98	79.63	1.04	6.53	−2.20	24.95
RAP	1.02	11.36	−3.14	80.97	1.03	4.09	−1.62	26.19
Treynor	1.00	11.36	−3.14	79.11	1.15	4.09	−1.62	26.27
Jensen	1.06	10.73	−3.02	81.68	0.95	5.73	−2.76	24.47
Omega	1.05	11.36	−3.85	48.22	0.78	2.09	0.03	59.86
D-ratio	1.03	11.36	−3.85	38.34	0.75	1.44	0.33	55.17
Hurst	1.02	11.36	−3.85	61.80	0.65	0.95	0.30	28.57
ROPS	1.03	11.35	−3.14	81.54	1.23	4.69	−1.49	25.66
ROAS	1.18	9.17	−2.71	88.91	0.83	6.72	−3.07	7.31
Sterling	1.17	8.85	−2.63	75.95	0.88	7.00	−3.14	23.97
Kalmar	1.18	8.91	−2.63	82.77	0.87	7.00	−3.14	13.01
Stutzer	1.01	11.16	−3.78	50.71	0.69	1.59	0.28	42.86
Kappa	1.10	10.45	−3.18	76.59	0.92	4.73	−2.07	8.72
Sharpe Omega	1.15	8.93	−2.58	78.01	0.89	6.92	−3.14	18.84

Note: % represents for the high (low) performers the ratio of funds with return higher (lower) than the mean value.
Source: Author's elaboration on data vendors' information.

The analysis presented above studies the mean return and the maximum/minimum results obtained for each year for the two subgroups of hedge funds created using the threshold of 50 per cent: the subgroup High is composed by the hedge funds that in the previous year have a value of the RAP higher than the mean value and the subgroup Low is the residual group (Table 2.2).

There is clear evidence of the dominance of new approaches proposed to select hedge funds: in fact, new RAPs define subgroups that, as with

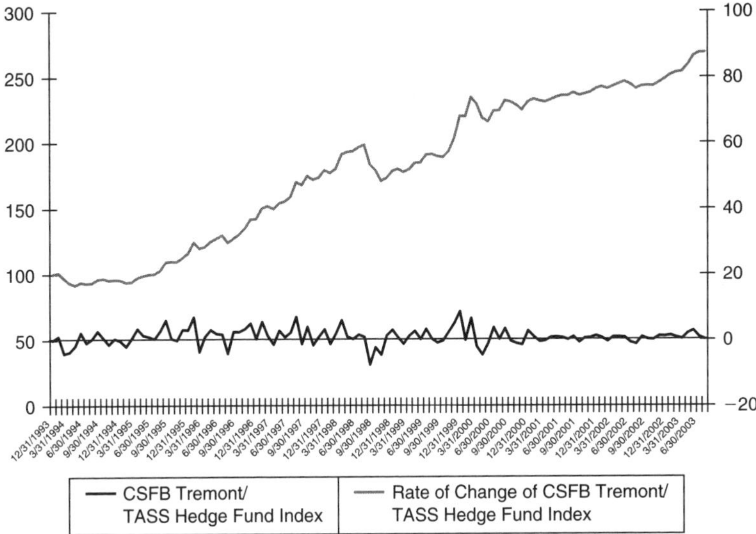

Figure 2.2   Hedge fund market performance in the evaluation period

the standard approach, are useful to separate the good performer from the bad one but the mean difference return is significantly higher if the two groups are identified using new measures.

Another interesting aspect is the capability of the new approaches to evaluate the future performances of funds in the different market phases. An analysis of this aspect could identify periods when an investment strategy founded on a more detailed analysis of hedge funds' dynamics makes the best gains.

To analyse this aspect it is necessary to identify phases of the hedge fund market considering, directly an hedge funds' index: in fact the hedge industry isn't similar to other financial assets (Sidani and Soueissy, 2003) and the lack of correlation could cause a misalignment between hedge funds' market dynamics and other assets' performances (Amec et al., 2002). In fact hedge funds' managers adopted strategies that are independent from market phases and they can assume opposite position to market dynamics (Boido, 2001).

In order to define the bull and bear periods for the hedge market we analyse the historical trend of a sectoral index, the CSFB Tremont Hedge Fund Index (Figure 2.2).[2]

Major trends are identified using a simple technical analysis approach that classifies the bull and the bear markets on the basis of index

Table 2.3   RAP analysis in bull and bear market

	% success bull market	Δ gains bull market	% success bear market	Δ gains bear market
Sharpe	57.14	−0.33	100.00	0.08
RAP	42.86	−0.26	100.00	−0.13
Information Ratio	71.43	−0.42	100.00	0.28
Sortino	57.14	1.19	100.00	0.55
Treynor	100.00	−1.33	100.00	−0.84
Jensen	42.86	−1.33	100.00	−0.84
Stutzer	57.14	−0.10	66.67	0.27
Omega	71.43	−0.12	100.00	−0.29
Sharpe Omega	85.71	0.01	0.00	0.36
Kappa	57.14	−0.18	0.00	−0.35
D-Ratio	42.86	−0.23	66.67	0.30
Roas	85.71	0.64	0.00	−0.28
Rops	57.14	0.10	100.00	−0.21
Hurst	57.14	−0.70	33.33	0.27
Kalmar	85.71	0.43	0.00	0.15
Sterling	100.00	0.82	0.00	0.61

variations recorded in the time horizon analysed. A simple approach founded on the rate of change allows us to identify two major trends: a bullish trend from the 1993 to 2000 and a bear trend for the period 2001–2003.[3] It is possible to verify the validity of different RAP measures to select investment opportunities in different scenarios and to evaluate the relative utility of these approaches in different scenarios.

The relative usefulness of the different approaches is tested by considering the mean difference of returns achieved by the best and worst classified funds and the mean percentage of success of each RAP in terms of identifying the best opportunities available (Table 2.3).

The results demonstrate that new RAPs are particularly useful in volatile markets, the bull markets, where a more detailed analysis of past performances is necessary to select hedge funds' best performers. In bear markets standard approaches are sufficient to identify best investment opportunities and a more detailed analysis realized using new RAPs couldn't be justified in the light of the differential gains related to these new measures.

The results achieved by hedge funds are often not time-persistent and a fund's classification based on historical performances could be less useful if it varies frequently in the period analysed (Boyson, 2003).

So the validity of a RAP measure can not be analysed without considering the temporal persistence of classifications based on the measure.

Table 2.4 Percentage of upgrade/downgrades in the subgroups using different RAP classifications

	Best portfolio			Worst portfolio		
	Mean (%)	Max (%)	Min (%)	Mean (%)	Max (%)	Min (%)
Sharpe	50.41	73.72	42.16	39.16	63.16	13.40
Modigliani's RAP	51.42	73.78	42.57	26.77	60.00	0.00
Information ratio	38.85	65.00	24.07	40.56	62.12	27.50
Sortino	59.10	77.11	49.16	29.92	75.00	0.00
Treynor	83.07	100.00	60.12	20.17	66.67	0.00
Jensen	55.88	77.78	50.82	47.43	68.26	27.91
Stutzer	70.17	93.45	66.67	34.37	51.52	12.50
Omega	73.67	96.53	71.30	50.96	100.00	0.00
Sharpe Omega	73.67	96.53	71.30	50.96	100.00	0.00
Kappa	51.28	74.69	41.72	28.48	60.00	0.00
D-ratio	23.00	46.37	8.33	47.93	74.19	36.00
ROAS	21.38	46.90	10.91	55.55	80.67	42.79
ROPS	21.59	35.10	15.38	53.46	77.97	40.84
Hurst	73.67	96.53	71.30	50.96	100.00	0.00
Kalmar	40.01	57.35	26.44	33.57	62.75	18.92
Sterling	20.88	53.33	0.00	49.06	74.80	35.05

One RAP could be preferred to another if the funds' classification obtained using this measure is stable over time and if the percentage of upgrades/downgrades of the funds included in a group is as small as possible. The analysis of new measures proposed is so completed with the persistence study of the classification realized with each RAP in the time horizon considered (Table 2.4).

The persistence seems not to be a characteristic that allows us to identify the more useful RAP. In fact, the mean percentage of revisions in group components is the same for classifications based on standard and new measures and the mean value is not low. If we conduct separate analyses of the new RAPs and old measures, it is possible to verify that:

- new measures have the capability to identify two groups, best and worst funds, that vary with the same frequency;
- old measures identify subgroups of worst funds that vary less in the time horizon analyzed;
- the failure of new measures is more evident in the bear market where the fund's selection reveals frequently erratic.

Unpredictability that characterized all group members could be explained considering hedge funds' characteristics that make less useful historical data to predict future performance when they are more time distant (Basile, 2002).

The higher variability that characterized this instrument makes also impossible to select a group of funds that can be over-performing for a long time period (Kat and Menexe, 2003) and it's necessary to monitor continually the market in order to understand when a particular hedge fund becomes an investment opportunity.

2.4 Conclusions

The new approaches proposed for the evaluation of hedge funds could be useful in defining investment strategy and the new measures may prove particularly useful in volatile markets where a more detailed analysis of hedge funds' performances makes it possible to select the best ones. New RAP approaches proposed do not eliminate problems related to the non-persistency of RAP-based classifications that must be considered a direct consequence of hedge funds' characteristics.

The results obtained are statistically significant for the European market, but there is no clear evidence of the validity of these conclusions for different markets. Before we can recommend the general acceptance of this approach, it is necessary to replicate these approaches in other financial markets.

The sample considers only a pool of successful funds that have survived throughout the time period analysed and it is probable that for different markets it is impossible to construct a numerous sample of funds that would not be affected by survivorship bias (Brown et al., 2004). The empirical analysis demonstrates that this phenomenon tends to overestimate the performance and/or to underestimate the risk exposure related to the market for hedge funds (Fung and Hsieh, 2002a). For these markets the choice either to include or not to include funds that expire before the end of the period analyzed can affect rankings realized with RAP measures and the interpretation of results must consider the impact of this choice (Baquero et al., 2004).

The analysis proposed in this work tries to verify the validity of new RAP approaches and evaluates the usefulness of these measures for an investor who has to select one of the funds available. The next step of the research could be to study the different dynamics of hedge funds that adopt different investment styles: this analysis could be useful in estimating the advantages related to the diversification among different hedge funds. In fact, a portfolio approach could make it necessary to reanalyse the RAP approach used to select hedge funds and to define a new measure that also considers possible correlations among different hedge funds included in the portfolio.

Notes

1. This chapter is the result of the authors' continuous cooperation. The Introduction and the conclusion can be attributed to Alessandro Carretta and other paragraphs to Gianluca Mattarocci.
2. Hedgefund.net does not offer a global aggregate index that could be used to analyse the market trend.
3. The bull market phase is identified as the period when the rate of change is double than the mean value registered on the overall time horizon.

References

Abernathy, J.D. and A.B. Weisman (2000) 'The Danger of Historical Hedge Fund Data', in L. Rahl, *Risk Budgeting*, London: Risk Books.

Ackermann, C., R. McEnally and D. Ravenscrat (1999) 'The Performance of Hedge Funds: Risk, Returns and Incentives', *Journal of Finance*, 53: 833–74.

Agarwal, V. and N.Y. Naik (2004) 'Risk and Portfolio Decisions Involving Hedge Funds', *Review of Financial Studies*, 17: 63–98.

Amenc, N., L. Martellini and M. Vaissié (2002) *Benefits and Risks of Alternative Investment Strategies*, EDHEC working paper, Nice.

Amenc, N., S. El Bied and L. Martellini (2005) *Evidence of Predictability in Hedge Fund Returns and Multi-Style Multi-Class Tactical Style Allocation Decisions*, USC FBE Working Paper no. 2, Los Angeles.

Amin, G.S. and H.M. Kat (2003) 'Hedge Funds Performance 1990–2000: Does the Money Machine Really add Value?', *Journal of Financial and Quantitative Analysis*, 38: 251–74.

Bacmann, J.F. and S. Scholz (2003) 'Alternative Performance Measures for Hedge Funds', *AIMA Journal*, 1: 1–9.

Baquero, G., J.T. Horst and M. Verbeek (2004) *Survival, Look-ahead Bias and the Persistence in Hedge Fund Performance*, RMS working paper, Netspar.

Basile, I. (2002) *Benchmark e performance dei portafogli azionari e obbligazionari*, Milan: Bancaria Editrice.

Bing, L. (1999) 'On the Performance of Hedge Funds', *Financial Analyst Journal*, 55: 72–85.

Blake, C.R., E.J. Elton and M.J. Gruber (1996) 'The Persistence of Risk Adjusted Mutual Fund Performance', *Journal of Business*, 69: 133–57.

Boido, C. (2001) 'Organizzazione e politiche di offerta degli hedge fund', *Analisi Finanziaria*, 1: 4–17.

Boido, C. and E. Riente (2004) 'Hedge fund: dal mito alla realtà', *Banche e Banchieri*, 5: 406–20.

Boyson, N.M. (2003) 'Why do Experienced Hedge Fund Managers Have Lower Returns?', EDHEC Working Paper, Nice.

Boyson, N.M. (2003) 'Do Hedge Funds Exhibit Performance Persistence? A New Approach', EDHEC Working Paper.

Braga, M.D. (2001) 'Problematiche di performance measurement nell'hedge fund industry', *Lettera Newfin*, 14.

Brooks, C. and H.M. Kat (2001) 'The Statistical Properties of Hedge Fund Index Returns and Their Implications for Investors', *Journal of Alternative Investments*, 5: 26–44.

Brown, S.H., W.N. Goetzmann and R.G. Ibbotson (1998) 'Offshore Hedge Funds: Survival & Performance 1989–1995', *Journal of Business*, 72: 91–117.

Brown, S.J., D.R. Gallagher, O. Steenbeek and P.L. Swan (2004) *Informationless Trading and Biases in Performance Measurement: an Examination of Sharpe Ratios*, Stern Asset Management Research Group working paper, New York.

Capocci, D., A. Corhay and G. Hubner (2003) *Hedge Funds Performance and Persistence in Bull and Bear Markets*, EDHEC Working Paper, Nice.

Carluccio, E.M. (1999) *Strategie, benchmarking e performance nell'asset management*, Milan: Bancaria Editrice.

Chen, K. and A. Passow (2003) *Quantitative Selection of Long-Short Hedge Funds*, FAME working paper, Geneva.

Colombini, F., A. Mancini and S. Mannucci (2003) *La performance dei fondi comuni di investimento*, Milan: Edibank.

Das, N., R.J. Kish, D.L. Muething and L.W. Taylor (2002) *An Overview of Hedge Fund Industry*, AIMA working paper, London.

Favre-Bulle, A. and S. Pache (2003) *The Omega Measure: Hedge Fund Portfolio Optimization*, EDHEC Working Paper, Nice.

Favre, L. and A. Ranaldo (2003) *How to Price Hedge Funds: From Two- to Four-Moment CAPM*, EDHEC Working Paper, Nice.

Fung, W. and D.A. Hsieh (1999) 'A Primer on Hedge Funds', *Journal of Empirical Finance*, 6: 309–31.

Fung, W. and D.A. Hsieh (2002) 'Asset-based Style Factors for Hedge Funds', *Financial Analyst Journal*, 58: 16–27.

Fung, W. and D.A. Hsieh (2002a) 'Benchmarks of Hedge Funds Performance: Information Content and Measurement Bias', *Financial Analyst Journal*, 58: 22–34.

Gehin, W. (2004) *A Survey of the Literature on Hedge Fund Performance*, EDHEC Working Paper, Nice.

Getmansky, M., A.W. Lo and I. Makarov (2004) 'An Econometric Model of Serial Correlation and Illiquidity in the Hedge Fund Returns', *Journal of Financial Economics*, 74: 529–609.

Goodwin, T. (1998) 'The Information Ratio', *Financial Analyst Journal*, 54: 34–43.

Gregoriou, G.N. and J.P. Gueyie (2003) 'Risk Adjusted Performance of Funds of Hedge Funds Using a Modified Sharpe Ratio', *Journal of Wealth Management*, 6: 77–83.

Gulko, L. (2003) 'Performance Metrics for Hedge Funds', *Journal of Alternative Investments*, 5: 88–95.

Hubner, G. (1999) *Horizon Risk and Asset Pricing*, Southern California – School of Business Administration papers 99-57, Los Angeles.

Jensen, M.C. (1968) 'The Performance of Mutual Funds in the Period 1945–1964', *Journal of Finance*, 23: 28–30.

Kaplan, P.D. and J.A. Knowles (2004) 'Kappa: a Generalized Downside Risk-adjusted Performance Measure', *Journal of Performance Measurement* 8: 52–4.

Kat, H.M. (2003) '10 Things That Investors Should Know About Hedge Funds', *Journal of Wealth Management*, 5: 72–81.

Kat, H.M. and F. Menexe (2003) 'Persistence in Hedge Fund Performance: the True Value of Track Record', *Journal of Alternative Investments*, 5: 66–72.

Kazemi, H., T. Schneeweis and R. Gupta (2003) *Omega as a Performance Measure*, University of Massachusetts Working Paper, Amherst.

Keating, C. and W.F. Shadwick (2002) 'A Universal Performance Measure', *Journal of Performance Measurement*, 6: 59–84.

Klemkosky, R.C. (1973) 'The Bias in Composite Performance Measurement', *Journal of Financial and Quantitative Analysis*, 8: 505–14.

Koh, F., W.T.H. Koh and M. Teoh (2003) *Asian Hedge Funds: Return Persistence, Style and Fund Characteristics*, Singapore Management University working paper, Singapore.

Koh, F., D. Lee and P. Kok Fai (2002) *Investing in Hedge Funds: Risk, Return and Pitfalls*, Ferrell Focus Working Paper, Singapore.

Kouwenberg, R. and W. Ziemba (2003) *Incentives and Risk Taking in Hedge Funds*, Erasmus University working paper, Rotterdam.

Liang, B. (2003) 'Hedge Fund Returns: Auditing and Accuracy', *Journal of Portfolio Management*, 29: 111–22.

Maugain, O. (2001) *The Evaluation of Hedge Funds*, University of St Gallen working paper, St Gallen.

Modigliani, F. and L. Modigliani (1997) 'Risk-adjusted Performance', *Journal of Portfolio Management*, 2: 45–54.

Moix, P. and C. Schmidhuber (2001) 'Fat Tail Risk: the Case for Hedge Funds (Part I)', *AIMA Newsletter*, 9.

Pedersen, C.S. and T. Rudholm-Alfvin (2003) 'Selecting a Risk-adjusted Shareholder Performance Measure', *Journal of Asset Management*, 4: 152–72.

Pia, P. (2002) *Hedge funds: fondi di copertura o fondi speculativi?*, Turin: Giappichelli editore.

Posthuma, N. and P.J. Van der Sluis (2003) *A Reality Check on Hedge Fund Returns*, Free University Amsterdam, Faculty of Economics, Business Administration and Econometrics Serie Research Memoranda, Amsterdam.

Schneeweis, T. and R. Spurgin (1996) *Multi-factor Models in Managed Futures, Hedge Funds and Mutual Fund Return Estimation*, University of Massachusetts working paper, Amherst.

Sharma, M. (2004) 'AIRAP – Alternative RAPMs for Alternative Investments', *Journal of Investment Management*, 2: 34–65.

Sharpe, W.F. (1966) 'Mutual Fund Performance', *Journal of Business*, 39: 119–38.

Sharpe, W.F. (1994) 'The Sharpe Ratio', *Journal of Portfolio Management*, 21: 49–58.

Sidani, R. and M. Soueissy (2003) *The Risk Underlying Hedge Fund Strategies*, University of Lausanne working paper, Lausanne.

Sortino, F.A. and H.J. Forsey (1996) 'On the Use and Measure of Downside Risk', *Journal of Portfolio Management*, 22: 35–42.

Tsatsaronis, K. (2000) 'Hedge Funds', *BIS Quarterly Review*, 61: 61–71.

Treynor, J. (1965) 'How to Rate Management of Investment Funds', *Harvard Business Review*, 44: 131–6.

3

Real Estate Investments: the Case of the Italian Market

Claudio Porzio and Gabriele Sampagnaro[1]

3.1 Introduction

With reference to the Italian market, in this chapter we discuss the results of an empirical survey that considers the size of real estate weight in a mixed-asset portfolio. The absence of data for the Italian public market has forced us to restrict the survey only to the impact of private segment inclusion in a portfolio invested in stocks and bonds (both short and long term). Although the Italian real estate public market officially started in 1994 with the institution of the specialized closed fund ('fondi comuni di investimento immobiliari', Law 86/1994), the illiquidity of the market and the limited number of listed funds determine the lack of a meaningful literature about the role of such investment's channel as portfolio diversifier. Previous studies on the public market from a portfolio approach point of view have referred only to the inclusion in an asset-mixed portfolio of Italian real estate company's shares and ABS derived from domestic properties securitization.

An investigation dealing with adding real estate to a financial portfolio according to a mean-variance framework raises some obvious and important issues such as: (a) the scarcity and the unrepresentative nature of the Italian real estate indexes that are currently available (either transaction-based or appraisal-based indexes); and (b) the methodological limits of the mean-variance model.

3.1.1 The choice of a representative real estate index

In relation to the lack of significance of indexes with respect to 'true' market values, it is important to point out that transaction-based indexes face a potential problem of fiscal elusion represented by the circumstance that property transactions can be recorded in the land registry office at a price below its 'true' market value; this phenomenon is widespread in Italy where it is common for real estate operators to reduce the price of a transaction in order to avoid paying transaction taxes.

Furthermore, and in a more general perspective, the adoption of appraisal indexes adds other issues concerning the use of a real estate index as a proxy of real market movements, such as sticky values and smoothing effects. If we observe the profile of property values we see that, depending on the frequency of valuation, there are often long periods when there is no change in values. One rationalization for the way in which values are adjusted is the presence of relevant costs associated with making changes in value, so that it may be optimal to adjust them by discrete amounts towards some underlying equilibrium level. There are a number of situations in which this might arise, for example: (i) large portfolios may be selectively valued by sample – within a large portfolio it may not be cost-effective formally to appraise each property when frequent valuations are required – in this case a representative sample of properties is valued and the average change is then applied to the remaining properties; (ii) many properties may be valued annually, with 'intermediate' values being recorded as showing no change; (iii) the value r may not consider small changes in information to be important enough to warrant a change in value. All of these reasons suggest that an index based on appraisal values may be sticky. In other words, valuations of a property can differ widely from market prices and be close to previous valuations, this aspect can write as follows:

$$V_t = k\overline{P_t} + (1 - k)V_{t-1} \tag{3.1}$$

with $0 < k < 1$ and where k represents the weight applied to the observed market prices, $\overline{P_t}$.

As k approaches one, more weight will be given to the observed market price; a value of k exactly equal to one means that the market is in equilibrium and then the valuations will equal current prices; as k approaches zero, more weights will be given to the previous valuation. This process is known as smoothing and usually happens at a time of bear markets when a smaller amount of comparable sales information is available. The presence of the smoothing effect in time series returns is very important because it contributes to a reduction of the volatility and, consequently, the correlation of real estate returns with other asset classes. This effect induces the investor seeking to optimize the mean-variance to prefer this specific asset class to the others, with a possible overestimation of its weight in any efficient portfolio. Moreover, if we use an appraisal index, we need to consider that this type of index also suffers from lagging and artificial seasonality which are due respectively to the partial adjustment in the index caused by the stale valuations, and to the bunching of the reappraisals in the same period – usually, the fourth calendar quarter.

3.1.2   The methodological limits of mean-variance optimization

Even using an index that is able to minimize the elements of distortion mentioned above, it is important to remark that surveys about the benefits of real estate investment in a mean-variance framework do not consider the impact of transaction costs (direct and indirect) related to investment in properties. This is also the case when these costs have a great relevance and could be considered as an important variable in deciding whether or not to realize the transfer of properties.

In addition to these specific aspects, there are other two general issues related to the adoption of the mean-variance approach for portfolio selection. First, the results of a portfolio optimization procedure very often show a tendency of the optimizer to select optimal portfolios that are only slightly diversified (strongly concentrated in a few asset classes). Such a phenomenon implies the recognition of some portfolios that are, in most cases, unacceptable for investors with a low risk tolerance. Secondly, one of the most serious problems regarding the practical adoption of the mean-variance model is to be found in the instability of optimal portfolios (Michaud, 1998). This instability shows up, firstly, because there are a sufficient number of small variations in the input set that cause significant changes in the shape of the efficient frontier (Pomante, 2004).

3.2   Data and distributional characteristics of real estate returns

With one exception, all of the asset classes are related to the Italian market. Monthly returns are derived for a series of domestic (Comit Globale Index) and foreign (S&P500 Index) stock, long-term Government bond (MTS BTP 10Y), Risk free-rate (MTS Bot), and real estate (SI Indexes, Scenari Immobiliari) for the time period from January 1997 to January 2004.

The SI indexes are monthly benchmarks provided by a private company since 1 January 1997. They are built following a mixed approach – that is, they are based on both transaction prices and appraisal values. In

Table 3.1 Distributional characteristic of Italian asset classes returns (monthly, 1997–2004)

	Domestic Stock (Comit)	Foreign Stock (S&P 500)	Dom. Bond (BTP 10Y)	Dom. Risk free (Bot 6m)	Real Estate (SI General Index)
Mean (monthly) (%)	0.91	0.41	0.06	0.33	1.11
Standard error	0.0078	0.0054	0.0043	0.0001	0.0007
Median	0.0029	0,0076	−0.0058	0.0030	0.0118
Mode	n.c.	n.c.	n.c.	n.c.	0.0123
Standard deviation (%)	7.22	4.97	3.95	0.13	0.63
Kurtosis (Fisher)	0.8552	−0.0024	−0.3463	−0.5320	−0.9361
Skewness	0.4065	−0.4297	0.3650	0.5135	−0.1156
Min. (%)	−16.87	−14.58	−8.55	0.11	−0.09
Max. (%)	23.15	9.67	8.98	0.64	2.31
Normality	*		*	*	*

particular, they consider: (1) the variation of rental values; (2) the variation of returns; and (3) the variations in the volume of transactions. The family of SI indexes consists of one general index (the SI General Index); one partial index (the SI General not residential Index), and four sectoral sub-indexes: SI commercial, SI residential, SI office and SI industrial.

The data shown in Table 3.1 and Figure 3.1 provide a brief description respectively of the movements and distributional characteristics of the four Italian asset class and S&P500 in our portfolio. As expected, stock markets exhibit return fluctuations that are higher than those observed in bond and real estate markets. The returns fluctuations of real estate market is higher than the volatility of the bond market and lower than the stock market, but the former measures are much smoother. Comparing the value of kurtosis, there is a tendency for stock market returns to be leptokurtic (the Italian stock market) and normal (the Usa stock market), while bond market, risk-free and, particularly, real estate are platycurtic. The sign of skewness is positive for all asset classes apart from S&P500 and real estate which, at this state of analysis, seems to be an asset class with very peculiar statistical characteristics.

Crucial to the application of the modern capital market theory is the assumption of normally distributed returns. In this case, we applied Jarque/Bera test and Anderson/Darling test; the results of which are shown in the final line of Table 3.1, where if both of these tests are not able to reject the null of normality at the 5% level, they are signed with '*'.

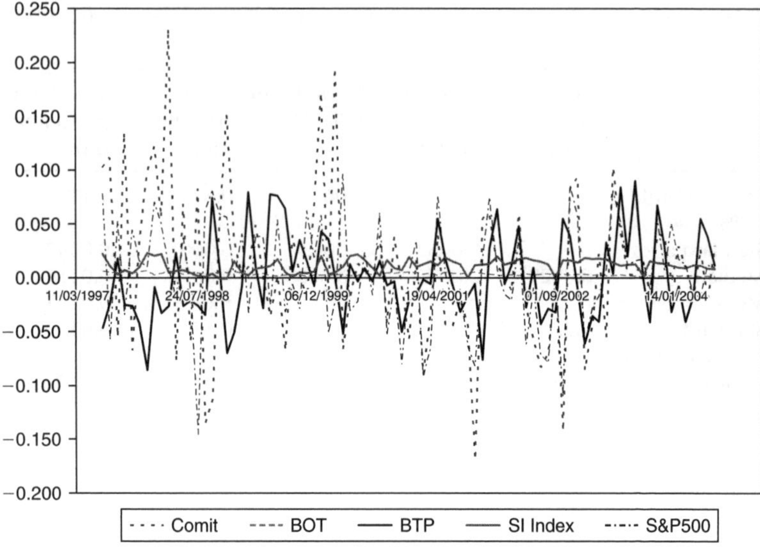

Figure 3.1   Monthly returns of asset classes, 1997–2004

Figure 3.2 contains the results for the ACF test which shows, for the real estate market, a strong link between the returns at time t and those at time t − 1 (lag 1) that suggests a presence of smoothing in the distribution of returns.

3.3   De-smoothing returns procedure

The appraisal-induced biases in the risk-return profile of the real estate series have been discussed thoroughly by many previous studies, including Quan and Quigley (1991), Geltner (1991, 1993) and Giacotto and Clapp (1992). In order to correct for bias in the appraisal-based data, we follow the 'unsmoothing' approach developed by Geltner (1993). This is different from the approach proposed by Ross and Zisler in that it does not assume that the true underlying series is efficiently priced so that the returns from period to period are uncorrelated. The approach followed by Geltner is based on the assumption that returns follow a first-order autoregressive process so that current observed returns are related to the returns in the previous period. In algebraic terms, the market return that would be observed if prices were correctly captured by valuations

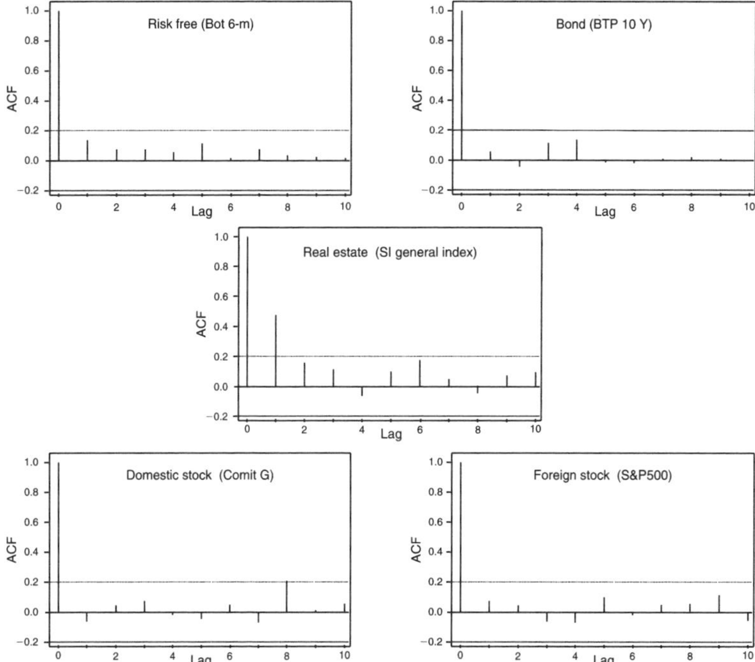

Figure 3.2 Autocorrelation of monthly returns

(and that we denote with R_{mt}), is described as follows:

$$R_{mt} = \frac{r_t^* - (1 - \alpha)r_{t-1}^*}{\alpha} \tag{3.2}$$

where r_t^* is the return derived from the valuation series publicly reported and α a constant lying in the range from 0 to 1.

Geltner assumes three equilibrium values of parameter α: a prudential value (lower bound), a normal value (best estimate), and an optimistic value (upper bound) respectively equal to $\alpha = 0.33$, $\alpha = 0.40$, $\alpha = 0.50$. In our case, we adopt the prudential value ($\alpha = 0.33$) attempting to reduce the risk of an 'over-preference' of the mean-variance optimizer for real estate investments. Thus, according to this procedure of unsmoothing, the annualized standard deviations of returns for SI Gen. Index increases from an original value of α smoothed $\cong 2.2$ to an unsmoothed value equal to α unsmoothed $\cong 6.4$. Furthermore, considering the correlation ratios between asset classes, Table 3.2 confirms the traditional role of real estate,

Table 3.2   Correlations among asset classes

	Domestic Stock	Foreign Stock	Bond	Risk free	RE (smoothed)	RE (unsmoothed)
Domestic Stock	1					
Foreign Stock	0.3349	1				
Bond	−0.1037	0.1279	1			
Risk free	0.094	−0.1219	−0.513	1		
RE (smoothed)	−0.0041	−0.0135	−0.0301	−0.037	1	
RE (unsmoothed)	−0.1265	−0.0713	−0.033	0.0488	0.761	1

either in a smoothing or an unsmoothing framework, as an asset class characterized by returns that are negatively correlated with the stock and bond market.

3.4   Portfolio selection and the measure of diversification

Using a mean-variance algorithm, we want to verify if a diversified portfolio shows the benefits of diversification for Italian investors holding direct real estate.

This benefit is realized in terms of the reduction of risk portfolio and is graphically illustrated by a translation towards the left of the frontier constructed with the inclusion of real estate investment. As is well known, in a general perspective, the addition of one (or more) asset class characterized by a low correlation with the others, produces a shift towards left of the frontier, allowing to choice more profitable portfolios at the same risk level.

This translation can follow two different paths: (a) the inclusion of a new (or more) asset class (scarcely correlated with others) determines a change of corner portfolios of the efficient frontier – that is, portfolios respectively with minimum and maximum variance – thus generating a 'raising effect' of the frontier; (b) the addition of a new (or more) asset class (scarcely correlated with others) does not modify the position of corner portfolios on the graph, but produces just an accentuation of curvature level of the frontier determining a sort of 'sling effect', because it is reminiscent of the behaviour of an elastic sling before the throw.

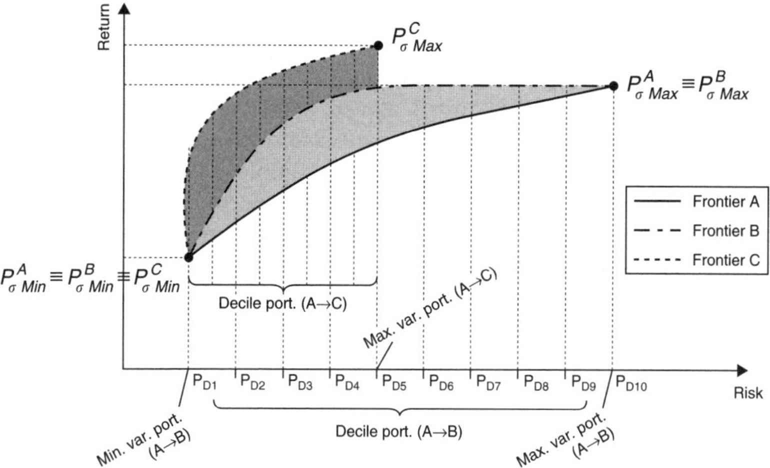

Figure 3.3   The inclusion of an asset class not correlated: the 'sling effect' and the 'raising effect'

These two effects are readily recognizable in Figure 3.3, where A represents the frontier of n asset class, and B and C the frontiers generated by the inclusion of a new asset (n + 1th) slightly correlated with the others n asset class (the n + 1th asset class in frontier B is different than in C).

The frontier A undergoes a sling effect and changes in B after the addition of an asset class characterized by: (1) a slight correlation with other asset classes; (2) a risk not too different from those of the other asset classes in the portfolio; (3) a return certainly lower than the highest return of the set of pre-existent asset classes.

Assertion (3) is related to the circumstance that the portfolio with the maximum variance is allocated entirely to the most profitable asset class: on the contrary, the inclusion of an asset class with a return higher than the return of the maximum variance portfolio (i.e., $P^A_{\sigma Max}$ in Figure 3.3), produces a translation from A to C, in consequence of a raising effect. In this case, the volatility interval of the frontier is wider or restricted if the new added asset class has respectively a risk higher or lower than the risk of portfolio with max. variance ($P^A_{\sigma Max}$).

After the analysis of this positive effect sprang from the inclusion in portfolio of an asset class that is only slightly correlated with the others, it is now necessary to consider how we can measure this benefit of diversification.

In the case of the 'sling effect', this measure can be provided by the breadth of shift of the new frontier with respect to its previous position: this shift can be calculated as the change (in the passage between the two set of portfolios) of the mean risk-adjusted performance of the frontier. The term 'mean risk adjusted performance of frontier', synthesized by the acronym MeRAPF, can be referred to a very simple measure of profitability represented by the mean of Risk Adjusted Performance of the optimal portfolios. Because the number of portfolios that compose an efficient frontier is unlimited, it is obvious that the MeRAPF must be elaborated only for a restricted number of cases. A solution could be provided by the calculation of the 'decile MeRAPF' – that is, the mean of the return to risk ratio of the 'decile portfolio', where with this term we indicate the portfolio with a risk equal to a decile of the volatility interval[2] (that is the portfolios PDi with i $= 1, \ldots, 10$, plotted in Figure 3.3). Formally:

$$\text{MeRAPF} = \frac{1}{10} \sum_{i=1}^{10} \frac{R_i^*}{\sigma_i} \tag{3.3}$$

where R_i^* is the return of optimal portfolio with a risk (σi) equal to the ith decile of the volatility interval of the frontier [$\sigma\text{min} - \sigma\text{max}$].

With regard to the frontiers A and B shown in Figure 3.3, the relation $\text{MeRAPF}_B > \text{MeRAPF}_A$ confirms that it is beneficial for the investor to move towards the new efficient frontier; graphically, the level of MeRAPF is proportional to the breadth of the segments in continuous lines plotted inside the grey area that delimits the differential area of efficiency between frontier A and B.

In the case of the 'raising effect', the calculation of MeRAPF follows the same methodology used for the 'sling effect', with only one, very important exception: the decile of volatility must be related only to a volatility interval common to the two frontiers[3] (the original and the translated). In this manner, the diversification benefit for the investor moving on the frontier raised (C) is commeasured to real levels of risk realizable with a positioning on the original frontier (A) too, and this to respect of homogeneous comparison.

3.5   Empirical results

The results of our analysis on portfolio allocation are shown in Figures 3.4, 3.5, 3.6 and 3.7, and are based on an assumption of past returns as a proxy of expected returns.

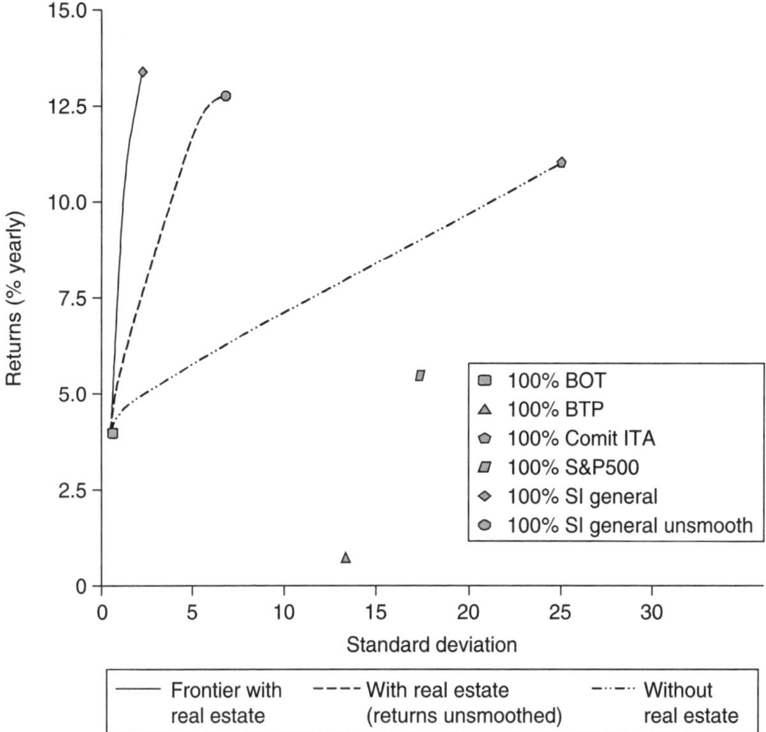

Figure 3.4   Efficient frontiers with and without real estate

Figure 3.4 shows the 'raising effect' caused by the inclusion of real estate in the portfolio, in this case approximated by the SI General Index for return smoothed and unsmoothed in accordance with the procedure previously indicated.

The subsequent figures – Figures 3.5, 3.6 and 3.7 – show the dynamic of the allocation respectively for the set of efficient portfolios without real estate, with real estate in the case of smoothed returns and with real estate after desmoothed returns.

The figures all show that every one of the portfolios lying on the efficient frontier hold a quote of real estate investment, and this independently of whether or not we use an unsmoothing procedure. Furthermore, the real estate weight prevails widely (in most cases extremely) over the weights related to the other asset class. The benefit of diversification is, in this case, very high: the change in MeRAPF moving from

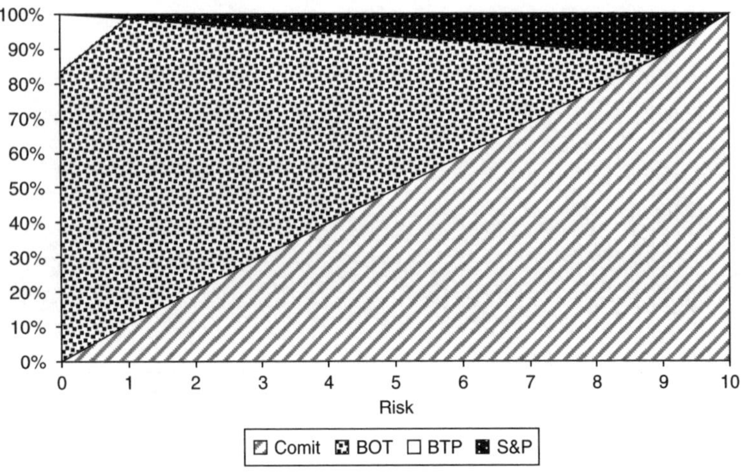

Figure 3.5   Portfolio allocation of the efficient frontier without real estate

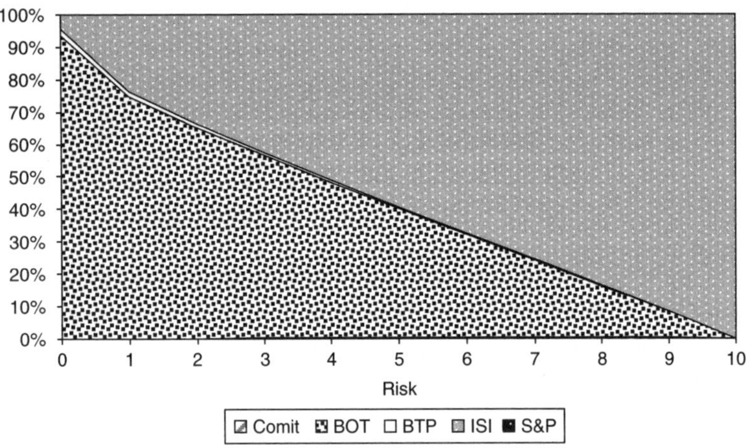

Figure 3.6   Portfolio allocation of the efficient frontier with real estate (SI general)

the frontier without to that with real estate (smoothed returns) is about ΔMeRAPF $= +91$ per cent while is equal to ΔMeRAPF $= +49.3$ per cent in case of unsmoothed returns.

Now we have to consider in detail the two results of our analysis – that is, the predominance of real estate in all portfolios along the efficient

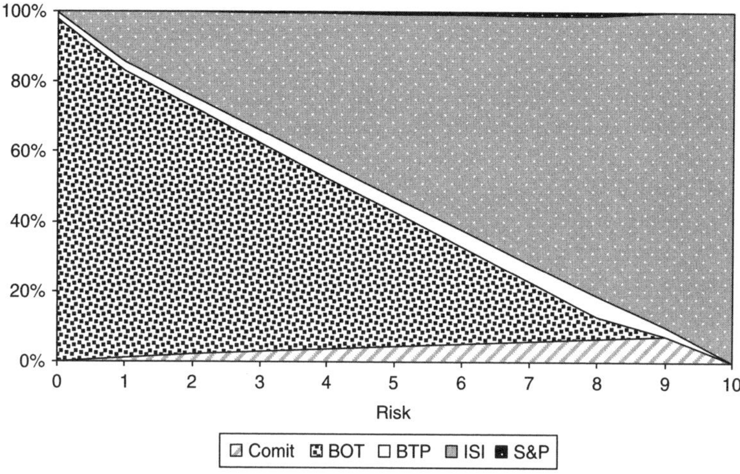

Figure 3.7   Portfolio allocation of the efficient frontier with real estate (SI general index, returns desmoothed)

frontier and the high levels of ΔMeRAPF – as excessive and misleading for at least two reasons strictly correlated between them: (1) the tendency of the mean-variance algorithm to concentrate the efficient frontier along a sequence of portfolios that is scarcely diversified; (2) a risk-adjusted return of the real estate index higher if compared to other asset classes, which causes a preference of optimizer for this type of investments (a remark consistent with point 1 above).

In order to minimize the impact of these factors on the efficient portfolio analysis, we consider it correct to face them respectively in the following two ways: (a) by making use of an alternative real estate index; (b) by making use of an alternative estimations procedure for the input of mean-variance optimization as under Bayes & Stein procedures and constrained allocations.

Regarding point (a), we substitute the 'SI General Index' for the 'SI General not Residential Index' composed of all sectors (Office, Commercial, Industrial) except the Residential. In this manner, we can use an index that is able both to sterilize the Italian residential sector that in recent years represented the sector mostly influenced by domestic speculative cycle of real estate prices, and to minimize the effects explained by previous point (2) remark. The adoption of an index with a lower risk-adjusted return should imply a set of more realistic efficient portfolios. In this case, we also tested the presence of a strong autocorrelation that

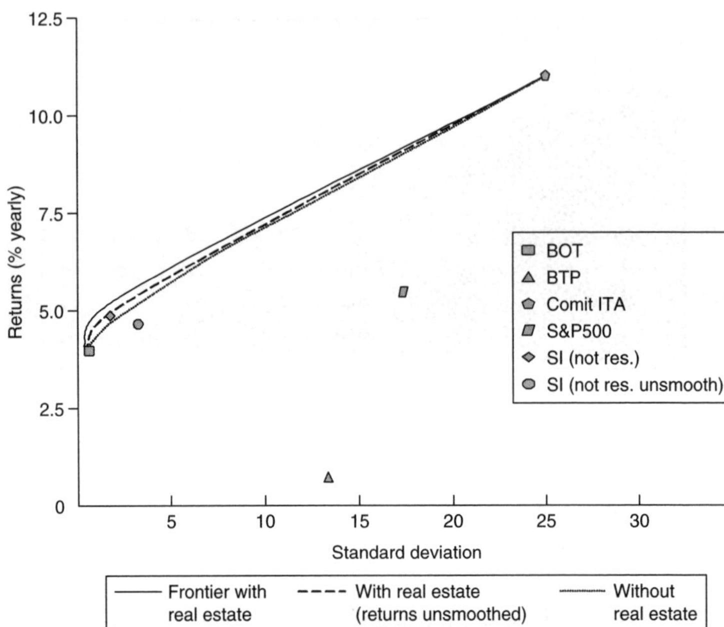

Figure 3.8   Efficient frontier with and without real estate (SI not residential)

induced the application of an unsmoothing procedure for the returns in conformity with the Geltner approach (see equation 3.2).

Concerning point (b) (the use of the alternative procedure of estimation of input of mean-variance optimization), we applied both the Bayes&Stein and the constrained portfolio procedures.

The translation to the left of the efficient frontier realized from the inclusion of real estate in a mixed-asset portfolio including domestic stock, bond and cash, also reflect a benefit in terms of the reduction of total portfolio risk for both smoothed and unsmoothed returns (see Figure 3.8).

Regarding changes in MeRAPF, the benefit realized by an investor moving from the frontier without real estate to the frontier with real estate (approximated by SI Not Residential Index, with returns smoothed) is approximately ΔMeRAPF $= +20.4$ per cent while if we use the de-smoothed returns, the benefit is reduced to ΔMeRAPF $= +12.7$ per cent. Although the exclusion of the residential component for the real estate index implies that there is a negative impact on portfolio

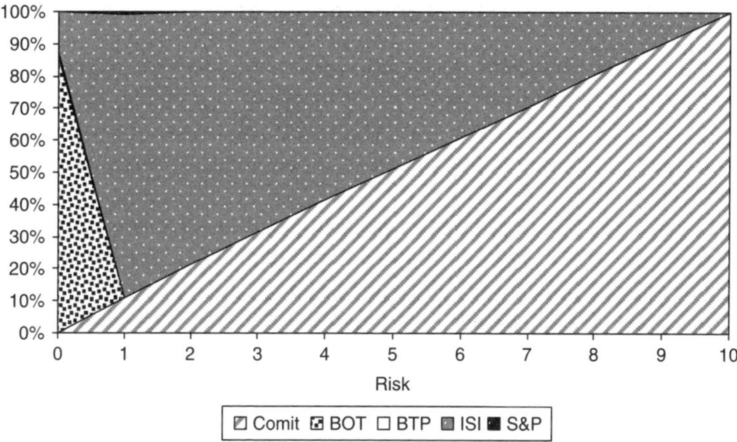

Figure 3.9   Portfolio allocation of the efficient frontier with real estate (SI not residential index, smoothed returns)

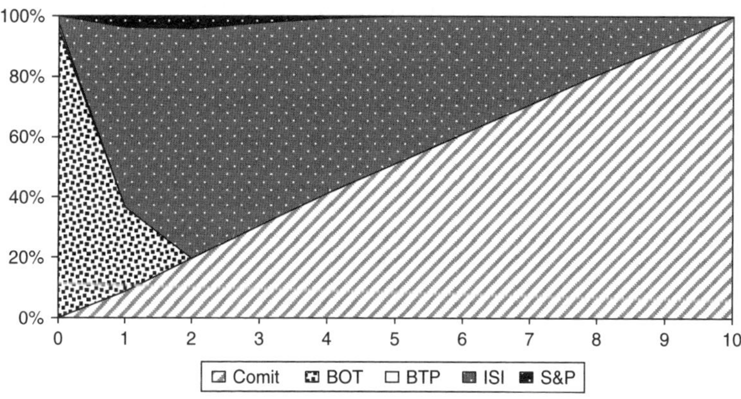

Figure 3.10   Portfolio allocation of the efficient frontier with real estate (SI not residential index, smoothed returns)

profitability, the adoption of a real estate 'Not Residential' Index (not influenced by the strong speculative movements of Italian residential real estate markets in recent years), generates, as expected, a greater diversification and, consequently, a low level of concentration of real estate in portfolio allocations – especially for the efficient frontier with unsmoothed returns (Figures 3.9 and 3.10).

3.6   Portfolio optimization and procedures of correction

Considering the need to modify the procedure adopted in traditional portfolio optimization, for improving the level of portfolio diversification along the efficient area, we proceeded following, separately, the Bayes&Stein estimators approach and the efficient frontier constrained approach.

The Bayes&Stein procedure for portfolio selection is able to reduce the dependence on pure statistically estimated data. There are many forms of Bayes&Stein procedures, all derived from well-known Bayesian theory and from the study of Stein (Stein, 1955), which shows that sample means are not an admissible statistic for a multivariate population mean under very general conditions. Stein's results implies that in many cases there are uniformly better methods for estimating optimization means than the sample mean.

Bayes&Stein estimators for mean-variance optimization are typically 'shrinkage' operators; the most widely used Bayes-Stein procedure is provided by James and Stein (1961): according to this approach, in the case of a portfolio with n assets, the estimators of a mean for each asset class may shrink sample mean toward the global mean (the means of N assets is the global mean) if they are dissimilar than if they are not. The formula for the Stein estimators of the expected value for the mean of the assets i, $E(r_i)$ is:

$$E(r_i) = \overline{r_g} + w_i(\overline{r_i} - \overline{r_g}) \tag{3.4}$$

where $\overline{r_g}$ is the global sample mean, $\overline{r_i}$ is the sample mean of asset i, and $w \geq 0$ is the 'shrink factor' of asset i whose value is derived from the following expression:

$$w_i = \max\left(0, \frac{1 - (k-3)\sigma_i^2}{\sum (\overline{r_i} - \overline{r_g})^2}\right) \quad \text{with k} \geq 3 \tag{3.5}$$

where k is the number of asset class and σ_i^2 asset i variance. The formula (3.4) shows as the estimators E(ri) shrink the sample mean ($\overline{r_i}$) to the global mean ($\overline{r_g}$), depending on asset variance (σ_i^2); shrinkage increases as a function of distance from the global mean and asset volatility (see also Efron and Morris, 1973).

Regarding the application of constraints to a portfolio, it is useful to remember that institutional portfolio optimization often includes many kinds of constraints. Generally, a constraint portfolio reflects investment

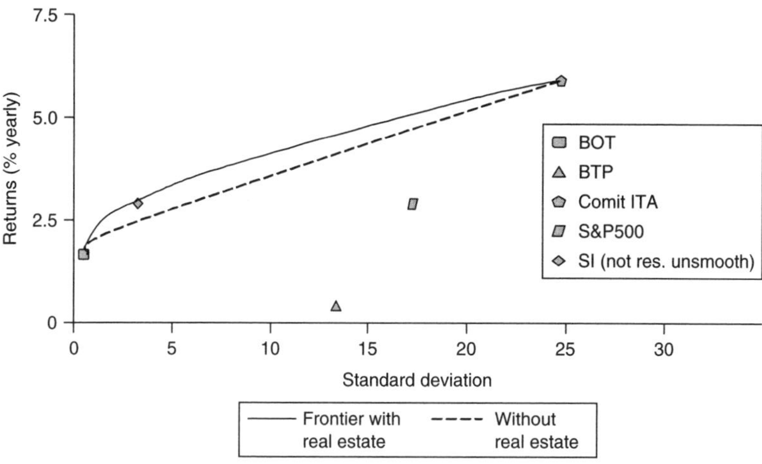

Figure 3.11   Efficient frontier with and without real estate (SI not residential index) in case of implementation of Bayes&Stein approach

strategies or market outlook information that is exogenous to return forecasts. In our case, constraints are used to control portfolio structure and avoid inadvertent risk exposures caused by an excessive size of real estate weight in portfolio.[4]

Now, concentrating our attention on the results of the application of these two procedures, Figures 3.11 and 3.12 indicate that the Bayes and Stein procedure does not solve the problem of the lack of diversification; on the contrary, It appears to accentuate this aspect. In addition, the benefit of diversification observed in this case is very limited and is equal to ΔMeRAPF $= +4.2$ per cent.

The conclusions based on the adoption of portfolio constraints are different from those given earlier. The constraints adopted in our analysis are related to those commonly used in previous studies (Lee and Stevenson, 2006) and allowing a wider diversification along the frontier (Figures 3.13 and 3.14). The presence of excessive discretionary power in the choice of portfolio constraints (in accordance with the risk tolerance of the investor), suggests however a form of caution if we using this approach. Nevertheless, the benefit of diversification is lower respect to that realized adopting Bayes&Stein (ΔMeRAPF $= +1.7$ per cent). This result is clearly due to the lower weight of real estate sector, which is upper limited to 20 per cent of the portfolio value.

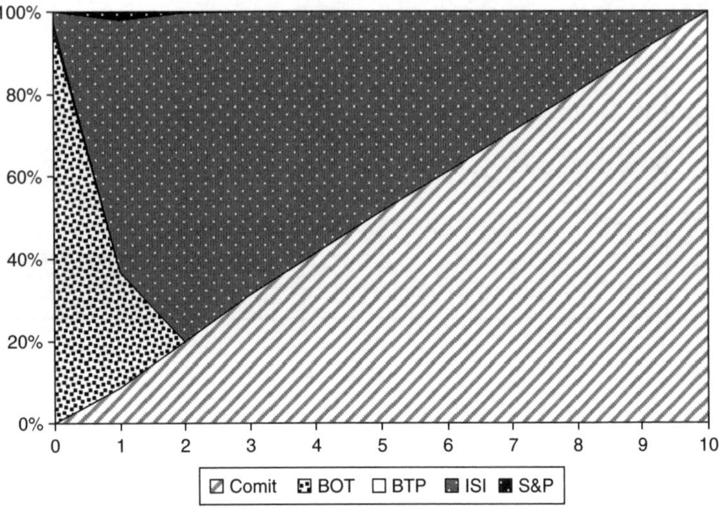

Figure 3.12   Portfolio allocation of the frontier with and without real estate (SI not residential index) – Bayes&Stein approach

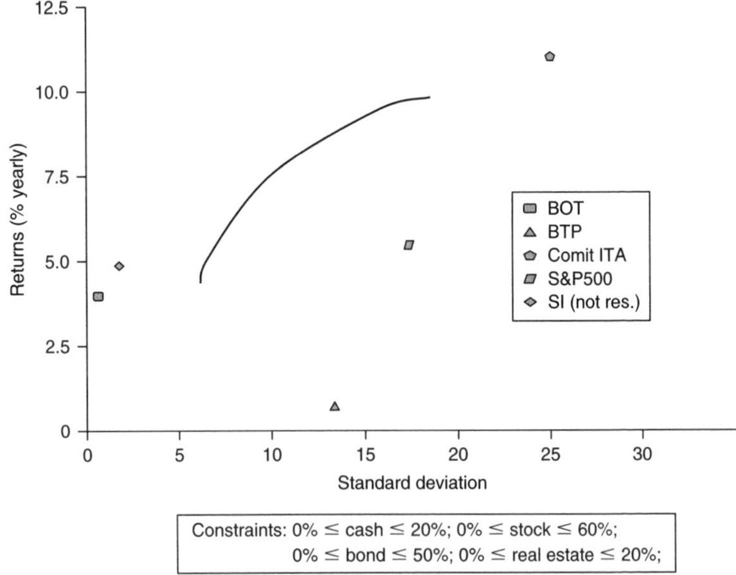

Figure 3.13   Efficient frontier constrained

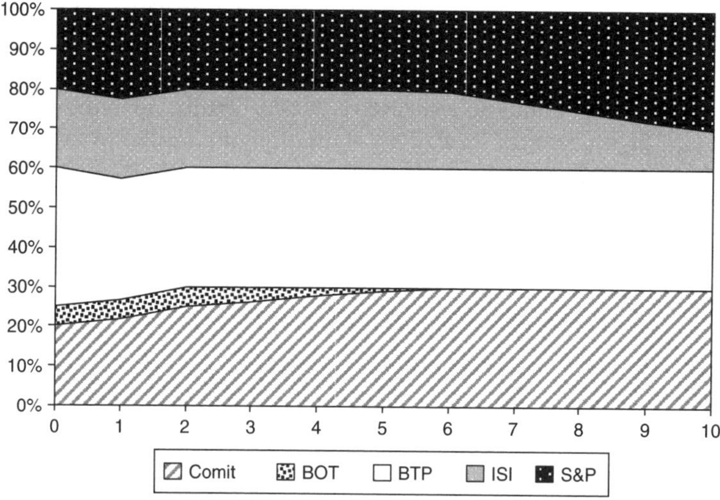

Figure 3.14 Allocation constrained

3.7 Final remarks

As an asset class, real estate features a number of fundamental characteristics that are useful and are widely accepted in most investment portfolios: the low volatility of real estate returns and the low correlation with other asset classes offer a powerful tool for portfolio diversification.

Using a traditional statistical approach, this study examines the effectiveness of MPT applied to a portfolio allocated to Italian financial asset class and also the private segment of the domestic real estate market. To determine the benefit arising from the inclusion of real estate in a specific mix portfolio of three asset classes (stock, long-term government bond, risk free rate), we adopt a measure of the shift of frontiers with and without real estate. This measure is very simple and is represented by the change of the mean risk adjusted performance of optimal portfolios (MeRAPF, Mean Risk Adjusted Performance of frontier).

The recent dramatic growth in the Italian private real estate market produces a superiority of real estate weights that is, in most cases, unacceptable for investors with low risk tolerance. To determine a more realistic (and diversified) efficient frontier, we proceed in different ways. First, we attempt to reduce the autocorrelation of real estate returns with a traditional procedure of de-smoothing; secondly, we substitute a 'general index' of the Italian real estate market with a 'not residential index' – that is, an index composed by all sectors (Office, Commercial, Industrial) except the Residential and this in the spirit of sterilizing the Italian residential sector that, in recent years, has been greatly affected by the domestic speculative cycle. Thirdly, to reinforce the attempt to mitigate the level of concentration of portfolio in real estate we use, separately, Bayes-Stein estimators and constrained portfolio optimization.

Although the results do differ, they do generally show the benefits of diversification that can result from the inclusion of real estate in a mixed portfolio. This represents a good chance for institutional investors, namely specialized closed funds: from this point of view the development of the private market can offer a further incentive to a definitive expansion of the Italian public market for real estate investments.

Notes

1. This chapter paper is the result of the authors' continuous cooperation. The Introduction and conclusion could be attributed to Claudio Porzio and other paragraphs to Gabriele Sampagnaro.
2. For example, for a frontier that moving along a continue volatility interval included between $\sigma min = 5\%$ (minimum variance) and $\sigma max = 15\%$ (maximum variance), the first portfolio decile will be that characterized by a standard deviation of $\sigma p = 6\%$, the second portfolio decile will have a volatility of $\sigma p = 7\%$, and so on until the risk of the tenth portfolio decile that, obviously, will correspond with the maximum variance ($\sigma p = 15\%$).
3. To clarify this concept we can note that, considering figure 3, the common interval correspond to $[\sigma min - \sigma max]$ of frontier C (i.e., the volatility interval of the two corner portfolios $P^C_{\sigma Max}$ and $P^C_{\sigma Min}$). If the frontier C is presented as a curve with a portfolio of max. variance ($P^C_{\sigma Max}$) and min variance ($P^C_{\sigma Min}$) respectively more and less risky of corner portfolio of the frontier A ($P^A_{\sigma Max}$ and $P^A_{\sigma Min}$), then the calculation of MeRAPF is extended to the interval $[\sigma min - \sigma max]$ of frontier A.
4. The downside of portfolio constraints is that they can lead to significant opportunity costs on investment performance if not properly used. Furthermore, overconstrained portfolios may be substantially riskier than they appear.

References

Addae-Dapaah, D., S.G. Wee and M.S. Ebrahim (2002) 'Real Estate Portfolio Diversification by Sources of Return', *Journal of Real Estate Portfolio Management*, 8: 1–15.

Banca Intesa (2001) 'Il mercato immobiliare corporate: competizione e convergenza con i mercati finanziari', *Servizio Studi – Pubblicazione Quadrimestrale*, 80.

Basile, I. and C. Porzio (eds) (2000) *La Finanza Immobiliare In Italia*, Milan: Fondazione Cariplo-Newfin Università Bocconi.

Beltratti, A. (2001) 'L'investimento nel settore immobiliare da parte degli investitori istituzionali: il caso italiano, *Ufficio Studi BNL, Problemi e Analisi*, 4.

Bond, S.A. and J.L. Glascock (2006) The Performance and Diversification of Benefits of European Public Real Estate Securities', *University of Cambridge Working Paper*.

Efron, B. and C. Morris (1973) 'Stein's Estimation and its Competitors – an Empirical Bayes Approach', *Journal of the American Statistical Association*, 68: 117–30.

Fischer, J.F. and D. Geltner (2000) 'De-lagging the NACREIF Index: Transaction Prices and Reverse Engineering', *Real Estate Finance*, 17: 7–22.

Fischer, J.F., D. Geltner and B. Webb (1994) 'Value Indices of Commercial Real Estate: a Comparison of Index Construction Methods', *Journal of Real Estate Finance and Economics*, 9: 137–64.

Frost, P.A. and J. E. Savarino (1988) 'For Better Performance: Constrain Portfolio Weights', *Journal of Portfolio Management*, 15: 29–34.

Gatzlaff, D. and D. Geltner (1998) 'A Transaction-based Index for Commercial Property and its Comparison to the NCREIF Index', *Real Estate Finance*, 15: 7–22.

Geltner, D. (1991) 'Smoothing in Appraisal-based Returns', *Journal of Real Estate Finance and Economics* 4: 327–45.

Geltner, D. (1993) 'Estimating Market Values from Appraised Values without Assuming an Efficient Market', *Journal of Real Estate Research*, 8: 325–45.

Geltner, D. (1998) 'How Accurate is the NCREIF Index as a Benchmark and Who Cares', *Real Estate Finance*, 14: 25–38.

Geltner, D. (2000) 'Benchmarking Manager Performance within the Private Real Estate Investment Industry', *Real Estate Finance*, 17: 23–34.

Geltner, D. and W.N. Goetzmann (2000) 'Two Decades of Commercial Property Returns: a Repeated-measures Regression-based Version of the NCREIF Index', *Journal of Real Estate Finance & Economics*, 21: 5–21.

Geltner, D., B.D. Macgregor and G.M. Scwann (2003) 'Appraisal Smoothing and Price Discovery in Real Estate Markets', *Urban Studies*, 40: 1047–64.

Giacotto, C. and J. Clapp (1992) 'Appraisal-based Real Estate Returns under Alternative Market Regimes', *AREUEA Journal*, 20: 1–24

Giannotti, C. and G. Mattarocci (2006) ' La costruzione di un portafoglio immobiliare e i criteri di diversificazione', in C. Giannotti, *La gestione del fondo immobiliare. Rischio, diversificazione e pianificazione*, Milan: EGEA.

Goetzmann, W.N. (1992) 'The Accuracy of Real Estate Indices: Repeat Sale Estimators', *Journal of Real Estate Finance & Economics*, 5: 5–53.

Goetzmann, W.N. (1990) 'The Performance of Real Estate as an Asset Class', *Journal of Applied Corporate Finance*, 3: 65–76.

Goetzmann, W.N. and K.G. Rouwenhorst (1999), *Global Real Estate Markets – Cycles and Fundamentals*, Yale School of Management Working Paper, New Haven.

Gyourko, J. and P. Linnemann (1988) 'Owner-occupied Homes, Income-producing Properties, and REIT as Inflation Hedges: Empirical Findings', *Journal of Real Estate Finance and Economics*, 1: 347–72.

Holsapple, E., T. Ozawa and J. Olienyk (2006) 'Foreign Direct Investment and Portfolio Investment in Real Estate. An Eclectic Paradigm', *Journal of Real Estate Management*, 12(1): 37–47.

James, W. and C. Stein (1961) 'Estimation With Quadratic Loss', *Proc. Fourth Berkeley Symp. Math. Statist. Prob.*, 1: 406–36.

Jorion, P. (1985) 'International Portfolio Diversification with Estimating Risk', *Journal of Business*, 58: 259–78.

Jorion, P. (1986) 'Bayes-Stein Estimation for Portfolio Analysis', *Journal of Financial and Quantitative Analysis*, 21: 279–92.

Kuhle, J.L. (1987) 'Portfolio Diversification and Return Benefits – Common Stock vs Real Estate Investment Trust (REIT)', *Journal of Real Estate Research*, 2: 1–9.

Lee, S. and S. Stevenson (2006) 'Real Estate in the Mixed-asset Portfolio: the Question of Consistency', *Journal of Property, Investment and Finance*, 24: 123–35.

Maspero, D. (2004) *Portfolio Selection for Financial Planners*, Newfin working paper, Milan.

Pagliari, J.L. (1995) *Handbook of Real Estate Portfolio Management*, Chicago, IL: Irwin Publishers.

Pomante, U. (2004) 'Global Asset Allocation: From the Efficient Frontier to the Reduction of the Instability due to Estimation Error', in G. De Laurentis (ed.), *Performance Measurements Frontiers in Banking and Finance*, Milan: EGEA.

Quan, D. and J. Quigley (1991) 'Price Formation and the Appraisal Function in Real Estate Markets', *Journal of Real Estate Finance and Economics*, 4: 127–46.

Richard, M. (1998) *Efficient Asset Management: a Practial Guide to Stock Portfolio Optimization*, New York: Oxford University Press.

Ross, S. and R. Zisler (1991) 'Risk and Return in Real Estate', *Journal of Real Estate Finance and Economics*, 4: 175–90.

Rubens, J.H., D.A. Louton and E.J. Yobaccio (1998) 'Measuring the Significance of Diversification Gains', *Journal of Real Estate Research*, 16: 73–86.

Saita, F. (2000) 'La valutazione delle performance dei portafogli mobiliari in gestione. L'impatto dell'orizzonte temporale', in P.L. Fabrizi (ed.), *La gestione del risparmio privato*, Rome: Bancaria Editrice.

Scenari Immobiliari (2003) *Metodologia di costruzione dell'indice ISI*, Reserved documentation.

Seiler, M.J. and V.L. Seiler (2005) 'Realistic Portfolio Allocation Decision-Making for the Small US Retail Investor', *Journal of Real Estate Finance and Economics*, 31: 319–30.

Stein, C. (1955) 'Inadmissibility of the Usual Estimator for the Mean of a Multivariate Normal Distribution', *Proc. 3rd Berkeley Symp. Math. Statist. Prob.* 1: 197–206.

Stevenson, S. (2000) 'International Real Estate Diversification: Empirical Tests Using Hedged Indices', *Journal of Real Estate Research*, 19: 105–31.

Webb, J.R. and J.H. Rubens (1987) 'How Much in Real Estate? A Surprising Answer', *Journal of Portfolio Management*, 14: 10–14.

Webb, J.R., R.J. Curcio and J.H. Rubens (1988) 'Diversification Gains from Including Real Estate in Mixed-asset Portfolio', *Decision Science*, 19: 434–52.

Yobaccio, E.J., J.H. Rubens and D.C. Ketcham (1995) 'The Inflation-hedging Properties of Risk Assets: the Case of REITS', *Journal of Real Estate Research*, 10: 279–96.

Ziobrowski, A.J. and B.J. Ziobrowski (1997) 'Higher Real Estate Risk And Mixed Asset Portfolio Performance', *Journal of Real Estate Portfolio Management* 6: 107–15.

Ziobrowski, A.J., R.W. Cairnes and B.J. Ziobrowski (1999) 'Mixed Asset Portfolio Composition with Long Term Holding Periods and Uncertainty', *Journal of Real Estate Portfolio Management* 2: 139–44.

4

Real Estate Selection and Portfolio Construction Model: Data Analysis from the Italian Market

Claudio Giannotti and Gianluca Mattarocci[1]

4.1 Introduction

The purpose of this chapter is to develop a real estate investment selection and a portfolio construction model, based on the main specific risk factors (tenant, exogenous, endogenous and financial risks).

This chapter takes into consideration the approaches used to evaluate real estate investments (section 4.2) and the main constraints of the application of the efficient frontier model to the property market (section 4.3). The assessment of real estate portfolios is completed with a study of risk profiles that are typical of a direct real estate investment (section 4.4) and an empirical test of the data drawn from a real estate sample provided by Fimit SGR (Unicredit group), whose purpose was to measure the weight of the different risk profiles in the selection and construction of a real estate portfolio (section 4.5).

4.2 Real investment valuation: characteristics and limits of the indicators

The economic evaluation of property investments can be made by applying the Discounted Cash Flow model and the summary indicators that are widely used in corporate and securities finance.

The financial sector's typical approach to investment evaluation provides for the calculation of differential (or incremental) cash flows – that is, cash flows that manifest themselves differentially, as a result of the investment, after tax and before the financial results. Debt service is not included in the calculation of significant cash flows because investment decisions must be kept separate from financing decisions, without a direct relationship between special investment and specific debt. Therefore, the weighted average cost of capital (WACC) is applied, as an expression of the target financial structure which the company aims at maintaining – or, indeed, achieving – over the years (Brealey, Myers Allen and Sandri, 2006; Pavarani, 2002; Ross, Westerfield and Jaffe, 1996).

The international literature on the property investments evaluation refers to principles that are typical of capital budgeting decisions, and show significant differences as regards their methodology and application (Damodaran, 2001, 2002; Geltner and Miller, 2001; Jaffe and Sirmans, 2001). Cash flows are differential, after tax and debt cash flow (the initial acquisition by the banks of monetary resources and the debt service in the following years). Property investment decisions, therefore, can be viewed according to an equity valuation model, wherein the positive and negative cash flows related to each single investment are regarded from the point of view of shareholders (or quotaholders), whose goal is to maximize their wealth.

In this specific case, there are two kinds of cash flows associated with property investments (Beretta, 2006; Lanzavecchia, 2007):

- annual cash flows (After Tax and Debt Cash Flow, ATDCF), corresponding to the difference between operating revenues and costs (Net Operating Income, NOI), minus capital improvements expenditure (CAPEX), debt service charges (interest and principal) and income tax;
- cash flows associated with the sale of the property (After Tax and Debt Equity Reversion, ATER), which takes account of the expected selling price and the related expenses minus taxes and the repayment of the residual debt.

The choice of the discount rate shall be consistent with the type of differential financial flows employed in the analysis. The evaluation,

Table 4.1 Expected cash flows associated with a property investment

After Tax and Debt Cash Flow (ATDCF)	After Tax Equity Reversion (ATER)
Net operating income	Expected selling price
– Capital expenditures (CAPEX)	– Selling expenses
– Debt service	– Unpaid mortgage balance
– Income tax	– Tax due on sale
= Annual net cash flow	= Net cash flow at sale of the property

therefore, must be conducted according to the cost of equity, that is, the return requested by the shareholders, based on the project's risk profile.

The most frequently used economic indicators are the Net Present Value of equity (NPV_e) and the Internal Rate of Return on equity (IRR_e).

$$NPV_e = \sum_{t=1}^{n} \frac{ATDCF_t}{(1+k_e)^t} + \frac{ATDER_n}{(1+k_e)^n} - (MV_0 - MD_0) \qquad (4.1)$$

$$\sum_{t=1}^{n} \frac{ATDCF_t}{(1+TIR_e)^t} + \frac{ATDER_n}{(1+TIR_e)^n} - (MV_0 - MD_0) = 0 \qquad (4.2)$$

where:

$ATCF_t$	is the periodic net cash flow at time t
$ATER_n$	is the net cash flow from the sale of the property at time n
n	is the expected period of investment
k_e	is the expected cost of equity
MV_0	is the market value of the property at time 0
MD_0	is the market value of the debt at time 0

Italian real estate investment funds are not subject to income tax. As a result, calculating the relevant cash flows is easier since the economic and financial impact of taxation on the investments can be ignored.

The periodic cash flows associated with the operating management of the property feature a degree of riskiness which, as a rule, is lower than the cash flow resulting from the sale of the property, the estimation of which appears to be an uncertain and complex matter. Therefore, it is easy to understand why investors with low-risk propensity primarily rely for return on their investment on rental income, while investors with a higher risk tolerance aim first and foremost to achieve capital earnings from the sale of the property (property development transactions, fractioning, and so on). The relative contribution made by the two income components (that is, the 'coupon income' paid at predetermined intervals and the 'incorporated income' made on the sale of the property) to the expected return on the investment determines the transaction's risk profile.

Thus, the investment becomes economically convenient if the VAN_e is higher than zero, i.e. if the current value of the annual net cash flows and of the cash flow resulting from the sale of the property exceeds the initial disbursement of financial resources, equal to the difference between the purchase price of the property and the financing used. The same result is obtained if the IRR_e is higher than the cost of equity.

In practice, the Internal Rate of Return on equity is preferred to the Net Present Value of equity, due to easier calculation and use. The IRR_e is a levered IRR, which also considers the debt cash flows, and differs from the unlevered IRR, which excludes all debt-related effects from the cash flows. Generally speaking, the levered IRR is higher than the unlevered IRR, as a result of the lower outlays for the shareholders, thanks to the obtaining of loans at a cost below the expected return on equity (Giannotti and Mattarocci, 2006).

In the case of the levered IRR, there is greater precision in the calculations and timing of the cash flows throughout the term of the investment, compared to the use of unlevered cash flows, which are discounted at the Weighted Average Cost of Capital (WACC), the expression of a target financial structure.[2] The analysis of the cash flow plan available to the providers of their own capital also allows a judgement on the financial viability of equity, as well as on its economic convenience (Liang, Neil and Terrance, 1998).

In the case of Italian real estate investment funds, the use of levered cash flows is unquestionably favoured by the widespread use of pertinent financing, with respect to the single properties, in which the loan repayment plan often proceeds in parallel with the property sale plan (so-called bullet loans) (Giannotti, 2005; Giannotti, 2006).

From the point of view of equityholders, the benefits of the financial leverage for a property portfolio are diverse, such as, for example, the higher returns, to the extent that the debt cost is lower than the return on investment. The debt burden also entails an increased financial risk – that is, the possibility that the real estate investment fund is incapable of meeting its payment obligations, as a result of the unexpected operating income. As a rule, it is necessary to assess whether the increased returns of the quotaholders compensates for the increased risk (Giannotti, 2006).

Despite the fact that the IRR method is more widespread in practice, it is widely known that it has certain limitations, especially with regard to the choice among alternative investments (Brearley, Myers, Allen and Sandri, 2006; Pavarani, 2002; Ross, Westerfield and Jaffe, 1996). The implicit hypothesis of reinvesting at the same IRR the positive cash flows generally entails greater problems in the case of long-term property investments with high levels of IRR. The indicator may therefore be adjusted by assuming the reinvestment of the financial resources at rates equal to the cost of equity (adjusted IRR) (Damodaran, 2001; Jaffe and Sirmans, 2001).

4.3 The application of the efficient frontier to real estate investments

The principles of the Markowitz model were used to analyse the effects of adding real estate investments to a portfolio that was initially composed of bonds and shares (multi-asset portfolios) (Adair et al., 2002; Biasin, 2005; Byrne and Lee, 2005; Hamelink and Hoesly, 1996; Lee, 2004; Muller and Muller, 2003; Sampagnaro, 2005), and then to find the efficient frontier of direct real estate investment portfolios. In the latter case, the portfolio was selected according to expected return (in terms of IRR) and expected risk (in terms of variance or standard deviation) (Del Casino, Pagliari and Webb, 1995; Friedman, 1971).

However, the application of mean-variance and efficient frontier approaches to direct real estate investments is biased by a number of constraints – partly inherent to the Markovitz theory and partly depending on the peculiarities of real estate investments and market.[3]

4.4 Diversification criteria

The analysis of real estate investments indicated that overall investment risk may be reduced by increasing the number of assets held and by investing in real estate whose value is not directly correlated to or depending on the same factors (Lee, 2005). Empirical tests showed that a diversified real estate management can give the best risk-return performance (Gyourko and Nelling, 1996).

The characteristics of real estate investments dictate that alternative criteria are identified other than the traditional geographical and sectoral segmentation that is used for financial assets in a portfolio (King, 1966). A review of the literature showed contrasting results with regard to the costs/benefits of geographical diversification (Wilson and Zurbruegg, 2003) and stressed that the efficiency of portfolio diversification based on sectoral types (office, housing, logistics, and so on) is only valid in some countries (Pagliari et al., 1997).

A number of studies in the literature agreed in classifying the main risk factors of real estate investments as tenant, exogenous, endogenous and financial risks (Cacciamani, 2003).[4]

4.5 The assessment of a real estate portfolio

Tenant, exogenous, endogenous and financial risks can impact differently on the risk-return ratio of each investment and/or the composition of a portfolio. Each risk profile can be investigated when assessing real estate investments both to obtain a fair risk-return trade-off and to maximize diversification benefits. The possibility to define an investment selection and a portfolio construction model based on the four risk profiles was tested through the construction of an efficient frontier and the use of cluster analysis, in order to assess the capability of risk profiles for sorting out investment clusters which are not correlated one another.

The efficiency of the above risk profiles was tested on a real estate sample supplied by Fimit SGR, containing individual assets with heterogeneous profiles and analysing data on the future evolution of the financial flows generated by individual real estate investments.[5]

4.5.1 Sample description

It was decided to construct a sample with different real estate with geographical area and target use criteria, trying to reproduce the same average composition of the Italian real estate market in the right proportions. The suggested analysis did not consider real estate as a whole; rather, it was focused on individual estate units in order to assess the different characteristics of individual tenants and/or the likelihood that different portions of the same building may be devoted to different uses. The analysis of this sample indicates 105 units (Figure 4.1).

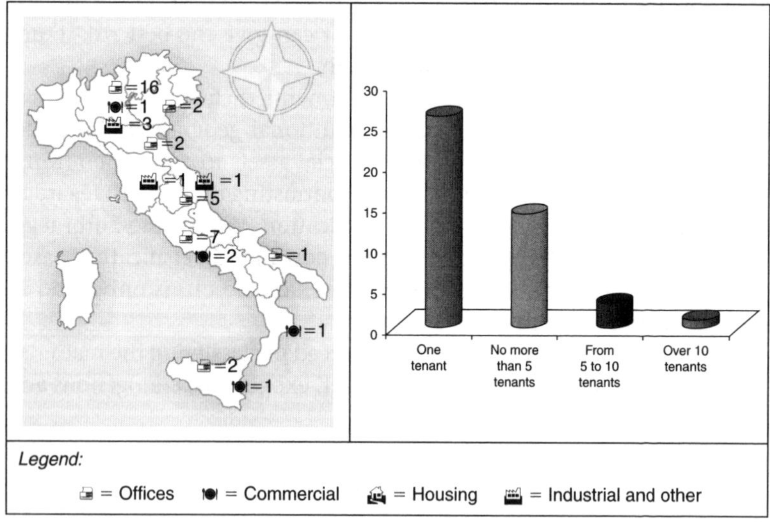

Figure 4.1   Geographical and sectoral estate distribution according to main use and number of tenants

4.5.2 The analysis of return/risk profiles in the real estate portfolio

Real estate investments were analysed using the most common approach for financial investments – namely the Discounted Cash Flow method. The risk-return ratio of a real estate investment was assessed according to the expected cash flows of the investment which may be drawn directly from the business plans of the inflows and outflows of each investment. The analysis considered a fictitious interval of time of six years, representing the predicted dismissal based on the business plan of the asset management company which had provided data.

The expected return of investment was calculated using the levered IRR (IRR_L), at the beginning assuming a scenario where investment is made without any borrowed capital and then with alternative scenarios where financial leverage is used (LTV from 0 per cent to 60 per cent).

Investment risk depends upon the uncertainty of future cash flows than can depend upon a change in the characteristics, context and/or reference market of the assets (Sivitanides et al., 1999). The lack of historical data relating to past rental evolutions and on the potential selling prices of the real estate before they are included in a real estate fund prevented any assessment of return and risk parameters with the traditional backward-looking approach. As a result, return variability was introduced by testing the impact of changing some assumptions on the real estate selling prices and – as a consequence – on the IRR of investment. A set of variability factors were investigated in detail, namely:

- the heterogeneity of the price trend of real estate in special geographical areas, which can affect the ability to sell assets in portfolio at the expected prices;
- the variableness of cap rate, that is the profit margins that can be made with a real estate investment, following external factors which are not associated with the price trend of an individual estate;
- the likelihood that the impact of any repairing work for the estate is overestimated or underestimated.

Having defined variability factors and calculated the IRR for all scenarios, the investment risk was measured as a standard deviation of the returns obtained in each scenario compared to the expected return in a case where there is a match between ex-ante flows and ex-post flows.

The efficient frontier, which was constructed with average IRR data and the covariance matrix for each rented unit, was exposed to the traditional optimizers' distortion – that is, the high concentration of investments on

Table 4.2   Aspects considered to assign risk classes to the various estate units

Risk category	Score	Main significant factors
Tenant risk	From A to D	Tenant's revenue, juridical status and financial liquidity
Endogenous risk	From A to D	Characteristics and fungibility of the real estate – Potential market replacement – Maintenance costs
Exogenous risk	From A to D	Local area characteristics – Facilities for tenant/owner – Potential use of adjacent areas
Financial risk	According to borrowing percentage	Loan characteristics – Financial leverage – Investment inflow characteristics

few asset classes. In order to obtain significantly diversified portfolios, a maximum investment limit was imposed for each estate unit with respect to total property value (6.93 per cent), which is in line with the strategies of Italian asset managers.

The approach included first of all an assessment of the individual criteria used to select the best investment opportunities (tenant, endogenous, exogenous and financial risk) (section 4.5.2.1) and then an analysis of the ability to discriminate among different risk-return ratios either by simply studying individual risk profiles (section 4.5.2.2) or by using an integrated model of several criteria (section 4.5.2.3).

4.5.2.1   *Analysis of the efficiency of selection criteria for individual real estate*

The efficiency of the criteria for investment selection – namely tenant, endogenous, exogenous and financial risks – was analysed using the efficient frontier obtained with the current risk-return values for all the real estate investments in portfolio. The real estate investments were divided into four classes, characterized by a similar tenant or exogenous or endogenous risk profile, and were given a score from A to D (Table 4.2).

By reviewing the relations between the characteristics of tenant, exogenous and endogenous risks for each estate, and the borrowing policy and investment return/risk ratio, a number of interesting connections of investment performance with some characteristics of real estate investment were found.

The first analysis of risk-return variables focused on the estate tenants' characteristics (10.77 per cent of real estate unit are vacant and are excluded from the analysis) (Figure 4.2).

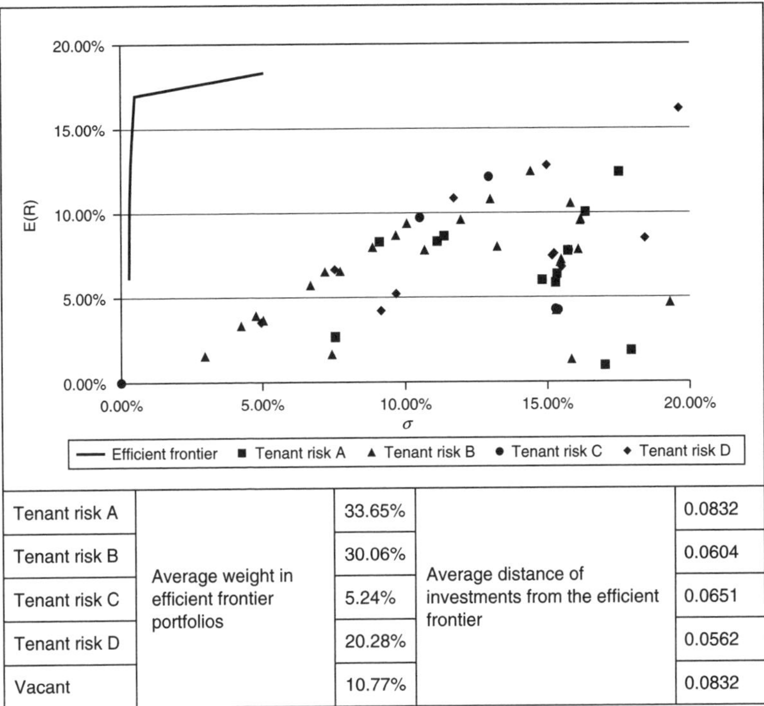

Tenant risk A	Average weight in efficient frontier portfolios	33.65%	Average distance of investments from the efficient frontier	0.0832
Tenant risk B		30.06%		0.0604
Tenant risk C		5.24%		0.0651
Tenant risk D		20.28%		0.0562
Vacant		10.77%		0.0832

Figure 4.2   Efficient frontier and tenant risk

The efficient frontier constructed by differentiating observations according to tenant risk evidenced that the real estates where tenant risk is high (mainly tenant risk C) are less efficient as an average than other rented real estates. In other words, their positioning is far from the efficient frontier. Conversely, we found that the subjects with high credit standing (tenant risks A and B) made up a very significant portion of the portfolios (more than 60 per cent) positioned on the efficient frontier.

The results relating to the weight of exogenous risk highlighted a significant prevalence of real estate with exogenous risk A in the portfolios positioned on the efficient frontier and a greater proximity of these assets to the efficient frontier itself (Figure 4.3).

These results, however, are biased by the poor weight of real estate with exogenous risks B and D that make up only 3 per cent of the sample and therefore can only play a marginal role in this analysis.

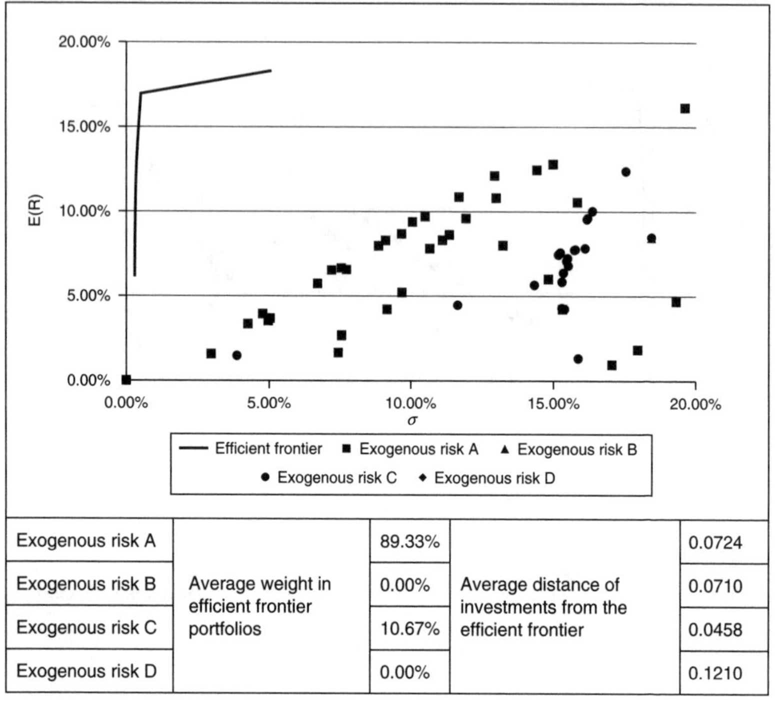

Exogenous risk A		89.33%		0.0724
Exogenous risk B	Average weight in efficient frontier portfolios	0.00%	Average distance of investments from the efficient frontier	0.0710
Exogenous risk C		10.67%		0.0458
Exogenous risk D		0.00%		0.1210

Figure 4.3   Efficient frontier and exogenous risk

The third risk profile is about the variability of the value of real estate devoted to special uses or with peculiar characteristics which make them hardly replaceable in the market (Figure 4.4).

Pure observation of the portfolios' composition on the efficient frontier and the proximity of individual real estate to the efficient frontier confirmed that more attention should be paid to those investments that are less exposed to endogenous risk (class A and mainly class B).

The analysis of the impact of leverage on real estate investments is realized considering the risk exposure for an established level of IRR_L and comparing the risk-return trade-off that could be achieved using different degrees of leverage (Boyd, Cheng, Ziobrowski and Ziobrowski, 1998). The weight of financial leverage was calculated by assuming a simplified financing pattern including a fixed-rate loan with capital repayments upon asset sales (bullet loan)[6] and using, for simplicity, an average interest rate in line with the sample of real estate secured loans.[7] The role of financial leverage was studied by calculating the expected IRR less

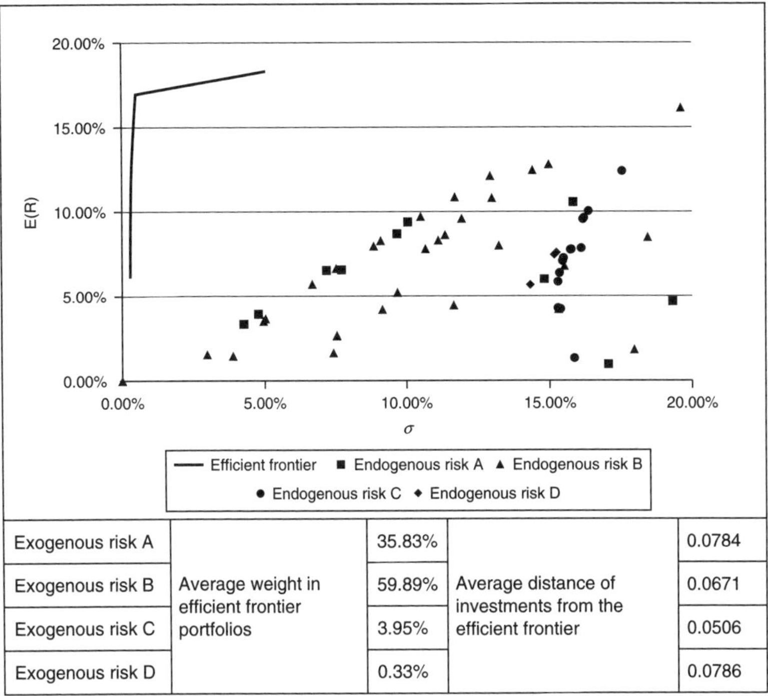

Exogenous risk A			35.83%		0.0784
Exogenous risk B	Average weight in efficient frontier portfolios		59.89%	Average distance of investments from the efficient frontier	0.0671
Exogenous risk C			3.95%		0.0506
Exogenous risk D			0.33%		0.0786

Figure 4.4   Efficient frontier and endogenous risk

debt service (IRR levered) and the variability of the new expected return for seven financial leverages from 0 to 60 per cent, assuming the same variability scenarios as the three prior analyses (cap rate variability, local price trends, pessimistic scenario where estate is sold at book value and the analysis of several scenarios with different repairing work benefits) (Table 4.3).

Looking at the results it seems clear that a higher level of leverage allows the achievement of a better risk-return trade-off, but this analysis has an important constraint about the interest rate: the cost of funding does not depend upon the debt amount.

The above studies about individual risk profiles did not prove the prevalence of either criterion in selecting the best investment opportunities. Therefore the four risk profiles must be taken jointly into consideration in order to minimize the event where one compiled portfolio deviates significantly from the investment combinations on the efficient frontier.

Table 4.3 Efficient frontier and leverage

IRR$_L$	Standard deviation					
	Leverage 10%	Leverage 20%	Leverage 30%	Leverage 40%	Leverage 50%	Leverage 60%
100%	0.59%	0.62%	0.73%	0.61%	0.52%	0.18%
105%	0.62%	0.64%	0.76%	0.65%	0.58%	0.19%
110%	0.65%	0.67%	0.79%	0.72%	0.69%	0.20%
115%	0.68%	0.70%	0.83%	0.88%	0.90%	0.21%
120%	0.71%	0.73%	0.87%	1.34%	2.14%	0.23%
125%	0.74%	0.75%	0.91%	4.05%	5.58%	0.25%
130%	0.77%	0.78%	0.96%	8.68%	10.50%	0.29%

4.5.2.2 Analysis of the criteria to construct real estate portfolios

The fact that no prevailing investment selection criterion can be found through either of the above risk factors does not rule out the benefits of using this approach to construct non-correlated investment portfolios, which reduce the overall level of investment risk (Markowitz, 1952).

The ability of quality criteria to identify investment types following different dynamics and having a significantly different risk/return ratio was tested by comparing the classifications made according to quality criteria with the results of cluster analysis. The results from the latter analysis, free from quality profiles, are therefore considered as the best diversification strategy and the clusters constructed are compared with the classifications based on the above quality profiles which can be used potentially ex-ante to construct a diversified portfolio.

Tenant, exogenous and endogenous risks were assessed using the qualitative classification supplied by Fimit SGR, and financial risk was broken down into four clusters similarly to the other criteria presented, as follows: investments with no capital borrowing (financial risk 1), 10 to 20 per cent leverage (financial risk 2), 30 to 40 per cent leverage (financial risk 3) and 50 to 60 per cent leverage (financial risk 4) (Table 4.4).[8]

A comparison of descriptive statistics and a check of the consistency of the ranking obtained from cluster analysis showed no absolute prevalence of either approach over the others, but it only allowed a relative hierarchy to be defined of individual segmentation criteria.

Among the portfolio segmentation criteria considered, tenant risk cannot be used to compile a diversified portfolio, because the clusters created with this criterion can hardly be defined as valid. Conversely, exogenous risk is the best criterion to diversify an investment portfolio, because

Table 4.4 Cluster analysis and comparison of qualitative diversification

	Degree of coherence for each risk level				Weighted average (%)
	A	B	C	D	
Tenant risk (%)	54.17	2.86	0.00	38.89	21.21
Exogenous risk (%)	57.53	0.00	0.00	2.74	44.44
Endogenous risk (%)	55.00	5.08	0.00	25.00	15.15
Financial risk (%)	100.00	0.69	0.00	33.70	19.64

the ex-ante classifications based on this quality profile coincide in 44.44 per cent of cases with the clusters constructed according to ex-post results. The other two quality criteria – namely endogenous and financial risks – provide good classification for extreme profiles (risks A and D), but not for middle profiles (risks B and C).

Lacking a prevailing segmentation criterion, it may be useful to investigate the relation among the various methods of investment selection and assess the efficiency of a joint evaluation method including several profiles.

4.5.2.3 The proposal of an integrated model for the assessment of real estate investment

Any change in the extent of leverage impacts directly on debt service cash flows and, consequently, on the amount of estimated IRR levered. The presence of more or less significant differences between levered and unlevered IRR in individual real estate can result in a greater or smaller ability of the other three quality criteria to support the efficient compilation of a real estate portfolio. As a matter of fact, a different financial leverage can affect the ex-post ranking based on cluster analysis and, consequently, it can result in a greater or smaller ability of individual quality profiles to provide classifications that are in line with the ex-post ranking.

The evaluation of the impact of financial leverage on the discriminating ability of quality criteria to select the best real estate investments can be tested by examining the consistency of cluster analysis results with quality-profile segmentation when the borrowing ratio changes. The aim of this analysis is to examine investment options and borrowing options simultaneously and see whether the management of a real estate portfolio requires that both options are managed together. This analysis was carried out by assuming the IRR levered and the standard deviation of

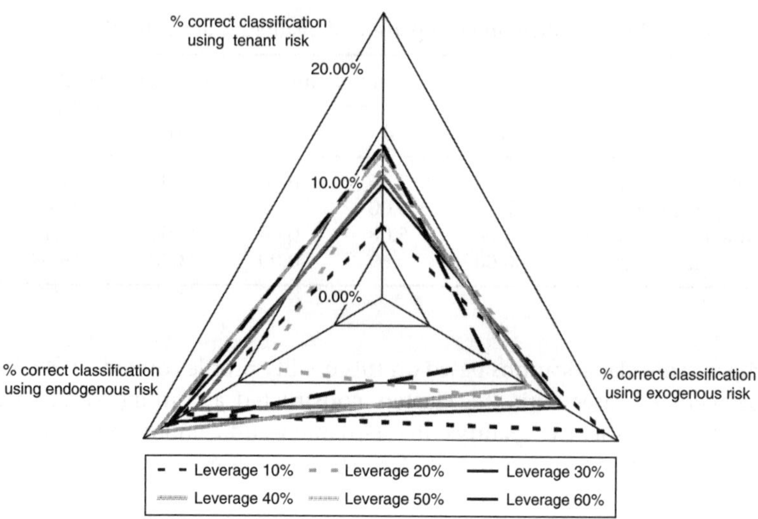

Figure 4.5   Relation of borrowing ratio and efficiency of real estate segmentation criteria

expected returns for each borrowing ratio and by repeating the cluster analysis explained above for the study on IRR unlevered (Figure 4.5).

The weight of exogenous risk and endogenous risk in the selection of real estate investments is higher than the weight of tenant risk. Any selection based on either one of these two criteria may be more or less efficient according to the borrowing ratio: for lower borrowing ratios (less than 20 per cent), a decision based on exogenous risk is the best solution, for higher borrowing ratios, endogenous risk is the best selection criterion.

Any analysis of financial investments cannot but include a careful review of the investor's financing options and the selection of the borrowing ratio will affect the criteria of portfolio composition. A correct real estate selection model should allow different weights to be assigned to the characteristics of an estate as a function of borrowing ratio and debt service costs: the greater the possibility of acting on financial leverage at arm's-length terms, the greater the likelihood that an investment portfolio providing an optimal risk-return trade-off is identified.

4.6   Conclusions

The debate on the possible application of portfolio theories to real estate investments is alive in the international literature, so much so that some authors support that real estate investments should be managed from a single-asset perspective rather than with a portfolio approach. However, the need for a formal model of portfolio optimization and investment selection is felt by sector operators.

No doubt the inefficiency of real estate markets and the peculiarities of real estate investments (high transaction costs, high unit cost, asset unevenness, and so on), as well as the scarcity of indispensable information to calculate the risk-return ratio (little disaggregate data, appraisal-based indexes, and so on), restrict the application range of portfolio theories. In particular, the use of the efficient frontier upon the initial selection of investments and a continual portfolio adaptation encounter a set of constraints, first of all the indivisibility of real estate investments and high transaction costs.

The likely developments of scientific research and practical application include the use of risk measures other than standard deviation and/or the introduction of investment constraints on the efficient frontier and/or the reduction in input estimate errors.

A study of the risk profiles that are deemed significant in the literature to explain the performance of real estate investments identified four main risk categories affecting the efficiency of investment. Correct and complete measures of tenant, exogenous, endogenous and financial risks are not yet available and some risk drivers can only be evaluated using qualitative criteria.

The empirical analysis suggested the presence of a number of peculiar characteristics that require consideration when assessing real estate investment both to obtain a fair risk-return trade-off and to maximize diversification benefits. When selecting real estate investments, the investor must focus on all risk profiles, and the best risk-return trade-off is obtained from investments where tenant, exogenous and endogenous risks are low.

When compiling a real estate portfolio, the greatest benefits can be obtained from investment diversification when investments are diversified according to exogenous risk. If the financial leverage ratio changes, the best compilation criterion for a diversified portfolio may no longer coincide with exogenous risk, so the portfolio must be constructed as a function of borrowing options.

The evolution of methods for the quantification of risk criteria and a larger availability of data on individual real estate are expected to increase the significance of the proposed assessment model and to solve some constraints and simplifications which characterise the model.

Notes

1. This chapter is the result of the authors' common efforts and continuous exchange of ideas. The individual parts of the chapter can be acknowledged as follows: sections 4.1–4.3 and 4.6 were contributed by Claudio Giannotti, and sections 4.4 and 4.5 by Gianluca Mattarocci. A preliminary edition of this work was published in C. Giannotti and G. Mattarocci, 'La costruzione di un portafoglio immobiliare e i criteri di diversificazione', in C. Giannotti (ed.) (2006), *La gestione del fondo immobiliare: rischio, diversificazione e pianificazione*, Milan: EGEA. The authors wish to thank Prof. Alessandro Carretta for his valuable advice.
2. An alternative calculation method of levered return (LR) which can be used when the unlevered return (UR), LTV and actual investment costs (i) are know is: RL = (RU − (LTV*i))/(1 − LTV). Cf. Boyd, Cheng, Ziobrowski and Ziobrowski (1998).
3. For the review of the literature, see, among the others, Giannotti and Mattarocci (2006b).
4. For a review of the literature about the efficiency of tenant, exogenous, endogenous and financial risk diversification, see Giannotti and Mattarocci (2006b).
5. Obviously, neither the data examined nor the method used nor the results obtained can be associated with a specific real estate fund or with the risk management service by Fimit SGR.
6. For further details see Giannotti (2005) and Giannotti (2006).
7. For simplicity, the model assumed that the amount of borrowed capital does not alter the cost for fund raising. By removing this simplifying method, achievable results may vary significantly, but the conclusions would be compliant with the results exposed in this chapter.
8. The upper borrowing limit is compliant to Italian laws on real estate funds.

References

Adair, A., M. Hoesli, B. MacGregor and S. McGreal (2002) *The Role of Property in Mixed Asset Portfolios*, RICS Foundation.

Beretta, S. 'Il business plan del fondo immobiliare', in C. Giannotti (ed.), *La gestione del fondo immobiliare: rischio, diversificazione e pianificazione*, Milan: EGEA.

Biasin, M. (2005) *L'investimento immobiliare*, Bologna: Il Mulino.

Boyd, J.W., P. Cheng, A.J. Ziobrowski and B.J. Ziobrowski, 'Leverage and Real Estate Investment in Mixed Asset Portfolios', *Journal of Real Estate Portfolio Management*, 4: 135–47.

Brealey, R.A., S.C. Myers, F. Allen and S. Zandri (2006) *Principi di finanza aziendale*, Milan: McGraw Hill.

Byrne, P. and S. Lee (2005) *The Impact of Real Estate on the Terminal Wealth of the UK Mixed-Asset Portfolios: 1972–2001*, London: University of Reading Business School.

Cacciamani, C. (ed.) (2003) *Il rischio immobiliare. Una soluzione di rating dell'investimento immobiliare*, Milan: EGEA.

C. Cacciamani (ed.) (2006) *I fondi immobiliari ad apporto specializzati*, Milan: EGEA.
Cacciamani, C. (ed.) (2007) *Real Estate. Economia, diritto e finanza immobiliare*, Milan: EGEA.
Damodaran, A. (2001) *Finanza aziendale*, Milan: APOGEO.
Damodaran, A. (2002) *Valuing Real Estate*, New York: John Wiley & Sons.
Del Casino, J.J., J.L. Pagliari and J.R. Webb (1995) 'Applying MPT to Institutional Real Estate Portfolios: the Good, the Bad and the Uncertain', *Journal of Real Estate Portfolio Management*, 1: 67–88
Friedman, H.C. (1971) 'Real Estate Investment and Portfolio Theory', *Journal of Financial and Quantitative Analysis*, 6: 861–74.
Geltner, D. and N.G. Miller (2001) *Commercial Real Estate Analysis and Investments*, Florence: South Western, Thompson.
Giannotti, C. (2005) 'La leva finanziaria nei fondi immobiliari ad apporto privato: vincoli, opportunità e rischi', *Bancaria*, 3 (2005): 82–96.
Giannotti, C. (2006a) 'La gestione finanziaria dei fondi immobiliari ad apporto', in C. Cacciamani (ed.), *I fondi immobiliari ad apporto specializzati*, Milan: EGEA.
Giannotti, C. (ed.) (2006b) *La gestione del fondo immobiliare: rischio, diversificazione e pianificazione*, Milan: EGEA.
Giannotti, C. and G. Mattarocci (2006a) *I finanziamenti ai fondi immobiliari: profili tecnici ed economici*, working paper del Dottorato di Ricerca in Banca e Finanza.
Giannotti, C. and G. Mattarocci (2006b) 'La costruzione di un portafoglio immobiliare e i criteri di diversificazione', in C. Giannotti (ed.), *La gestione del fondo immobiliare: rischio, diversificazione e pianificazione*, Milan: EGEA.
Gyourko, J. and E. Nelling (1996) 'Systematic Risk in the Equity REIT Market', *Real Estate Economics*, 24: 493–515.
Hamelink, F. and M. Hoesli (1996) 'Diversification of Swiss Portfolios with Real Estate: Results Based on a Hedonic Index', *Journal of Property Valuation and Investment*, 14: 59–75.
Jaffe, A.J. and C.F. Sirmans (2001) *Fundamentals of Real Estate Investment*, Florence: South Western Thompson.
King, B.F. (1966) 'Market and Industry Factors in Stock Price Behaviour', *Journal of Business*, 39: 139–90.
Lanzavecchia, A. (2007) 'L'analisi finanziaria degli investimenti immobiliari', in C. Cacciamani (ed.), *Real Estate. Economia, diritto e finanza immobiliare*, Milan: EGEA.
Lee, S.L. (2004) *When Does Direct Real Estate Improve Portfolio Performance?*, Paper presented at the annual meeting of the Pacific-Rim Estate Society, Bangkok, Thailand.
Lee, S.L. (2005) *The Marginal Benefits of Diversification in Commercial Real Estate Portfolios*, London: University of Reading Business School.
Liang, Y., M.F.C. Neil and A. Terrance (1998) 'Leverage in a Pension Fund Real Estate Program', *Real Estate Finance*, 15: 53–77.
Markowitz, H. (1952) 'Portfolio Selection', *Journal of Finance*, 7: 77–91.
Muller, A.G. and G. Muller (2003) 'Public and Private Real Estate in a Mixed-Asset Portfolio', *Journal of Real Estate Portfolio Management*, 9: 193–203.
Pagliari, J.L., A.C. Todd, J.R. Webb and F. Lieblich (1997) 'Fundamental Comparison of International Real Estate Returns', *Journal of Real Estate Research*, 13: 317–47.
Pavarani, E. (ed.) (2001) *Analisi finanziaria*, Milan: McGraw Hill.

Ross, S.A., R.W. Westerfield and J.F. Jaffe (1996) *Finanza aziendale*, Bologna: Il Mulino.

Sampagnaro, G. (2005) 'Il caso del Real Estate', in C. Porzio and E. Basile (eds), *Gli investimenti alternativi: asset allocation, strategie di gestione, valutazione delle performance*, Ricerca Newfin, no. 94.

Sivitanides, P.S., J. Southward, R.G. Torto and W.C. Wheaton (1999) 'Evaluating Risk in Real Estate', *Real Estate Finance*, 16: 15–22.

Wilson, P.J. and R. Zurbruegg (2003) *Does it Pay to Diversify Real Estate Assets? A Literary Perspective*, University of Adelaide working paper, Adelaide.

5

Funds of Funds Portfolio Composition and its Impact on Performance: Evidence from the Italian Market

Alessandro Carretta and Gianluca Mattarocci[1]

5.1 Introduction

Funds of Funds (FoF) are financial instruments that have been traded on the American market since the 1980s. In the 1990s they experienced significant growth in the United States, but only at the beginning of the new millennium did they become an actively traded financial instrument in Europe (Davidson, 2003).

The rapid growth registered in recent years could be explained in light of the high level of financial innovation that has characterized these markets. In fact, some of the proposed new instruments do achieve higher performances, but they are more complex and investors are unable to evaluate the risk profile of these financial products. As a result, the choice of delegating the selection and management of these instruments represents an alternative that is used frequently by retail and institutional investors (Liang, 2004).

The FoF manager selects investment funds using information and skills that are not likely to be possessed by investors. This selection service is remunerated by the investor, who hopes to profit from accessing this specialist financial advice (Lai, 2005).

The chapter is structured in two sections: the first explains the characteristics of the FoFs and the portfolio construction criteria (section 5.2), while the second provides an assessment of the relationship between the funds' diversification strategy and the results achieved (section 5.3).

5.2 Fund of Funds and the diversification strategies adopted

5.2.1 Definition of Funds of Funds

Mutual funds are complex financial instruments characterized by the complete – or partial – independence of the fund's manager from the investor. Some instruments are developed to reduce the information gap between the manager and the investors, but it is impossible to say that investors know everything about a particular mutual fund and they can correctly select the funds that respond better to their objectives. The lack of transparency that characterizes FoF investments, and the difficulties related to their selection, are hypotheses that justify the existence of this type of instrument (Mattoo, 2004).

FoFs are open-ended funds that differ from other mutual funds because they invest resources in individually managed funds (Bisogni, 2000). The FoF's approach is founded on the principles presented in Markowitz's (1952) work about the benefits of diversification and represents an application of the theoretical results about the relationship between the size and the variance of a portfolio (Elton and Gruber, 1977). Earlier works consider the effect of diversification on a portfolio of stocks and/or bonds (Evans and Archer, 1968) but, more recently, some authors have presented studies about the impact of diversification among different mutual funds (Statman, 2004). The higher benefits related to the diversification of the portfolio could be explained as an effect of the reduction of the unsystematic risk that characterized a well-diversified portfolio (Lhabitant and Learned, 2002) and higher benefits are related to FoFs that invest in actively managed funds, where the opportunity to reduce active risks allows the extension of the potential subscriber base (Warning et al., 2000).

The FoF offers the opportunity to diversify investment by selecting a range of portfolio managers with different investment styles that select financial instruments ranging across different geographical areas or different industrial sectors (Still, 2004). The main advantage of investing in a FoF must be identified in the possibility of increasing the capabilities of selection using a multi-manager approach: in fact, good results could be achieved more easily if the FoF manager chooses to hire managers that are specialized in investing in particular assets and compose a portfolio with funds managed by these managers (Barry and Starks, 1984).

This type of instrument represents a high-risk investment opportunity, because the final composition of a portfolio is the result of choices realized by different managers, each of whom have different objectives and strategies. In fact, investors can select the FoF manager, but they do not control the manager's choices about the diversification level and criteria adopted in the selection of mutual funds (Cardani et al., 2003). Furthermore, the FoF manager defines the portfolio's composition in terms of selecting mutual funds, but he does not control investments made by single portfolio managers, and it could be that the expected strategies/performances of the mutual fund managers do not respond to the ex-post results (Jerome, 2004).

FoF managers are paid for this selection service, like other mutual fund managers, according to different types of fees: a management fee that represents a fixed remuneration for the funds' selection and an incentive fee that is related to the performance of the fund (Colombini et al., 2003). Investors thus pay a double commission for investing in FoFs, commissions to individual fund managers and fees to FoF managers, and so these instruments could be more expensive than a self-made portfolio of mutual funds (Liang, 2002). The higher level of commissions that characterized these funds could only be justified if the portfolio composition service secures an extra performance that the investor cannot achieve with other financial instruments (Brown et al., 2004).

5.2.2 Types of diversification strategies and portfolio's heterogeneity constraints

The main characteristics of a FoF can be identified in: (i) the number of funds included in the portfolio; (ii) the criteria adopted for the selection; and (iii) the selection constraints that managers are subject to.

The choice of the number of funds to include in the FoF portfolio must consider that the benefits related to the introduction of a fund in a diversified funds' portfolio are lower for more highly diversified portfolios (O'Neal, 1997). The number of funds must be defined taking into account the pay-off between risk diversification and trading costs: a high number of funds increases the likelihood of high performance stability, but it also causes higher transaction costs and lower net gains (Statman, 2004). Empirical analysis shows that greater benefits are obtained by portfolios that invest in ten or twenty funds, as a function of the correlation between single portfolios (Farrell and Gregoriou, 2000), but there is evidence that, in certain markets, the number of funds is significantly lower (Brands and Gallagher, 2003). The reduction of benefits related to the diversification could be explained by analysing the inefficiencies of multi-fund portfolios: a higher segmentation of wealth on different fund managers increases the probability of the duplication of holdings and it is also likely that strategies adopted by different fund managers are not finely tuned (Connelly, 1997). The number of funds to include in a hypothetical portfolio depends upon a number of factors, including the risk profile of a typical subscriber, the sectoral and geographical specialization and the covariance between different sectors and geographical areas (Moultrup, 1998).

The FoF's results are influenced by the criteria that are adopted to build the portfolio and investors select the FoF that best fits their risk-return preferences (Amenc et al., 2004). The criteria adopted could be classified into four main strategies: the naïve approach, the style approach, the past performance analysis and the reputation approach.

The naïve approach assumes that all of the different investment opportunities have the same trend and that the investment selection does not provide an improved performance. Portfolio managers that adopt this strategy do not assess different investment opportunities and are interested only in selecting the correct number of funds to include in the portfolio (Park and Staum, 1998). This approach could be acceptable if the FoF manager assumes that the results achieved by fund managers are independent from the managers' capabilities and so a random selection represents the best solution to minimize the impact of unpredictable events that could cause a negative performance for a single fund (Sharpe, 1981).

The style approach selects funds based on the style adopted by the fund manager and defines a portfolio that includes funds characterized by different investment styles (Moultrup, 1998). Empirical studies demonstrate that managers who adopt the same investment style achieve results that are highly correlated, and so a fund selection based on the investment style could be useful in constructing a well-diversified portfolio (Brands and Gallagher, 2005).

The assumption of the persistence in time of the results achieved by a fund manager mean that it is rational to consider past performance when selecting funds (Grinblatt and Titman, 1992). FoF managers that adopt this approach analyse the performances achieved in previous years, and the risks related to particular portfolios, and they also try to identify the best current managers (Bird and Gallagher, 2002). The higher results obtained by fund managers that have had positive performances in the past could offer an explanation of investors' choices: in open-ended funds investors are likely to withdraw their money from poorly performing mutual funds (Berk and Xu, 2004) and these choices could cause a lack of liquidity for the fund manger that had to change investment decisions made in order to take account of the less money available (Carhart, 1997).

The analysis of past performance is influenced strictly by the time period analysed and so some FoF managers prefer to integrate this approach considering other specific factors related to the manager's characteristics. This approach, called the reputation approach, also analyses other managers' characteristics such as experience or instruction

(Chevalier and Ellison, 1999) that could influence the level of performance achieved. The analysis of qualitative and quantitative aspects is realized using the rating attributed to each fund (Sharpe, 1998): this instrument represents an useful tool to select investment opportunities especially when the results achieved by a manager are heavily influenced by a particular market trend, because past results do not represent a good proxy of future performances if the market conditions vary (Black and Morey, 2000).

The FoF could be constituted by selecting either from among all of the investment opportunities or only in a restricted pool of investment funds offered by the same investment company that creates the FoF, or by a company from the same group (Linciano and Marrocco, 2002). These types of investment products are built considering a smaller set of investment opportunities, and offer only partial diversification, which does not consider the opportunity of a diversification of judgement (Cucurachi, 2005): better results achieved by this strategy could be a consequence of lower fees applied by the investment companies within the group (Lazzari, 2003).

5.3   Research design

The proposed analysis considers the impact of the diversification level and funds' selection strategy on the portfolio results. The study is released considering both the performance achieved and the risk exposure of the FoF portfolios using the standard RAP approach.

The choices of FoF managers in portfolio composition can impact upon the performance and criteria adopted in the fund selection process and allow for the achievement of better results compared to other funds. The analysis proposed considers the main differences in FoF results that could be explained analysing the different criteria adopted in portfolio composition. The analysis of the FoF is possible only for those funds that invest in standard financial instruments that are obliged to give information about investments released.

5.3.1   Data

The FoF analysis is based on the instruments offered in Italy, a new market featuring a significant growth in recent years. The study considers all of the FoF traded in the Italian market since the launch of the first such fund – by Arca SGR in 2000. The complete database consists of 137 funds offered by 25 different investment companies (Figure 5.1).

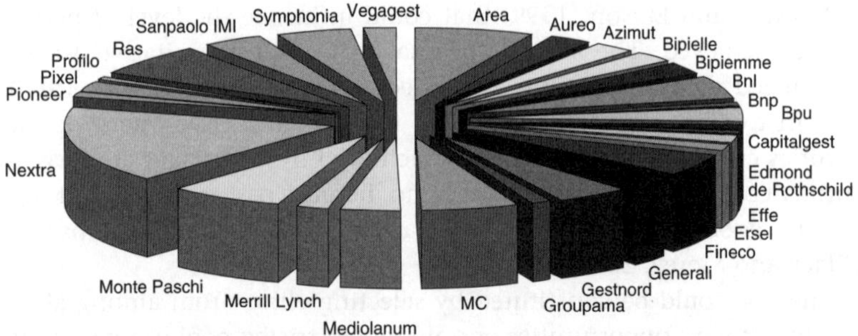

Figure 5.1   Funds of Funds' investment companies in the Italian market
Source: Assogestioni data processed by authors

The market is highly concentrated, but products offered by each investment company are heterogeneous and so it is possible to verify whether the different criteria impact on the performance achieved.

The performance time series data are collected using the Morningstar database and the qualitative data relating to the FoF investment choices are collected from the fund analyses issued by Bluerating for each FoF.

5.3.2   Methodology

The study analyses different aspects related to the remuneration mechanism and fund selection mechanism. The aspects considered in the paper are the management and incentive fee, the level of industrial and sectoral diversification of the funds selected and the criteria adopted for fund selection purposes by the FoF managers.

Firstly, the performance analysis is carried out using a descriptive approach that tries to point out if there is a relationship between gains and type of FoF remuneration. A more detailed analysis is proposed using the standard RAP approach and the persistence analysis of the results achieved; in this second analysis the main purpose is to identify the best criteria to construct a portfolio of mutual funds. For the analysis we use only RAPs that employ standard deviation or Beta as a measure of risk, because the main objective of the work is to study the relationship between portfolio composition and the FoF risk/return profile and so, as in Markowitz's paper (Markowitz, 1952), we do not use alternative risk measures.

5.3.3   Results

The analysis of the FoF's convenience for investors must consider the returns of these types of instruments in the period concerned.

Table 5.1 Performance of Funds of Funds

		Bear market		Bull market	
		2001	2002	2003	2004
Gross Gain	Mean (%)	−7.05	−15.45	6.39	6.39
(GG)	Maximum (%)	3.80	20.60	41.80	13.40
	Minimum (%)	−22.50	−36.60	−4.90	−5.40
Management	Mean (%)	1.00	1.11	1.11	1.17
Fee	Maximum (%)	1.60	2.50	2.50	2.75
	Minimum (%)	0.00	0.00	0.00	0.00
Incentive	Mean (%)	0.01	0.31	0.37	0.18
Fee	Maximum (%)	0.01	5.6	5.50	2.80
	Minimum (%)	0.00	0.00	0.00	0.00
Net Gain	Mean (%)	−8.05	−16.87	4.91	2.34
(NG)	Maximum (%)	2.879	12.50	39.71	11.50
	Minimum (%)	−23.48	−36.60	−5.60	−7.50

Source: Bluerating data processed by authors.

The simple analysis of the results achieved by the FoF highlights that the period concerned is characterized by both a bull and a bear market phase (Table 5.1). The first two years (2001–2002) are the worst years for the FoF market and in the last two years under consideration (2003–2004) there was clear evidence of a new upturn in the market.

The strategies adopted to remunerate FoF managers can influence the results obtained by the FoFs. The choice to adopt a remuneration mechanism linking fees with results achieved could encourage managers to achieve better performance. The following table analyses separately the results achieved by FoFs that use an incentive fee and the results of those that do not apply this type of remuneration (Table 5.2).

The analysis of performance highlights the point that the funds that offer incentive fees cause extra positive performances in the bull market (years 2003–04), but also higher losses in the bear market (years 2001–02) (Elton et al., 2003). This result could be explained by considering that a fund manager who is paid according to an incentive fee mechanism is liable to be more active in the market and this approach makes the best benefits when there are profitable opportunities, but is a failure when the high frequency of portfolio re-balances causes only higher transaction costs, due to the relative absence of good investment opportunities (Wermers, 2000).

The analysis of the impact of portfolio characteristics on the results achieved by FoFs is a partial analysis because it considers only one of

Table 5.2   Performance of Funds of Funds and incentive fees

		FoFs with incentive fees	FoFs without incentive fees	
2001	Mean Gross Gain (%)	−13.03	−7.05	BEAR MARKET
	Mean Net Gain (%)	−11.05	−8.05	
2002	Mean Gross Gain (%)	−20.86	−14.23	BEAR MARKET
	Mean Net Gain (%)	−23.83	−15.31	
2003	Mean Gross Gain (%)	10.56	5.03	BULL MARKET
	Mean Net Gain (%)	7.88	3.94	
2004	Mean Gross Gain (%)	4.43	3.52	BULL MARKET
	Mean Net Gain (%)	2.29	2.36	

Source: Bluerating data processed by Authors.

the aspects considered by investors to select investment opportunities. A more detailed analysis of the results achieved by the FoFs is issued using the RAP approach and analysing the extra-return per unit of risk exposure. RAPs considered in the study are a measure grounded on the same criteria adopted by Markowitz to define diversification benefits and, in particular, the RAP selected are the Sharpe ratio (Sharpe, 1994), the Information ratio (Goodwin, 1998), the Treynor index (Treynor, 1965) and the Jensen's alpha (Jensen, 1968).

The analysis on the overall sample highlights that results achieved in the 2002 are, on average, lower than the results achieved in other years. This trend in the Italian FoF market is not strange because all the most important world financial markets achieved, in this year, low results and all investment products traded in Italy registered the same result (Assogestioni, 2004) (Table 5.3).

To make a more detailed study of the results achieved by FoFs, an analysis of the results achieved by some sub-samples, characterized by different remuneration mechanisms and different fund classification in the Assogestioni database and different exposure to geographical/sectoral risk, has been issued (Table 5.3).

The first interesting finding from the study is the relationship between the remuneration mechanism and the results achieved: FoFs that applied incentive fees, as demonstrated for other mutual funds (Brown et al., 1996), achieved higher results in terms of return per unit of risk, compared to the mean result obtained in the overall sample.

Another possible criteria used to select FoFs is the type of investment released and there some studies in literature that demonstrate that differences in the funds' style influence the results achieved (Grinblatt and

Table 5.3   RAP for Funds of Funds classified on the basis of fees and portfolio composition.

	All sample	Subsample				
		FOFs with incentive fees	Specialized stocks	Specialized bonds	Flexible	Balanced
S_{2002}	−7.60	−8.82	−1.38	−1.43	−4.33	−2.26
	(0.0389)	(0.0345)	(0.0299)	(0.0631)	(0.0423)	(0.0288)
SO_{2002}	−1.93	−4.29	−16.16	9.79	−27.33	−10.53
	(0.0402)	(0.0627)	(0.0553)	(0.0244)	(0.0582)	(0.0256)
TR_{2002}	−10.41	−14.59	0.84	−0.79	−3.67	−3.02
	(0.2327)	(0.0725)	(0.0752)	(0.5084)	(0.3629)	(0.0469)
IR_{2002}	−1.33	−3.63	3.78	−1.33	−0.25	0.93
	(0.0661)	(0.0641)	(0.0403)	(0.0906)	(0.0942)	(0.0644)
S_{2003}	1.67	3.16	2.63	−0.27	−2.13	−1.28
	(0.0547)	(0.0727)	(0.0467)	(0.0915)	(0.0757)	(0.0292)
SO_{2003}	0.31	2.96	8.83	0.33	25.38	1.30
	(0.0521)	(0.0878)	(0.0680)	(0.0116)	(0.0694)	(0.0274)
TR_{2003}	5.82	8.88	1.61	0.27	−5.13	−3.23
	(0.2029)	(0.1502)	(0.117)	(0.0669)	(0.6847)	(0.029)
IR_{2003}	−0.93	1.01	4.94	7.86	2.80	5.46
	(0.0733)	(0.0876)	(0.057)	(0.1007)	(0.0999)	(0.0609)
S_{2004}	5.48	5.72	−0.02	−0.19	−0.90	−1.28
	(0.0597)	(0.0439)	(0.0438)	(0.1038)	(0.0808)	(0.0402)
SO_{2004}	−0.62	0.08	7.47	2.95	1.10	3.80
	(0.0406)	(0.0689)	(0.0581)	(0.0169)	(0.0401)	(0.0266)
TR_{2004}	4.75	7.21	−0.36	−1.57	−3.10	−4.15
	(0.0598)	(0.0777)	(0.0693)	(0.0672)	(0.0728)	(0.0316)
IR_{2004}	−2.31	0.12	−1.38	−1.43	−4.33	−2.26
	(0.0884)	(0.0797)	(0.0667)	(0.1538)	(0.0706)	(0.0716)

Notes: Data presented are mean values in italics and the standard deviation in brackets.
S = Sharpe Index; SO = Sortino Index; TR = Treynor Index; IR = Information ratio.
Source: Fondionline data processed by authors.

Titman, 1993). FoFs are classified into four classes, based on the basis of the relative importance of risky and unrisky assets in the portfolio (stocks, obligations, flexible and balanced) and the RAP analysis points out some difference among these classes. The results obtained do not highlight that there is a best class of FoFs for all the time period considered and the unique result is that mean higher performances are obtained by the stock FoFs, but maximum results aren't obtained by funds classified in this group.

Table 5.4   RAP for Funds of Funds classified on the basis of geographical and sectoral concentration

RAP measures	All sample	Subsample			
		Geographical concentrated	Geographical not concentrated	Sectoral concentrated	Sectoral not concentrated
S_{2002}	−7.60	−8.09	−7.35	−6.69	−7.94
	(0.0389)	(0.0419)	(0.0373)	(0.0457)	(0.0358)
SO_{2002}	−1.93	−1.91	−1.94	−2.65	−1.66
	(0.0402)	(0.0204)	(0.0476)	(0.0579)	(0.0314)
TR_{2002}	−10.41	−13.36	−8.86	−10.73	−10.29
	(0.2327)	(0.1689)	(0.2598)	(0.0797)	(0.2687)
IR_{2002}	−1.33	−1.15	−1.43	−2.62	−0.86
	(0.0661)	(0.0661)	(0.0666)	(0.0741)	(0.0628)
S_{2003}	1.67	0.18	2.32	1.79	1.62
	(0.0547)	(0.0473)	(0.0568)	(0.036)	(0.0604)
SO_{2003}	0.31	−1.09	0.93	−1.10	0.84
	(0.0521)	(0.0238)	(0.0596)	(0.0315)	(0.0572)
TR_{2003}	5.82	6.82	5.39	3.41	6.71
	(0.2029)	(0.3379)	(0.1004)	(0.0582)	(0.2344)
IR_{2003}	−0.93	−2.88	−0.07	−2.59	−0.32
	(0.0733)	(0.0686)	(0.0741)	(0.0597)	(0.0771)
S_{2004}	5.48	6.09	5.16	5.20	5.58
	(0.0597)	(0.0728)	(0.0516)	(0.0563)	(0.0611)
SO_{2004}	−0.62	−0.76	−0.55	−1.77	−0.21
	(0.0406)	(0.0288)	(0.0457)	(0.0511)	(0.0355)
TR_{2004}	4.75	3.54	5.39	4.89	4.70
	(0.0598)	(0.0477)	(0.0646)	(0.0559)	(0.0614)
IR_{2004}	−2.31	−3.57	−1.64	−2.80	−2.13
	(0.0884)	(0.1033)	(0.0793)	(0.0902)	(0.0882)

Notes: Data presented are mean values in italics and the standard deviation in brackets.
S = Sharpe Index; SO = Sortino Index; TR = Treynor Index; IR = Information ratio.
Source: Fondionline data processed by author.

Another aspect considered in the standard analysis of a mutual fund is the sectoral and geographical concentration (Potter, 2001). The importance of these two aspects is related to the traditional debate presented in literature about the useful criteria for maximizing portfolio diversification (King, 1966) (Table 5.4).

The RAP analysis highlighted that there is no clear superiority of one criteria of selection, and the only conclusion that can be drawn from the data is that the diversification benefits are higher during a bear market phase, when a well-diversified portfolio minimizes losses.

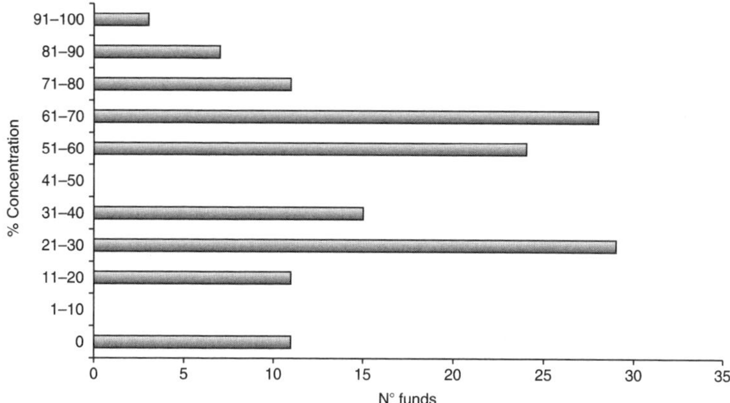

Figure 5.2   Funds of Funds portfolio concentration
Source: Fondionline data processed by authors.

The impossibility of defining suitable criteria for selecting FoFs, using the standard approach adopted to evaluate other investment funds, makes it clear that other aspects are relevant in an FoF evaluation. A more detailed analysis is released using information collected by reports of each FoF and the focus is on aspects that seem to be more relevant in the Italian market.[2]

The first aspect considered in the analysis is the percentage of funds bought that are created by the same SGR, or by related investment companies, and the number of funds where the manager invests (Figure 5.2). In fact, the analysis of information available reveals that FoF portfolios are very heterogeneous: less than 10 per cent of the FoFs analysed could be considered non-concentrated and others feature a different level of concentration that indicates different strategies adopted by FoF managers (Figure 5.2).

Another difference can be identified in the constraints applied to the portfolio selection. The Italian FoF market does not feature a clear prevalence of one type of FoF: fewer than 0.5 per cent of the available FoFs do not invest in funds issued by the same company, or by companies of the same group, and less than 5 per cent invest only in related funds (Figure 5.3).

In the evaluation of FoFs, the strategy adopted for fund selection purposes is also relevant. The analysis of the diversification strategy is released analysing each FoF prospect and the selection strategy declared by the FOF manager. Clustering FoFs on the basis of four main strategies

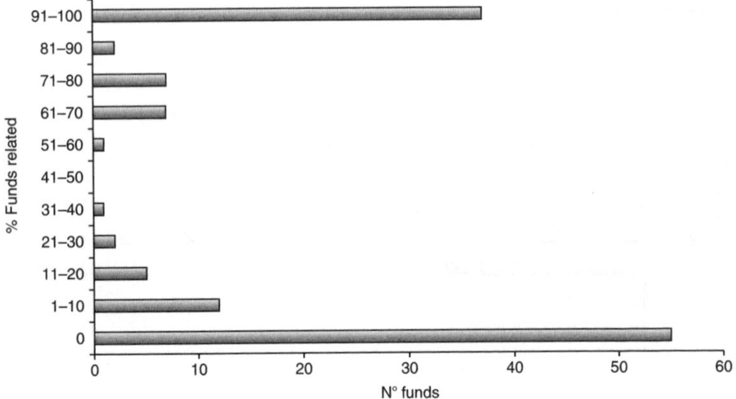

Figure 5.3   Funds of Funds portfolio percentage invested in related funds
Source: Fondionline data processed by authors.

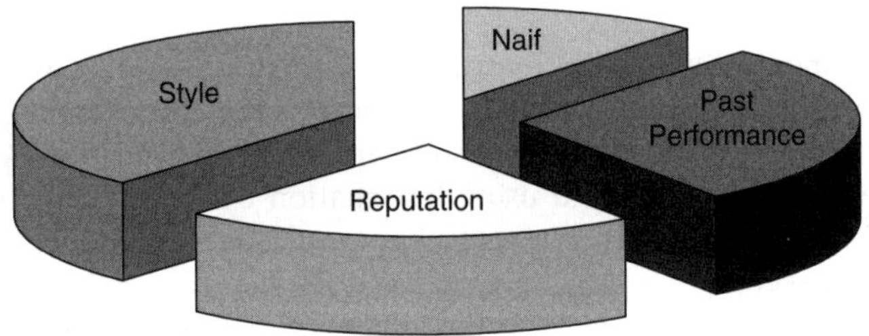

Figure 5.4   Funds of Funds' diversification strategies
Source: Fondionline data processed by authors.

of selection analysed in the previous section, it becomes clear that there is no leading strategy adopted by the Italian FoF managers[3] (Figure 5.4).

This brief analysis highlights clearly that the FoF market is characterized by a high degree of heterogeneity, and it could be useful to check whether the different aspects that are analysed have a clear impact on the performance achieved. The analysis of the choices made by FoF managers reveals a relationship between the criteria adopted, the relevant constraints and the results achieved (Table 5.5).

The analysis of the constraints and strategies adopted for the purposes of fund selection highlights some interesting aspects that could be useful in the selection of a FoF. In more than 80 per cent of cases, FoF managers who invest a significant amount of the money managed[4] in a small number of funds issued by the same investment company, or by related companies, achieve a lower result than other FoFs. This result could be

Table 5.5 RAP for Funds of Funds on the basis of linkage and concentration

RAP measures	All sample	Subsample			
		Funds linked	Funds not linked	Funds concentrated	Funds not concentrated
S_{2002}	−7.60	−8.16	−7.24	−6.06	−7.99
	(0.0389)	(0.0396)	(0.0383)	(0.0358)	(0.0389)
SO_{2002}	−1.93	−1.92	−1.93	−1.06	−2.17
	(0.0402)	(0.0196)	(0.0494)	(0.0365)	(0.0409)
TR_{2002}	−10.41	−13.21	−8.57	3.59	−13.56
	(0.2327)	(0.1583)	(0.2703)	(0.4738)	(0.1213)
IR_{2002}	−1.33	−1.37	−1.31	0.88	−0.14
	(0.0661)	(0.0649)	(0.0675)	(0.0715)	(0.1718)
S_{2003}	1.67	0.32	2.40	2.94	−4.47
	(0.0547)	(0.0445)	(0.0586)	(0.0412)	(0.5599)
SO_{2003}	0.31	−1.08	1.07	0.88	6.01
	(0.0521)	(0.0225)	(0.0615)	(0.0154)	(0.5582)
TR_{2003}	5.82	6.13	5.66	4.18	7.64
	(0.2029)	(0.3148)	(0.1034)	(0.0622)	(0.2605)
IR_{2003}	−0.93	−2.82	0.10	3.00	2.52
	(0.0733)	(0.064)	(0.0763)	(0.0602)	(0.417)
S_{2004}	5.48	5.52	5.46	8.33	6.12
	(0.0597)	(0.0705)	(0.0515)	(0.0651)	(0.1399)
SO_{2004}	−0.62	−0.91	−0.43	0.33	−0.80
	(0.0406)	(0.0274)	(0.0476)	(0.0511)	(0.0383)
TR_{2004}	4.75	3.35	5.71	7.19	6.23
	(0.0598)	(0.0458)	(0.0663)	(0.0711)	(0.2115)
IR_{2004}	−2.31	−4.17	−1.04	3.33	−3.38
	(0.0884)	(0.1005)	(0.0773)	(0.0941)	(0.084)

Notes: Data presented are mean values in italics and the standard deviation in brackets.
S = Sharpe Index; SO = Sortino Index; TR = Treynor Index; IR = Information ratio.
Source: Fondionline data processed by authors.

considered rational if the benefits related to lower fees are not sufficient to justify a selection realized on a restricted set of mutual funds, and this result is the same obtained by similar analyses carried out on the Italian market (Cinquemani and Siciliano, 2001).

Compared to other studies in the literature, portfolio concentration is analysed using an unusual approach. Previous studies consider the number of funds included in the portfolio managed (Connelly, 1997) and they do not evaluate that it is possible to differentiate investments not only using a different set of funds, but also investing a higher/lower percentage of wealth in a particular fund. The analysis presented considers the percentage of wealth invested in the five most important funds and classifies as concentrated each FoF that invests more than the 70 per cent of money managed in this set of funds. The results obtained highlight that more concentrated funds achieve higher results, on average, than less concentrated funds and so there is clear evidence that too much diversification does not achieve extra-performances.

The criteria adopted in the selection of funds influenced results achieved by the FoFs, and it is possible to identify a hierarchy in the criteria adopted (Table 5.6).

The performance analysis seem to be the best criteria to construct portfolio managed and there is clear evidence that the best performing

Table 5.6   RAP for Funds of Funds on the basis of the portfolio's composition criterion

RAP measures	All sample	Subsample			
		Naïve diversification	Performance diversification	Style diversification	Reputation diversification
S_{2002}	−7.60	−7.40	−7.39	−7.30	−8.32
	(0.0389)	(0.0566)	(0.0324)	(0.0404)	(0.036)
	−7.60	−7.40	−7.39	−7.30	−8.32
	(0.0389)	(0.0566)	(0.0324)	(0.0404)	(0.036)
SO_{2002}	−1.93	−3.00	−1.04	−1.68	−2.76
	(0.0402)	(0.0298)	(0.031)	(0.0376)	(0.0534)
TR_{2002}	−10.41	−9.90	−6.65	−11.41	−12.84
	(0.2327)	(0.0659)	(0.4638)	(0.0766)	(0.0656)
IR_{2002}	−1.33	−4.90	0.30	−1.41	−1.40
	(0.0661)	(0.098)	(0.0498)	(0.0655)	(0.0647)
S_{2003}	1.67	0.75	1.15	3.20	−0.16
	(0.0547)	(0.0328)	(0.0608)	(0.0551)	(0.0521)
SO_{2003}	0.31	−1.92	−0.46	1.84	−0.52
	(0.0521)	(0.0332)	(0.0286)	(0.0695)	(0.036)
TR_{2003}	5.82	1.92	9.46	6.55	2.80
	(0.2029)	(0.0476)	(0.3776)	(0.1197)	(0.0702)
IR_{2003}	−0.93	−5.75	−1.54	0.57	−0.80
	(0.0733)	(0.0739)	(0.0605)	(0.0785)	(0.0699)
S_{2004}	5.48	7.25	6.34	5.51	3.21
	(0.0597)	(0.0594)	(0.0765)	(0.0464)	(0.0511)
SO_{2004}	−0.62	−1.44	−0.16	−0.55	−0.93
	(0.0406)	(0.0324)	(0.0385)	(0.045)	(0.0411)
TR_{2004}	4.75	4.88	4.66	5.18	4.10
	(0.0598)	(0.0432)	(0.0609)	(0.0605)	(0.0677)
IR_{2004}	−2.31	−2.88	−1.63	−1.98	−3.52
	(0.0884)	(0.0852)	(0.0969)	(0.0838)	(0.091)

Notes: Data presented are mean values in italics and the standard deviation in brackets.
S = Sharpe Index; SO = Sortino Index; TR = Treynor Index; IR = Information ratio.
Source: Fondionline data processed by authors.

ones are never those that adopt the simpler strategy of selection, the 'naive' strategy. These results make clear that a more detailed analysis of funds to include in the FoF's portfolio determines a higher performance and/or lower risk, and so higher costs related to this type of FoF could be economic rationale.

The FoFs' risk-return profile cannot be studied without considering the time persistence of the results achieved and the usefulness of the historical data to predict returns (Cucurachi, 1999).

In order to study the Italian market of FoFs we constructed the quartiles of the return distribution for the whole of the sample considered. We then tested to see if some particular types of FoFs are now more persistent over time. In our classification of FoFs we considered all of the criteria proposed in previous analysis (Table 5.7).

Table 5.7 Performance persistence for different types of FoFs

Classification Criterion (%)	Time period considered			
	2001–2004	2001–2002	2002–2003	2003–2004
Incentive fee	22.22	44.44	6.25	56.25
Specialized stocks	22.22	59.09	10.53	56.25
Specialized bonds	16.67	72.22	17.65	58.82
Flexibles	23.08	46.15	13.79	38.81
Balanced	12.50	50.00	13.04	45.83
Geographic concentrated	13.04	65.22	8.70	41.56
Geographic nonconcentrated	25.00	55.00	14.89	51.02
Sectoral concentrated	18.18	45.45	13.33	61.54
Sectoral nonconcentrated	12.50	37.50	12.00	44.00
Funds linked	25.00	50.00	0.00	39.13
Funds not linked	25.00	75.00	21.62	40.91
Concentrated	50.00	0.00	16.67	75.00
Not concentrated	55.56	22.22	28.13	35.00
Naïve diversification	0.00	50.00	15.38	23.08
Performance diversification	0.00	50.00	50.00	85.71
Style diversification	14.29	71.43	21.95	53.66
Reputation diversification	22.22	44.44	6.25	56.25

Source: Fondionline data processed by authors.

The incentive fees could be considered to be a reasonable criterion in the selection of FoFs, because these funds are significantly stable over time with a quartile variability over time lower than 16 per cent.

The analysis of fund classifications allows us to identify the higher persistence of ranking for low-risk profile investments, Specialized bonds, and, if the aim is to construct ranking stable over time, the sectoral diversification is better than the geographical one.

The choice to buy FoFs that invest only in funds realized by the same investment company, or by companies of the same group, represents an efficient criterion to select investment opportunities, otherwise the choice to invest only in concentrated funds does not determine a higher probability to achieve the best results in the future in all years considered.

Analysing the criteria adopted in the funds' selection is possible to identify only the worst criterion that is the naïf criterion: in fact results obtained are significantly different from empirical evidence proposed in literature[5] and rankings obtained with this approach are not coherent if we compare ranking at the beginning and at the end of the overall time period (2001–2004) and the percentage of coherence year by year is never more than 50 per cent.

5.4 Conclusions

FoFs are complex financial investments which offer an opportunity to achieve risk-return results that could not be obtained using other instruments. The past results determine a significant diffusion of the instrument that, over the past few years, is beginning to be traded in new markets.

The popularity of the instrument makes it necessary to study the FoF's distinctive characteristics to be in the assessment of its risk-return profile. The standard segmentation that considers geographical/sectoral concentration or type of fund, based on the Assogestioni classification, does not seem to be useful to identify the best investment opportunities.

Among the relevant aspects in the selection of FoFs are the number of funds included in the portfolio, the selection strategy adopted and the constraints in the selection of mutual funds. The best results are achieved by FoFs that do not have too fragmented a portfolio and are not obliged to invest in funds issued by related investment companies. Portfolio construction criteria are another factor affecting the results achieved by FoF managers and the empirical analysis makes it clear that resources invested in fund selection achieve better results.

The analysis proposed in this chapter could be extende to consider Funds of Hedge Funds (FoHF), which have been excluded from this analysis (Goodworth and Jones, 2004). To achieve that result it is necessary to collect information directly from the FoHF managers, because the transparency of the available information is lower for this type of funds (Kat, 2002). At this step, the proposed approach could not be applied for lack of information and so there is no clear evidence of the relationship between portfolio composition and performance achieved for this particular type of FoF (Davies et al., 2004). An empirical analysis for this type of instrument could be very interesting because it also had to take into account the fact that the returns' distribution of hedge funds is not normal (Davies et al., 2005) and it could be an opportunity to test new approaches for the assessment of FoHF portfolio construction criteria, which must be different from the standard RAP approach (Carretta and Mattarocci, 2005).

Notes

1. The chapter is the result of the authors' continuous cooperation. The Introduction and conclusion could be attributed to Alessandro Carretta and the other paragraphs to Gianluca Mattarocci.
2. Detailed data about the composition of FoFs are collected using www.fondionline.it.
3. All of the FoFs that adopt a naïve diversification declare particular criteria in the selection of mutual funds.
4. The threshold used in the analysis is 50 per cent of the portfolio managed, but the same results can also be obtained using a lower threshold.
5. In fact, other studies on Italian mutual funds demonstrate that historical performance is a useful tool to predict results achieved by funds' manager. See Campanelli and Trovato (2001).

References

Amenc, N., L. Martellini, M. Vaissié and J.R. Giraud (2004) *An Overview of European Multimanagement Practice*, EDHEC working paper, Nice.
Assogestioni (2004) *Guida Italiana al Risparmio Gestito*, Rome: Fact Book.
Barry, C.B. and L.T. Starks (1984) 'Investment Management and Risk Sharing with Multiple Managers', *Journal of Finance*, 39: 477–91.
Berk, J.B. and J. Xu (2004) *Persistence and Fund Flows of the Worst Performing Mutual Funds*, NBER working paper, Cambridge.
Bird, R. and D. Gallagher (2002) 'The Evaluation of Active Manager Returns in a Non-symmetrical Environment', *Journal of Asset Management*, 2: 303–24.
Bisogni, G.B. (2000) 'Il fondo di fondi', in Assogestioni, *La disciplina delle gestioni patrimoniali*, Rome: Bancaria Editrice.

Black, C.R. and M.R. Morey (2000) 'Morningstar Ratings and Mutual Funds Performance', *Journal of Financial and Quantitative Analysis*, 35: 451–83.

Brands, S. and D.R. Gallagher (2005) 'Portfolio Selection, Diversification and Fund of Funds: a Note', *Accounting and Finance*, 45: 185–97.

Brown, K.G., W.V. Harlow and L.T. Starks (1996) 'Of Tournaments and Temptations: an Analysis of Managerial Incentives in the Mutual Funds Industry', *Journal of Finance*, 51: 85–110.

Brown, S.J., W.N. Goetzmann and B. Liang (2004) *Fees on Fees on Funds of Funds*, Yale ICF working paper, New Haven.

Campanelli, F. and G. Trovato (2001) *Performance Evaluation and Classification of Italian Equity Mutual Funds*, EFMA paper, Lugano.

Cardani, A., E. Comi and V. Lazzari (2003) *L'offerta dei fondi di fondi speculativi in Italia*, LIUC papers, Castellanza.

Carhart, M.M. (1997) 'On Persistence in Mutual Fund Performance', *Journal of Finance*, 52: 57–82.

Carretta, A. and G. Mattarocci (2005) *The Performance Evaluation of Hedge Funds: a Comparison of Different Approaches*, University of Rome Tor Vergata working paper, Rome.

Chevalier, J. and G. Ellison (1999) 'Are Some Mutual Fund Managers Better Than Others? Cross Sectional Patterns in Behavior and Performance', *Journal of Finance*, 54: 875–99.

Chevalier, J. and G. Ellison (1999) 'Career Concerns of Mutual Fund Manager', *Quarterly Journal of Economics*, 114: 389–432.

Cinquemani, G. and G. Siciliano (2001) *Quanto sono grandi i vantaggi della diversificazione? Un'applicazione alle gestioni patrimoniali in fondi e ai fondi di fondi*, Quaderni di finanza della CONSOB no. 47, Rome.

Colombini, F., A. Mancini and S. Mannucci (2003) *La performance dei fondi comuni d'investimento*, Milan: Edibank.

Connelly, T.J. (1997) 'Multi-fund Diversification Issues', *Journal of Financial Planning*, 8: 34–7.

Cucurachi, P.A. (1999) 'L'analisi delle performance e la valutazione degli asset manager', in E.M. Carluccio, *Strategie, benchmarking e performance nell'asset management*, Rome: Bancaria Editrice.

Cucurachi, P.A. (2005) 'I fondi di fondi: una verifica empirica', in L. Anderloni, *L'innovazione finanziaria. Osservatorio Newfin 2004*, Rome: Bancaria Editrice.

Davidson, C. (2003) *The Fund of Funds Market: a Global Review*, London: AltAsset research.

Davies, R., H.M. Kat and S. Lu (2004) *Single Strategy Funds of Hedge Funds*, University of Reading working paper, Reading.

Davies, R., H.M. Kat and S. Lu (2005) *Funds of Hedge Funds Portfolio Selection: a Multiple Objective Approach*, Cass Business School research paper, London.

Elton, E.J. and M.J. Gruber (1977) 'Risk Reduction and Portfolio Size: an Analytical Solution', *Journal of Business*, 50: 415–37.

Elton, E.J., M.J. Gruber and C.R. Blake (2003) 'Incentive Fees and Mutual Funds', *Journal of Finance*, 58: 779–804.

Evans, J.L. and S.H. Archer (1968) 'Diversification and the Reduction of Dispersion: an Empirical Analysis', *Journal of Finance*, 23: 761–7.

Farrell, M. and G.N. Gregoriou (2000) 'Funds of Funds: When More Definitely Means Less', *Canadian Business Economic*, 8: 82–5.

Goodwin, T. (1998) 'The Information Ratio', *Financial Analyst Journal*, 54: 34–43.

Goodworth, T.R.J. and M.C. Jones (2004) *Building a Risk Measurement Framework for Hedge Funds and Funds*, University of Cambridge working paper, Cambridge.

Grinblatt, M. and S. Titman (1992) 'The Persistence of Mutual Fund Performance', *Journal of Finance*, 47: 1977–84.

Grinblatt, M. and S. Titman (1993) 'Performance Measurement without Benchmarks: an Examination of Mutual Fund Returns', *Journal of Business*, 66: 47–68.

Jensen, M.C. (1968) 'The Performance of Mutual Funds in the Period 1945–1964', *Journal of Finance*, 23: 28–30.

Jerome, S. (2004) *Quantitative Analysis of Asset Allocation in a Multi-manager Fund: an Application to the Gold Mining Sector*, HEC working paper, Paris.

Kat, A. (2002) *Portfolios of Hedge Funds*, Alternative Investment Research Centre working paper, London.

King, B.F. (1966) 'Market and Industry Factors in Stock Price Behavior', *Journal of Business*, 39: 139–90.

Lai, R. (2005) *Why Funds of Funds?*, Harvard Business School working paper.

Lazzari, V. (2003) *Modelli organizzativi ed operativi delle SGR speculative italiane*, LIUC papers, Castellanza.

Lhabitant, F.S. and M. Learned (2002) *Hedge Funds Diversification: How Much is Enough?*, FAME research paper, Geneva.

Liang, B. (2002) *Hedge Funds, Funds of Funds and Commodity Trading Advisor*, CWRU working paper, Cleveland.

Liang, B. (2004) 'On the Performance of Alternative Investments: CTAs, Hedge Funds and Funds of Funds', *Journal of Investment Management*, 2: 76–93.

Linciano, N. and E. Marrocco (2002) *Fondi di fondi e accordi di retrocessione*, Quaderni di Finanza CONSOB, Rome.

Markowitz, H. (1952) 'Portfolio Selection', *Journal of Finance*, 7: 77–91.

Mattoo, M. (2004) 'Structured Alternative Investment Products', in Euromoney Institutional Investors, *Euromoney Alternative Investments Handbook 2004/05*, Essex: Euromoney yearbooks.

Moultrup, J. (1998) 'The Multiple-equity Fund Portfolio Investment Strategy, Part I', *Journal of Financial Planning*, 8: art. 11.

Moultrup, J. (1998) 'The Multiple-equity Fund Portfolio Investment Strategy, Part II', *Journal of Financial Planning*, 8: art. 13.

O'Neal, E.S. (1997) 'How Many Mutual Funds Constitute a Diversified Mutual Funds Portfolio?', *Financial Analyst Journal*, 2: 37–46.

Park, J.M. and J.C. Staum (1988) 'Funds of Funds Diversification: How Much is Enough?', *Journal of Alternative Investment*, 1: 39–42.

Potter, M.E. (2001) *What You See is Not What You Get: Mutual Fund Tracking Error and Fund Diversification Properties*, Babson College working paper, Babson Park.

Sharpe, W.F. (1981) 'Decentralized Investment Management', *Journal of Finance*, 36: 217–34.

Sharpe, W.F. (1994) 'The Sharpe Ratio', *Journal of Portfolio Management*, 21: 49–58.

Sharpe, W.F. (1998) 'Morningstar Risk Adjusted Rating', *Financial Analyst Journal*, 7–8: 21–33.

Statman, M. (2004) 'The Diversification Puzzle', *Financial Analyst Journal*, 60: 44–53.

Still, L. (2004) 'Why are Funds of Funds Increasingly Popular?', *Equinox Newsletter*, 6: 690.

Treynor, J. (1965) 'How to Rate Management of Investment Funds', *Harward Business Review*, 44: 131–6.

Waring, B., D. Whitney, J. Pirone and C. Castille (2000) 'Optimizing Manager Structure and Budgeting Manager Risk', *Journal of Portfolio Management*, 26: 90–104.

Wermers, R. (2000) 'Mutual Fund Performance: an Empirical Decomposition into Stock Picking Talent, Style, Transaction Costs and Expenses', *Journal of Finance*, 55: 1655–95.

6
Market Characteristics and Chaos Dynamics in Stock Markets: an International Comparison

Gianluca Mattarocci

6.1 Introduction

Capital markets are characterized by significant differences in investors' attitudes and expectations that, as a rule, determine unusual price dynamics that are unlike those suggested by classical linear models (Westerhoff, 2005).

International evidence proves the relevance of chaos dynamics to explain the dynamics of the most actively traded financial instruments, especially in well-organized markets (Mucley, 2004). Quite a few of these works have merely considered a single market and, frequently, paid considerable attention to well-developed economies. There are not many works focusing on undeveloped countries (Assaf and Cavalcante, 2005) and/or comparing different countries (Huang and Yang, 1995) and, therefore, there is no clear evidence of the main reasons for the difference in chaos level in different markets.

This chapter analyses the role of the financial market characteristics in the degree of chaotic dynamics using the standard approach proposed in the literature in order to evaluate stock markets. It starts with a brief analysis of the literature dealing with chaos in general, its estimation measures and its application to the stock market (section 6.2). The analysis being proposed focuses on several major stock markets and tries to verify if differences in the degree of chaos can be explained based on a number of market characteristics. International evidence shows that the role of a few market characteristics is not residual in the selection of the best statistical model to predict future dynamics (section 6.3). The conclusions endeavour to evaluate the impact of these results on the stock market predicting models and the future prospects for the best model to predict stock dynamics in different market scenarios.

6.2   Chaos theory and the stock market

The nonlinear models are a heterogeneous set of econometric approaches that allow higher predictability levels, but not all of the approaches may be applied easily to real data (Schreimber, 1998). Deterministic chaos represents the best trade-off to establish fixed rules in order to link future dynamics to past results of a time series without imposing excessively simplified assumptions (Peitgern, Jurgens and Saupe, 2004). In essence, chaos is a nonlinear deterministic process that looks random (Hsieh, 1991) because it is the result of an irregular oscillatory process influenced by an initial condition and characterized by an irregular periodicity (Brown, 1995).

The chaos theory assumes that complex dynamics may be explained if they are considered as a combination of simpler trends (Devaney, 1990): the higher the number of breakdowns, the higher the probability of identifying a few previously known basic profiles (Mandelbrot, 1987).

Chaotic trends may be studied considering some significant points that represent attractors or deflectors for the time series being analysed and the periodicity that exists in the relevant data (Arnold, 1992).

The next two subsections analyse in detail the stock market and try to point out the main approaches suggested in literature to evaluate stock dynamics (subsection 6.2.1) and evidence of the effect of market characteristics on chaotic dynamics (subsection 6.2.2).

6.2.1   Estimation procedures for chaotic dynamics

The nonlinear dynamics assumption calls for the definition of a few aspects that are required to understand the rationality of past trends and to define the expected dynamics. The main characteristics may be identified in Eckmann (1985):

- the type of randomness;
- the fractal dimension;
- the duration of the cycle;
- the relevance of past results.

The first analysis considers the time series noise and attempts to verify whether it may be considered a classical 'white noise' or a 'chaotic noise' (Liu, Granger and Heller, 1992). The test adopted to analyse this aspect is the Brock, Dechert and Scheinkman test (BDS), which tries to ascertain whether a time series may be considered random or if it actually presents a hidden structure (Brock, Dechert and Scheinkman, 1987). Mathematically:

$$W_{nT}(\varepsilon) = \sqrt{T}[C_{n,T}(\varepsilon) - C_{1,T}(\varepsilon)^n]/\sigma_{n,T}(\varepsilon) \tag{6.1}$$

where the statistic represents a ratio between the spread of error terms with respect to the normality assumption $(C_{n,T}(\varepsilon) - C_{1,T}(\varepsilon)^n)$ and the asymptotic standard error $(\sigma_{n,T}(\varepsilon))$ (Olmeda and Perez, 1995). A zero value of the statistic is obtained only when the time series' error $(C_{n,T}(\varepsilon))$ is IID and in all the other scenarios it is possible (not necessary) to identify chaos dynamics (Hsieh, 1991).

The fractal dimension represents the number of basis elements (fractals) necessary to define an object that is similar to the trend being analysed (Falconer, 1990) and, mathematically, it represents the number of degrees of freedom necessary to define a polynomial function that fits the real dynamics correctly (Kuguimtzis, Lillekjendlie and Christopherses, 1995). The higher the complexity of the time series being analysed, the higher the estimated fractal dimension (Greenside, Wolf, Swift and Pignataro, 1982).

In nonlinear models, the role of long-term dependence may not be considered by studying the simple covariance or autocovariance and more complex approaches have to be used (McCauley, 1994). One of the most commonly used approaches is the rescaled range analysis (R/S analysis) that tries to check the role of past dynamics considering the maximum and minimum range with respect to the standard deviation (Mouck, 1998). In formulae (Sadique and Silvapulle, 2001):

$$H = \lim_{n \to \infty} \frac{RS}{\ln(n)} \tag{6.2}$$

where the value of H is estimated considering an approximately infinite horizon (n) and the results of an autoregressive estimate of the role of past results (RS). The RS factor is estimated considering residuals of a standard linear model using this formula:

$$RS = \frac{1}{\frac{1}{T}\sum_{t=1}^{T} x(t) - E[x(t)]} \left\{ \max_{0 < \tau < T} \left[\sum_{t=1}^{\tau} x(t) - E(x(t)) \right] \right.$$

$$\left. - \min_{0 < \tau < T} \left[\sum_{t=1}^{\tau} x(t) - E(x(t)) \right] \right\} \tag{6.3}$$

where the R/S measure is constructed considering the maximum spread observed in the period $(\max_{0<\tau<T} [\sum_{t=1}^{\tau} x(t) - E(x(t))] - \min_{0<\tau<T}$

$(\sum_{t=1}^{\tau} x(t) - E(x(t)))$ with respect to the classical standard deviation measure $(\sum_{t=1}^{\tau} x(t) - E(x(t)))$. The index varies from zero to one and measures the role of past performance in predicting future dynamics (Los, 2004).

The approach being proposed represents a simplified approach to evaluate the degree of chaotic dynamics but, even if some adjustments were proposed in literature (Lo, 1991), there is no clear evidence of the higher forecasting capability of these new approaches (Willinger, Taqqu and Teverovsky, 1999).

One of the major applications of this approach is related to the possibility of also using these statistics to study the length of cycles that are relevant to a market. This approach assumes the possibility of defining the reversal point considering the point to be the ratio between R/S estimated for different time periods and the number of observations and looking for the period when the natural growing trend of the ratio is interrupted (Hurst, 1991). In formulas:

$$\text{if } H_n = \frac{RS_n}{\ln(n)} < H_{n-1} = \frac{RS_{n-1}}{\ln(n-1)} \qquad \text{market cycle duration} = n \quad (6.4)$$

Results obtained by this test are influenced strictly by the variability of the time series and may call for the definition of a threshold to differentiate wrong signals from inversions.

The relevance of nonlinear trends with respect to randomness is assessed by studying the relevance of previous history on the results. The long-term dependence is considered by comparing the results achieved with the results obtained by the same statistics estimated on the scrambled series. The scrambled series is constructed using a random criterion that allows defining a new time series that is very different from the original time series (Peters, 1996). After estimating these two time series, the relevance of the fractal dimension is higher if the results achieved are worse for the scrambled series than for the original time series (Scheinkman and LeBaron, 1989).

All of these approaches work on a series of error estimates that could be obtained using different filtering criteria. This characteristic allows the application of these models to different scenarios but implies that the results are strictly influenced by the type of data used and by the criteria adopted in filtering the time series (Connelly, 1996).

6.2.2   The relationship between market characteristics and stock price dynamics

Stock market transactions are characterized by irregular dynamics in prices and volumes that may not be predicted by standard linear forecasting methods (Day, 1993). In fact, the trends identified by different linear models are not stable over time (Henry, 2002) and a significant increase or decrease in volatility causes the uselessness of previously estimated models (LeBaron, 1993).

The lack of predictability of stock market returns demonstrated by classical linear methodologies led to the development of studies that attempted to demonstrate the randomness of stock markets (Fama, 1970). Random approaches are not useful for predicting market dynamics and better results may be obtained if the analyst assumes that there is an underlying relationship in the stock price historical trends that cannot be analysed using such simple models as linear approaches (Brock, Hsieh and LeBaron, 1993).

The hypothesis that history is not relevant to predict future stock price dynamics cannot be correct since all of the investors define their investment strategy based results obtained in the past. Even if there are differences in the information available (Broze, Gourieroux and Szafarz, 1990) and/or it may be assumed that response functions to the same information are different for each investor (Brock and Cars, 1998), it may be useful to define models to predict future performance.

The usefulness of the approach being proposed is linked to a few market characteristics that are likely to influence the impact of investors' choices on stock market dynamics. The main aspects identified in literature as a significant explanation of chaos dynamics are:

- asymmetric transaction costs;
- type of orders;
- type of investors;
- transactions volume.

All of the factors that are likely to influence the net results obtained by investors may affect the market price dynamics and/or volume of transactions (Pesaran and Potter, 1992). The portfolio optimization process is more complex for the trade-off between transaction costs and volume/opportunity of trading (Davis and Norman, 1990) and, as a rule, high transaction costs determine a lower frequency of portfolio re-balances and a lower volume of transactions (Costantinides, 1986).

Market price dynamics are influenced by investors' choices and constraints in the implementation of the strategies being adopted (Cunningham, 2000). All the world markets are electronically based but differences may be identified in the type of orders that may be used (Banfi, 2004). Different types of admitted orders may influence price dynamics because the effectiveness of a few trading strategies is related to the possibility of defining limits to the validity of buying and/or selling orders and to the presence/absence of liquidity providers (Seppi, 1997). The opportunity to define time or price-related conditions for the transactions reduces the impact of randomness on the stock price dynamics (Iori, Daniels, Famer, Gillemot, Krishnamurty and Smith, 2003) and causes different market dynamics (Famer and Joshi, 2002) because investors can select in which scenario the order will be executed. Markets where this possibility is offered are characterized by a partial independence of the investors' strategies from short-term variations (Tyurin, 2003) and the trends observed seem to be significantly independent by noise and substantially related to investors' strategies and expectations (Maslow, 2000). The decision to define a few conditions for the execution of orders allow making price dynamics independent of a transitory lack of demand or supply for each type of stock and ensuring that the price dynamics reflects in an improved manner the long-term expectations of investors (Lillo and Farmer, 2004).

The role of institutional investors in the market could be relevant because these traders are usually more capable of identifying investment opportunities and defining the best type of order that allows them to achieve the best results (Linnainmaa, 2005). This advantage with respect to individual investors is related to the experience that allows them to predict future dynamics and to reduce the risk exposure that characterizes stock investments (Seru, Shumway and Stoffman, 2005). Considering the institutional investors, a special role is played by dealers and/or market makers, traders that are likely to influence the variability of price in each day of trading and to reduce the market risk (Zanotti, 2006). Markets with liquidity providers are usually characterized by a more stationary price envelope (Grossman and Miller, 1988) or, more generally, by a hidden trend that is clearer than in other markets (Bouchaud, Gefen, Potters and Wyart, 2004).

Stock price dynamics are influenced by the number of investors that are active traders in the market and a significant variability in the number of investors could influence the proximity of the trading price to the fundamental value (Cass and Shell, 1983). In fact, markets characterized by a low number of traders and/or transactions achieve equilibria that could be significantly different from the optimal scenario based on the stocks' fundamental value and price dynamics for this type of market could be difficult to forecast. The nonlinearity of the stock price dynamics is influenced by the number of transactions relative to each stock (Antoniou, Ergul and Holmes, 1997). Therefore, with reference to each time period being considered, it may be ascertained that a higher (lower) level of transactions implies a lower (higher) capability of the linear model to explain the dynamics of the market (Hinich and Patterson, 1990).

6.3   The impact of stock market characteristics on chaos theory: empirical evidence

6.3.1   The sample

The aim of this contribution is to study the market efficiency of each country; hence, it stands to reason that the chaos theory principles and methodologies apply directly to the stock market indexes (Pandey, Kohers ann Kohers, 1998). In fact, the alternative of considering each stock listed in each stock market could produce results that are strictly affected by the criteria adopted in the selection of stocks.

The proposed analysis attempts to analyse some of the main world markets and to study markets that present significant differences in market characteristics. The sample is constructed by considering indexes that are characterized by the availability of data for a time period that has to be long enough to be useful in analysing chaos dynamics and, based on results presented in the literature (Jaditz and Sayers, 1993), the indexes considered are those for which data have been available for not less than ten years (Figure 6.1).

The sample is constructed considering at least one index – the most representative – for each country, for a total of fifty indexes. The data are collected daily for a ten-year time period (1996–2005) using the Datastream database.

6.3.2   The characteristics of world stock markets

The relevance of the previously evidenced variables may only be tested by defining rules that allow collecting data for all or a relevant percentage of the countries being considered. All of the assumptions made afterwards represent a simplification of the approach, but they may be considered the best solution based on the data available for the analysis.

At an aggregate level, the transaction costs may be considered only in part, because a quote is characterized by a fixed transaction cost that is independent of the type of stock considered and the bid–ask spread that is typical for each stock (Atkins and Dyl, 1990). Hence, the decision to consider only the mean transaction costs applied to the transaction during the time period being considered.

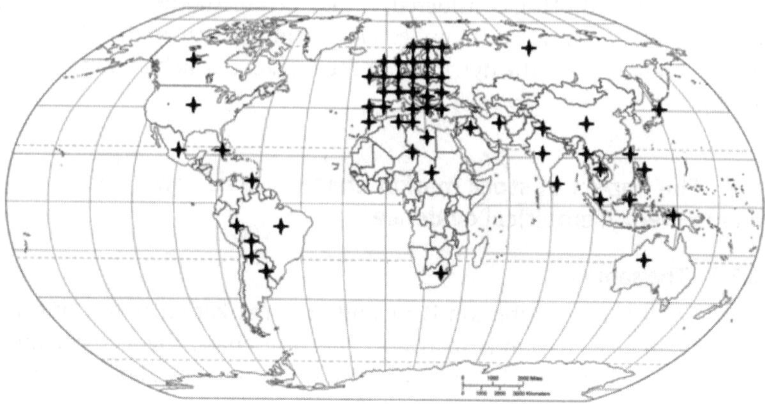

Figure 6.1   The sample

The trading mechanism may be examined considering market statements and the possibility of defining different types of orders. The adoption of an international comparison of strategies in different markets requires the definition of a standard classification that may be applied to all the markets. The choice is to define the most general one that discriminate orders only on the basis of the type of constraint imposed: time, quantity and price.

The relative importance of institutional investors with respect to individuals can hardly be evaluated by comparing the number and/or volume of trades because the activism of these investors is related strictly to the available information and expectations, and no data about these aspects are on hand. The only unquestionable datum that may be used to evaluate the potential role of institutional investors is the presence or absence of dealers or market makers established by law.

The study of liquidity considers a standard proxy such as the number of trades in the period being analysed. In more detail, the suggested approach studies daily trades and, considering the high variability of volumes related to market anomalies (Chordia, Roll and Subrahmayam, 2001), tries to define a classification of stock markets breaking them down into four categories based on the mean amount of trades for all of the periods under consideration.[1]

Figure 6.2 summarizes the selected characteristics with respect to the countries considered in the analysis.

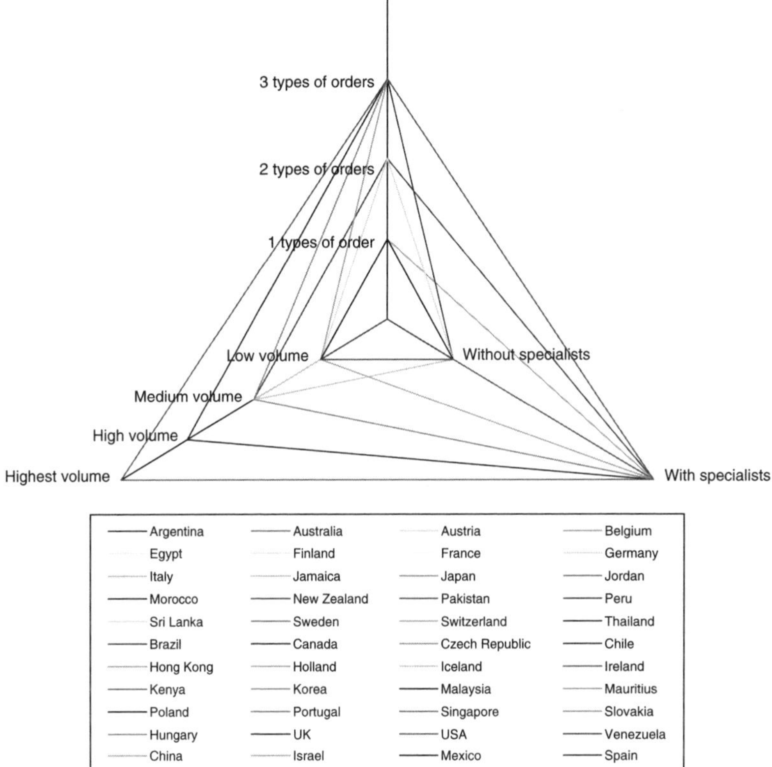

Figure 6.2   Main characteristics of the markets being considered

Even if the aggregation of all order types into only three macro categories reduces the variability between the countries, the analysis of the sample allows a singling out of differences because only 51 per cent of the markets present a complete set of orders. A simple data analysis shows that there is no predominant solution and so it is possible to verify if different choices in type of orders admitted impact on stock price dynamics.

The resulting sample considers markets with different degrees of stability related to the presence or absence of market makers and by different degrees of liquidity. In fact, the available data allow us to ascertain that more than 35 per cent of the markets have no market maker and, even if it is clear that some of the markets being considered are very small, the big markets are highly heterogeneous with respect to the degree of activism of the investors.

Transaction costs data are more difficult to collect since the decision to delegate to the market the definition of the proper price may have a negative impact upon the ability to monitor correctly the amount of the fee applied to market participants.

With reference to all of the data taken into consideration, this allows us to ascertain the existence of differences among the countries being considered that permit the analysis of whether or not these characteristics may influence the degree of chaotic dynamics of each type of market.

6.3.3 The model

Markets dynamics are studied considering the stock index value and estimating the daily returns using the standard logarithmic approach. In formulae:

$$_j r_t = \ln \left(_j I_t / _j I_{t-1} \right) \tag{6.5}$$

where $_j I_t$ represents the stock market index considered for the country j.

The analysis of the chaotic degree considers likely methods of estimation of the hidden basic linear function and tries to verify whether there are results independent of the methodology used and/or methodologies that are better suited. The role of past forecast results in forecasting is evaluated considering very simple approaches that could replicate results obtainable by standard technical analysis tools: moving average and trends. The selected econometric models are (Hamilton, 1995):

$$r_t = AR(n) = c + \phi_1 r_{t-1} + \ldots + \phi_n r_{t-n} \tag{6.6}$$

$$r_t = MA(m) = c + \psi_i \varepsilon_{t-1} + \ldots + \psi_n \varepsilon_{t-m} \tag{6.7}$$

$$r_t = ARMA(n, m) = c + \phi_1 r_{t-1} + \ldots + \phi_n r_{t-n} + \psi_i \varepsilon_{t-1} + \ldots + \psi_n \varepsilon_{t-m} \tag{6.8}$$

The high level of heterogeneity in the sample does not permit the identification of a model suited to all of the markets under consideration. Hence, it is necessary to estimate the lag that enables us to achieve the best result for each market. The decision to use more than one model in order to estimate hidden trends leads to results that are partially independent of the assumption made in the construction of the hidden model.

All of the previously suggested tests about the type of randomness and all of the statistics related to the degree of chaotic dynamics need to be estimated with reference to all of the filters being proposed and for all of the de-trend time series under consideration. The cycle lengths identified with the Hurst index are only estimated in respect of the time series showing chaotic dynamics.

6.3.4 Results

The analysis of the degree of randomness of the series filtered with different criteria is conducted for all of the filters proposed above and the results obtained permit to reject the hypothesis of a random dynamics also for all the proposed criteria. The results that have been obtained show that, as a rule, residuals are not identically distributed for a large majority of filters and, in respect of a few countries, this relationship may be verified independently of the selected filter (Table 6.1).[2]

The analysis of randomness in error time shows that there are a number of scenarios where the chaos dynamics are likely to explain some of the errors relative to the standard linear model. The degree of chaotic dimension is analyzed looking for the best specification of the three models being proposed and comparing the results with the scrambled one (Table 6.2).

The markets being considered seem to point to the presence of chaotic dynamics because the results obtained through the AR filter and the ARIMA filter identify a Hurst index that is higher than the random scenario (H = 0.5) and bigger than the scrambled one in more than 65 per cent of the countries.

In more detail, the markets exhibiting more chaotic characteristics show high order type heterogeneity (more than 65 per cent of these markets seem chaotic) and, in more than a half percentage of cases, chaotic markets are characterized by the presence of a market maker. The degree of chaotic dynamics is also clearer for markets with lower trade volumes, but there seems to be no relationship with the amount of the transaction costs (Figure 6.3).

If we consider only the indexes showing chaotic patterns for one of the criteria being proposed, it becomes possible to study the mean duration of the cycles that characterize these markets and to look for other relationships between market characteristics and chaos dynamics (Figure 6.4).

Cycles estimated with more complex models (ARIMA) vary more frequently during the period analysed with respect to all the countries being considered. A comparison of the cycles of different countries clearly suggests that the liquidity not only affects the degree of chaos, but also the type of cyclicality. In fact, as a rule, highly liquid markets have a higher frequency of reversion. This could be considered a direct consequence of the high number of investors that interact in the market.

Table 6.1   BDS statistics for each country

Countries	BDS worst filter		
	AR (n)	MA (n)	ARIMA
Argentina	9.87**	26.32***	9.23***
Australia	8.41**	24.71***	8.54***
Austria	8.38**	25.23***	8.49***
Belgium	12.24***	22.89***	12.19***
Brazil	12.93***	26.24***	12.34***
Canada	9.30**	24.28***	9.07**
Czech Republic	8.19**	24.73***	8.25**
Chile	12.22***	16.72***	12.45***
China	11.06***	28.34***	10.97***
Egypt	15.18***	20.51***	14.82***
Finland	12.69***	24.75***	12.12***
France	9.20***	27.02***	8.92**
Germany	11.43***	28.01***	11.47***
Hong Kong	14.91***	24.95***	−1.02
Holland	13.73***	28.00***	13.39***
Iceland	12.52***	24.17***	12.39***
Ireland	8.41**	26.25***	8.35***
Israel	3.76*	24.77***	3.58*
Italy	11.31***	26.70***	11.04***
Jamaica	−1.06	25.13***	−1.07
Japan	−0.03	25.52***	−0.04
Jordan	9.81**	21.52***	9.88**
Kenya	23.46***	25.52***	26.22***
Korea	6.49**	26.14***	6.30**
Malaysia	16.70***	20.68***	0.16
Mauritius	8.07**	26.92***	8.85**
Mexico	9.30**	24.28***	9.07**
Morocco	19.20***	23.79***	18.83***
New Zealand	9.39**	24.82***	9.10***
Pakistan	15.26***	25.92***	15.36***
Perù	9.48***	23.86***	9.79*
Poland	11.31***	26.70***	11.04***
Portugal	−9.95**	−0.21	−11.09***
Singapore	14.35***	25.18***	14.16***
Slovakia	6.74**	26.75***	6.63**
Spain	10.11**	27.97***	10.15***
Sri Lanka	20.24***	21.76***	19.57***
Sweden	11.15***	24.80***	11.06**
Switzerland	13.86***	27.15***	13.96***
Thailand	22.75***	26.13***	26.38***
Hungary	12.74***	26.27***	13.39***
UK	12.05***	26.47***	−0.21
USA	7.15**	26.52***	7.22**
Venezuela	13.26***	22.77***	13.19***

Notes: * Statistically significant at 90%.
** Statistically significant at 95%.
*** Statistically significant at 99%.

Table 6.2 Hurst index and scrambled hurst

	AR (n) best filter		MA (n) best filter		ARIMA (n) best filter	
	Hurst	Hurst scrambled	Hurst	Hurst scrambled	Hurst	Hurst scrambled
Argentina	0.56	0.33	0.12	0.43	0.56	0.45
Australia	0.46	0.46	0.10	0.39	0.51	0.48
Austria	0.55	0.43	0.03	0.40	0.55	0.47
Belgium	0.54	0.47	0.10	0.46	0.54	0.48
Brazil	0.46	0.38	0.09	0.42	0.46	0.42
Canada	0.46	0.40	0.02	0.49	0.45	0.45
Czech Republic	0.55	0.35	0.15	0.47	0.54	0.46
Chile	0.53	0.45	0.21	0.42	0.53	0.45
China	0.50	0.38	0.02	0.42	0.49	0.46
Egypt	0.60	0.45	0.16	0.43	0.59	0.44
Finland	0.55	0.42	0.08	0.46	0.54	0.41
France	0.54	0.39	0.09	0.48	0.54	0.43
Germany	0.51	0.43	0.01	0.49	0.52	0.38
Hong Kong	0.40	0.42	0.17	0.53	0.53	0.49
Holland	0.53	0.44	0.09	0.42	0.55	0.40
Iceland	0.61	0.39	0.23	0.50	0.60	0.45
Ireland	0.54	0.49	0.05	0.47	0.49	0.46
Israel	0.49	0.34	0.18	0.47	0.51	0.44
Italy	0.51	0.36	0.01	0.49	0.50	0.45
Jamaica	0.49	0.45	−0.21	0.39	0.49	0.40
Japan	0.48	0.47	−0.07	0.52	0.49	0.49
Jordan	0.64	0.43	0.02	0.36	0.64	0.49
Kenya	0.61	0.40	0.45	0.51	0.60	0.47
Korea	0.55	0.37	0.16	0.43	0.55	0.38
Malaysia	0.51	0.51	0.42	0.51	0.49	0.50
Mauritius	0.60	0.44	0.20	0.41	0.57	0.39
Mexico	0.46	0.41	0.02	0.42	0.45	0.46
Morocco	0.58	0.36	0.13	0.46	0.56	0.49
New Zealand	0.48	0.48	0.16	0.45	0.45	0.48
Pakistan	0.53	0.43	0.04	0.47	0.49	0.41
Peru	0.56	0.41	0.16	0.40	0.56	0.39
Poland	0.49	0.41	0.01	0.37	0.50	0.39
Portugal	1.00	0.45	0.48	0.51	0.98	0.49
Singapore	0.53	0.37	0.18	0.42	0.53	0.40
Slovakia	0.61	0.41	0.19	0.48	0.61	0.47
Spain	0.53	0.49	0.11	0.51	0.52	0.40
Sri Lanka	0.55	0.38	0.36	0.47	0.53	0.38
Sweden	0.53	0.44	0.03	0.41	0.54	0.40
Switzerland	0.51	0.41	0.09	0.45	0.52	0.46
Thailand	0.67	0.45	0.52	0.48	0.67	0.44
Hungary	0.55	0.49	0.12	0.47	0.52	0.34
UK	0.50	0.39	0.02	0.43	0.54	0.42
USA	0.47	0.48	−0.05	0.34	0.48	0.43
Venezuela	0.59	0.42	0.31	0.48	0.55	0.44

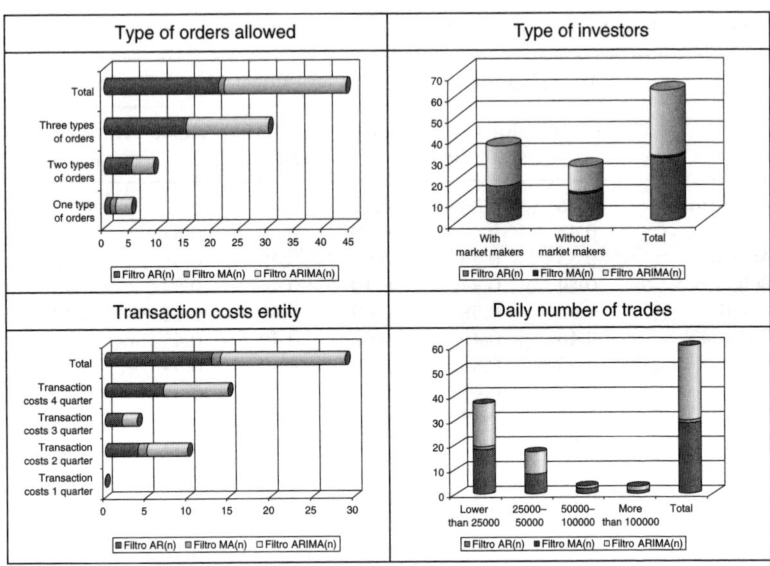

Figure 6.3   Market characteristics and degree of chaotic dynamics

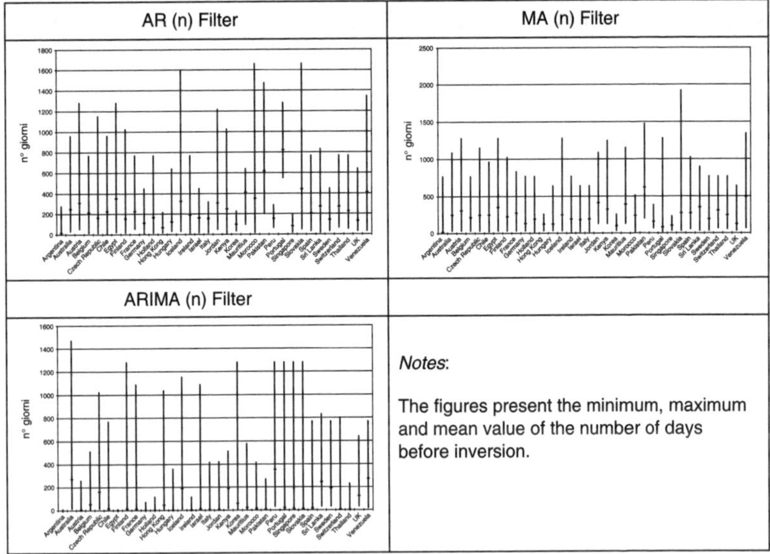

Figure 6.4   Duration of cycles (number of days)

6.4 Conclusions

An international comparison shows that the forecasting methods are likely to be influenced significantly by the characteristics of the market that are being analysed and the interpretation of the results by each forecasting process could be re-thought based on the evidence suggested in this chapter.

In fact, the differences identified in the degree of nonlinearity for different market structures clearly point to the impossibility of assuming that a single methodology is best, irrespective of the market being analysed. In fact, the different degree of nonlinearity implies a different length of the cycles that are relevant for all the forecasting methodologies and are likely to affect to a significant extent the results.

The next step of the analysis could be the search of the best technique to predict the future performance of stock markets that are homogenous in respect of one or more variables identified in this chapter.[3] The recourse to more complex approaches, such as e-GARCH (Abhyankar, Copeland and Wong, 1995), could prove useful for future developments as they allow us to study not only day or monthly dynamics, but also the impact of chaos on strategies adopted by investors examining intraday data (Bayracatar, Poor and Sircar, 2003).

Another future development of the analysis could be identified in the analysis of chaotic dynamics in the trend of individual stocks (Barkoulas and Baum, 1996). This different approach could be useful because the degree of chaotic dynamics is not necessarily independent of firm characteristics (Skarandzinski, 2003) and it could be interesting to analyse which are the main characteristics of stocks that demonstrate a more chaotic dynamic (Hiemstra and Jones, 1997).

The results obtained from a comparison of different markets could be useful in an analysis of stock markets, even if the world markets tend to achieve a high level of integration. A few differences – such as the mean volume of trades and the relative incidence of institutional investors (Sewell, Stansell, Lee and Below, 1996) – are not likely to disappear with the finalization of the integration process. Hence, it could prove useful to replicate the analysis considering new market characteristics that allow us to discriminate between different stock markets.

Notes

1. The high heterogeneity of the sample causes the uselessness of a non arbitrary approach to define a threshold with respect to the distribution of the number of trades.
2. The table only shows the results of the worst criteria that may be adopted to construct residual series. Results obtained with other lag and/or time periods are better than those shown in the table and will be available on request.
3. For a review of different methodologies proposed in literature see Kugiumtzis, Lillekjendlie and Christophersen (1995).

References

Abhyankar, A., L.S. Copeland and W. Wong (1995) 'Non Linear Dynamics in Real Time Equity Market Indices: Evidence from the United Kingdom', *Economic Journal*, 105: 864–80.

Antoniou, A., N. Ergul and P. Holmes (1997) 'Market Efficiency, Thin Trading and Nonlinear Behaviour: Evidence from an Emerging Country', *European Financial Management*, 3: 175–90.

Arnold, V.I. (1992) *Catastrophe Theory*, Berlin: Springer-Verlag.

Assaf, A. and J. Cavalcante (2005) 'Long Range Dependence in the Returns and Volatility of the Brazilian Stock Market', *European Review of Economic and Finance*, 4: 1–19.

Atkins, A.B. and E.A. Dyl (1990) 'Price Reversal, Bid Ask Spreads and Market Efficiency', *Journal of Financial and Quantitative Analysis*, 25: 535–47.

Banfi, A. (2004) *I mercati e gli strumenti finanziari. Disciplina e organizzazione della borsa*, Turin: ISEDI.

Barkoulas, J.T. and C.F. Baum (1996) *Long Term Dependence in Stock Returns*, Boston College Working Papers in Economics no. 314, Boston.

Bayracatar, E., V.H. Poor and K.R. Sircar (2003) 'Estimating the Fractal Dimension of the S&P 500 Using Wavelet Analysis', Princeton University working paper, Princeton.

Bouchaud, J.P., Y. Gefen, M. Potters and M. Wyart (2004) 'Fluctuations and Response in Financial Markets: the Subtle Nature of Random Price Change', *Quantitative Finance*, 4: 176–90.

Brock, W.A. and H.H. Cars (1998) 'Heterogeneous Beliefs and Routes to Chaos in a Simple Asset Pricing Model', *Journal of Economic Dynamics and Control*, 22: 1235–74.

Brock, W.A., W. Dechert and J.A. Scheinkman (1987) *A Test for Independence Based Correlation Dimension*, University of Wisconsin working paper, Madison.

Brock, W.A., D.A. Hsieh and B. LeBaron (1993) *Nonlinear Dynamics, Chaos and Instability: Statistical Theory and Economic Evidence*, Cambridge, MA: MIT Press.

Brown, C. (1995) *Chaos and Catastrophe Theories*, Thousand Oaks, CA: Sage Publications.

Broze, L., C. Gourieroux and A. Szafarz (1990) 'Speculative Bubbles and Exchange of Information on the Market of a Storable Good', in W.A. Barnett, J. Geweke and K. Shell (eds), *Economic Complexity: Chaos, Sunspots, Bubbles and Nonlinearity*, New York: Cambridge University Press.

Cass, D. and K. Shell (1983) 'Do Sunspots Matter?', *Journal of Political Economy*, 91: 193–207.

Chordia, T., R. Roll and A. Subrahmayam (2001) 'Market Liquidity and Trading Activity', *Journal of Finance*, 56: 501–30.

Connelly, T.J. (1996) 'Chaos Theory and the Financial Markets', *Journal of Financial Planning*, 36: 26–30.

Costantinides, G.M. (1986) 'Capital Market Equilibrium with Transaction Costs', *Journal of Political Economy*, 94: 842–62.

Cunningham, L.A. (2000) *From Random Walks to Chaotic Crashes: the Linear Genealogy and the Efficient Capital Market Hypothesis*, Boston College of Law Working Paper, Boston.

Davis, M.H.A and A.R. Norman (1990) 'Portfolio Selection with Transaction Costs', *Mathematics of Operation Research*, 15: 676–713.

Day, R.H. (1993) 'Complex Economic Dynamics: Obvious in History, Generic in Theory, Elusive in Data', in N.H. Pesaran and S.M. Potter (eds), *Nonlinear Dynamics, Chaos and Econometrics*, Chichester: John Wiley and Sons.

Devaney, R.L. (1990) *Caos e frattali*, Milan: Addison-Wesley.

Eckmann, J.P. (1985) 'Ergodic Theory of Chaos Dynamics and Strange Attractors', *Review of Modern Physics*, 57: 617–56.

Falconer, K. (1990) *Fractal Geometry: Mathematical Foundations and Applications*, Chichester: John Wiley and Sons.

Fama, E. (1970) 'Efficient Capital markets: A Review of the Theory and Empirical Works', *Journal of Finance*, 25: 383–417.

Famer, J.D. and S. Joshi (2002) 'The Price Dynamics of Common Trading Strategies', *Journal of Economic Behaviour and Organization*, 49: 149–71.

Greenside, H.S., A. Wolf, J. Swift and T. Pignataro (1982) 'Impracticability of a Box Counting Algorithm for Calculating the Dimensionality of Strange Attractors', *Physical Review A*, 25: 3453–6.

Grossman, S.J. and M.H. Miller (1988) 'Liquidity and Market Structure', *Journal of Finance*, 43: 617–33.

Hamilton, J.D. *Econometria delle serie storiche*, Bologna: Monduzzi Editore.

Henry, O.T. (2002) 'Long Memory in Stock Returns: Some International Evidence', *Applied Financial Economics*, 12: 725–9.

Hiemstra, C. and J.D. Jones (1997) 'Another Look at Long Memory in Common Stock Returns', *Journal of Empirical Finance*, 4: 373–401.

Hinich, M.I. and D.M. Patterson (1990) 'Evidence of Nonlinearity in the Trade-by-trade Stock Market Return Generating Process', in W.A. Barnett, J. Geweke and K. Shell (eds), *Economic Complexity: Chaos, Sunspots, Bubbles and Nonlinearity*, New York: Cambridge University Press.

Hsieh, D.A. (1991) 'Chaos and Non Linear Dynamics: Applications for Financial Markets', *Journal of Finance*, 46: 1839–77.

Huang, B.N. and C.W. Yang (1995) 'The Fractal Structure in Multinational Stock Returns', *Applied Economic Letters*, 2: 67–71.

Hurst, H.E. (1991) 'The Long Term Storage Capacity of Reservoirs', *Transactions of the American Society of Civil Engineers*, 116: 770–99.

Iori, G., M.G. Daniels, J.D. Famer, L. Gillemot, S. Krishnamurty and E. Smith (2003) 'An Analysis of Price Impact Function in Order Driven Markets', *Phisica A*, 324: 146–51.

Jaditz, T. and C. Sayers (1993) 'Is Chaos Generic in Economic Data?', *International Journal of Bifurcations and Chaos*, 3: 745–55.

Kugiumtzis, D., B. Lillekjendlie and N. Christophersen (1995a) *Chaotic Time Series, Part I: Estimation of Some Invariant Properties in State Space*, University of Oslo Working Paper.

Kugiumtzis, D., B. Lillekjendlie and N. Christophersen (1995b) *Chaotic Time Series. Part II: System Identification and Prediction*, University of Oslo Working Paper.

LeBaron, B. (1993) 'Forecast Improvements Using Volatility Index', in N.H. Pesaran and S.M. Potter (eds), *Nonlinear Dynamics, Chaos and Econometrics*, Chichester: John Wiley and Sons.

Lillo, F. and J.D. Farmer (2004) 'The Long Memory Effect of the Efficient Market', *Studies in Nonlinear Dynamics and Econometrics*, 8: 1–32.

Linnainmaa, J. (2005) *The Limit Order Effect*, UCLA Working Paper, Los Angeles.

Liu, T., C.W.J. Granger and W.P. Heller (1992) 'Using the Correlation Exponent to Decide Whether an Economic Series is Chaotic', *Journal of Applied Econometrics*, 7: 525–39.

Lo, A.W. (1991) 'Long Term Memory in Stock Market Prices', *Econometrics*, 5: 1279–313.

Los, C.A. (2004) *Measuring the Degree of Financial Market Efficiency*, Kent State University Working Paper, Kent.

Mandelbrot, B.B. (1987) *Gli oggetti Frattali*, Milan: Giulio Einaudi Editore.

Maslow, S. (2000) 'Simple Model of Limit Order Driven Market', *Phisica A*, 278: 571–8.

McCauley, J.L. (1994) *Chaos, Dynamics and Fractals: An Algorithmic Approach to Deterministic Chaos*, Cambridge: Cambridge University Press.

Mouck, T. (1998) 'Capital Markets Research and Real World Complexity: the Emerging Challenge of Chaos Theory', *Accounting, Organizations and Society*, 23: 189–215.

Mucley, C. (2004) 'Empirical Asset Return Distributions: Is Chaos the Culprit?', *Applied Economic Letters*, 11: 81–6.

Olmeda, I. and J. Perez (1995) 'Non Linear Dynamics and Chaos in the Spanish Stock Market', *Investigaciones Economicas*, 19: 217–48.

Pandey, V., T. Kohers and G. Kohers (1998) 'Deterministic Non Linearity in the Stock Returns of Major European Equity Markets in the United States', *Financial Review*, 33: 45–64.

Peitgen, H.O., H. Jurgens and D. Saupe (2004) *Chaos and Fractals: New Frontiers of Science*, Berlin: Springer-Verlag.

Pesaran, N.H. and S.M. Potter (1992) 'Nonlinear Dynamics, Chaos and Econometrics: an Introduction', *Journal of Applied Econometrics*, 7: 51–7.

Peters, E. (1996) *Chaos and Order in the Capital Markets: A New View of Cycles, Prices and Market Volatility*, Chichester: John Wiley and Sons.

Sadique, S. and P. Silvapulle (2001) 'Long Term Memory in Stock Market Returns: International Evidence', *International Journal of Finance and Economics*, 6: 59–67.

Scheinkman, J.A. and B. LeBaron (1989) 'Nonlinear Dynamics in Stock Returns', *Journal of Business*, 62: 311–37.

Schreimber, T. (1998) 'Interdisciplinary Application of Nonlinear Time Series Methods', *Physics Reports*, 308: 1–64.

Seppi, D.J. (1997) 'Liquidity Provisions with Limit Orders and Specialists', *Review of Financial Studies*, 10: 103–50.

Seru, A., T. Shumway and N. Stoffman (2005) *Learning by Trading*, Stephen Ross School of Business Working Paper, Ann Arbor.

Sewell, S.P., S.R.I. Stansell Lee and S.D. Below (1996) 'Using Chaos Measures to Examine International Capital Market Integration', *Applied Financial Economics*, 6: 91–101.

Skarandzinski, D.A. (2003) *The Non Linear Behavior of Stock Prices: the Impact of Firm Size, Seasonality and Trading Frequency*, Virginia Polytechnic Institute Working Paper, Blacksburg.

Tyurin, K. (2003) *High Frequency Principal Components and Evolution of Liquidity in a Limit Order Market*, Indiana University Working Paper, Bloomington.

Westerhoff, F.H. (2005) 'Heterogenous Traders, Price Volume Signals and Complex Asset Price Dynamics', *Discrete Dynamics in Nature and Society*, 1: 19–29.

Willinger, W., M.S. Taqqu and V. Teverovsky (1999) 'Stock Market Prices and Long Range Dependence', *Finance and Stochastics*, 3: 1–13.

Zanotti, G. (2006) 'Organizzazione e struttura dei mercati mobiliari', in P.L. Fabrizi (ed.), *Economia del mercato mobiliare*, Milan: EGEA.

Part II
Determinants of Value Creation in Banking

7
The Profit Generation Process in Banking

Franco Fiordelisi

7.1 Introduction

This chapter examines the determinants of profit and shareholder value creation for a large sample of European listed and unlisted banks between 1995 and 2002. There is a substantial literature that focuses on various factors that influence the performance of banks (see Molyneux and Thornton, 1992; Berger, 1995; Berger and Hannan, 1997; Berger and Mester, 2003; and Berger and Bonaccorsi di Patti, 2006). Few of these studies, however, consider the shareholder value creation indicators as measures of bank performance, which is surprising given that creating value for shareholders (generating returns in excess of the opportunity cost of capital) has been the main strategic objective of quoted banks over the last decade or so (Fiordelisi and Molyneux, 2006).

A number of studies (see, for example, Beccalli et al., 2006; Fernàndez et al., 2002; Eisenbeis et al. 1999; Chu and Lim, 1998) have sought to link measures of banks' productive efficiency to stock returns, and have generally found there to be a positive relationship. However, these studies tell us little about the determinants of shareholder value creation because they typically ignore the costs of capital considerations. Others have investigated the relationship between operational risk and bank stock price reactions (Cummings et al., 2004) and the role played by corporate risk management in the shareholder value creation process (see Bartram, 2000, 2002). Overall, however, it can be seen that the existing empirical literature on the determinants of shareholder value creation in banking is somewhat esoteric and limited.

This chapter aims to extend the established literature by examining whether or not various factors (such as market concentration, the bank's market share, efficiency, financial structure and exposures) impact on profit and shareholder value creation in banking. The contribution of this chapter is fourfold:

1. As far as we are aware, this is the first study to analyse the determinants of shareholder value creation in banking.
2. It explicitly compares the processes of profits and shareholder value creation.
3. It considers the impact of the most important types of risk on bank's performance.
4. It assesses if banks from different countries (namely, France, Germany, Italy and the UK) which have different ownership features (namely, commercial, cooperative and savings bank) have advantages\disadvantages in generating profits and\or shareholder value.

7.2   The determinants of profit and shareholder value creation in banking

Shareholder value and profitability are two different measures of bank performance. While profits express the ability of a bank to achieve an income that is superior to its costs over a given time period, a bank creates value for shareholders when the return on invested capital is greater than its opportunity cost, or than the rate that investors could earn by investing in other securities with the same level of risk.

The established empirical banking literature highlights a variety of bank- and market-specific factors that influence the level of performance. Bank-specific determinants of performance include features such as efficiency, risk and the bank's financial structure. The most common market-specific measures include indices of market structure (for example, concentration ratios) and the bank's competitive strength.

Regarding the first potential driver of profit and shareholder value creation, we focus both on cost efficiency (that is, the ability of a firm to choose inputs and/or output levels and to mix these in order to minimize cost) and profit efficiency (that is, the bank's ability to produce at the maximum possible profit given a particular level of input prices and output prices and other variables).[1]

There is a large literature dealing with bank efficiency which focuses on methodological issues (for example, Berger, 1993; Altumbas and Chakravarty, 2001), compares estimates from different methodologies (for example, Berger and Mester 1997, 2003; Bauer et al., 1997), examines bank efficiency focusing on countries and/or financial sectors that have been poorly analysed by previous studies (for example, Sathye, 2001; Green and Segal, 2004; Beccalli, 2004), and/or assesses the source of inefficiency and the role of environmental factors (for example, Dietsch and Lozano-Vives, 2000; Berger and De Young, 2001; Chaffai et al., 2001; Carbo Valverde et al., 2007). Following on from Berger (1995) and Berger and Mester (2003), we recognise that efficiency is likely to have an impact on bank performance, but we have no clear expectations about the relationship between bank efficiency and shareholder value created over a period.[2] One may expect improvements in efficiency (cost and profit) to have a positive influence on present and expected future cash flows (by reducing costs, keeping constant outputs, and/or improving profits, keeping inputs constant). Beccalli et al. (2006), for example, finds a positive relationship between bank cost efficiency and stock returns which suggests a positive relationship between efficiency and shareholder value creation. However, high efficiency levels (or efficiency improvements) may result in various externalities that may have a negative influence on expected free cash flow and, therefore, on bank's returns. For example, 'aggressive' efficiency programmes may result in a reduced level of customer satisfaction and have an adverse impact on workforce motivation. As such, the impact of cost and profit efficiency on bank's profit and shareholder value creation cannot be confidently identified ex-ante. In addition, bank's improvements in efficiency may have a different influence upon bank's profits and shareholder value – for example, 'aggressive' efficiency programmes may also increase risk with a negative effect on shareholder value created (by increasing the opportunity cost of the capital invested), while this would not necessarily influence the profit created in the same period.

The risk-taking propensity of banks is another factor that is expected to have a significant influence on the ability to generate returns. We consider the main type of risk in banking, such as credit, market, operational and liquidity risk. Credit risk (that is, the potential that a bank borrower or counterparty will fail to meet its obligations in accordance with agreed terms[3]) is the major risk faced by banks engaged in deposit-taking and lending. The number of studies dealing with credit risk is again substantial and deals with a variety of issues, including: measurement methodologies (for example, Duffie, 2005; Lucas and Klaassen, 2006; Galluccio and Roncoroni, 2006); the adequacy of new capital requirements to credit risk management practices in banking (for example, Jacobson et al., 2006); relationships with other risks (for example, Zheng, 2006; Jobst et al., 2006) and so on. Following the deregulation process in European banking, commercial banks are free to undertake financial markets activities so shareholder value and bank's profits are also increasingly influenced by market risks (that is, the risk of losses in on- and off-balance sheet positions arising from movements in market prices). The number of studies dealing with market risk in banking is again large and deals with a variety of issues including measurement methodologies (for example, Lopez, 1999; Berkovitz and O'Brien, 2002); the adequacy of capital requirements to market risk in banking (for example, Kupiec and O'Brien, 1995; Marchall and Venkataraman, 1998); relationships with other risks (for example, Barnhill et al., 2000) and so on. More recently, various studies have also focused on operational risk (that is, the risk of loss resulting from inadequate or failed internal processes, people and systems of from external events[4]) mainly looking at measurement issues (Scandizzo 2005; De Fontnouvelle et al., 2005). Finally, liquidity risk is the risk that banks hold insufficient liquid assets and are unable to meet these short-term obligations.

A bank's financial structure can also influence performance and therefore it may be an important determinant of profit and\or shareholder value creation. Barth et al. (1998) provide evidence that companies having a bond rating (or the authors' fitted bond rating) above the S&P investment grade (labelled as financially healthy) tend to have higher price multiples to net income and lower pricing multiples to book value relative to less healthy firms (that is, companies having a bond rating below investment grade). Focussing on US banks, Berger and Bonnacorsi di Patti (2006) recently investigate the hypothesis under which high leverage reduces the agency costs of outside equity and increases firm value (since managers tend to act more in the interests of shareholders). The authors find strong evidence that higher leverage (or a lower equity capital ratio) is associated with higher profit efficiency, all else being equal. As such, we use a bank leverage measure total liabilities over equity capital) to account for financial structure.

Up to this point we have only discussed bank-specific determinants of shareholder value creation. However, there is a substantial literature[5] that suggests that market structure features can impact on firm performance. Typically, the literature seeks to examine whether factors such as industry concentration (a test of the traditional structure–conduct–performance hypothesis) or individual market shares (a test of Berger's (1995) relative market power hypothesis) impact on bank performance.[6] Some of the recent research[7] allows for the possibility that the different sizes of banks may affect competitive conditions. Some other studies[8] test the hypothesis that state-owned banks may compete in different ways from privately-owned institutions, while others[9] suggest that foreign-owned banks may compete in different ways from domestically-owned banks. A few papers also investigate the effects of the US market structure on bank risk-taking.[10] Most of the current literature that examines structure/competition issues typically focuses on the US banking markets with a few exceptions, namely Panetta and Focarelli (2003), Beck, Demirgüç-Kunt and Levine (2003) and La Porta, Lopez-de-Silanes and Shleifer (2002). By using a large sample of European banks, this chapter analyses the possibility that banks which have larger market shares, or those that operate in more concentrated markets, have an advantage in generating profits and shareholder value. In addition, we also consider the possibility that listed banks may have an advantage\disadvantage in creating shareholder value and\or profits.

7.3   Methodology and data

We specify a model similar to that proposed by Molyneux and Thornton (1992), Berger (1995) and Berger and Bonnacorsi di Patti (2006), where bank performance indicators are regressed against a number of potential determinants. We estimate the following model so as to deal with the panel dimensions of our dataset:[11]

$$\psi_{i,t} = \partial + \sum_{k=1}^{3} \alpha_k T_k + \sum_{j=0}^{2} \beta_j x - eff_{i,t-j} + \sum_{j=0}^{2} \chi_j \pi - eff_{i,t-j} + \sum_{j=0}^{2} \delta_j CR_{i,t-j}$$

$$+ \sum_{j=0}^{2} \phi_j OR_{i,t-j} + \varphi MR_{i,t} + \gamma LR_{i,t} + \sum_{j=0}^{2} \omega_j LEV_{i,t-j} + \sum_{j=0}^{2} \iota_j MS_{i,t-j}$$

$$+ \sum_{j=0}^{2} \kappa_j CONC_{i,t-j} + \sum_{k=1}^{m} \lambda_k Z_k + \mu L_{i,t} + e_{i,t} \tag{7.1}$$

where $\psi_{i,t}$ is the variable representing bank performance (we use both ROA and an Economic Value Added measure – EVAbkg[12]), ∂ is a constant (capture missing variables); T_k ($k=1$, 2, 3) are dummy variables for the years considered (namely, 2000, 2001 and 2002); x-eff$_{i,t-h}$ is the cost efficiency for the bank i over the period $t-j$ ($j=0$, 1, 2);[13] π-eff$_{i,t-h}$ is the profit efficiency for the bank i over the period $t-j$ ($j=0$, 1, 2);[14] CR$_{i,t-h}$ is the unexpected credit risk losses for the bank i over the period $t-j$ ($j=0$, 1, 2);[15] OR$_{i,t-h}$ is the operational risk exposure (calculated using the Basle simple indicator approach for the bank i over the period $t-j$ ($j=0$, 1, 2); MR$_{i,t}$ is the market risk exposure (measured as the total amount of

Table 7.1 Number of banks in samples used for estimating shareholder value drivers in European banking

	1997	1998	1999	2000	2001	2002	Total
France							
Commercial banks	199	208	213	218	235	227	1300
Cooperative banks	95	97	101	100	111	98	602
Savings banks	25	25	25	29	31	28	163
Total	319	330	339	347	377	353	2065
Germany							
Commercial banks	140	149	151	167	170	170	947
Cooperative banks	832	930	1102	1220	1371	1381	6836
Savings banks	568	587	600	609	616	604	3584
Total	1540	1666	1853	1996	2157	2155	11367
Italy							
Commercial banks	87	106	117	127	132	144	713
Cooperative banks	132	262	386	464	505	520	2269
Savings banks	63	64	64	66	64	66	387
Total	282	432	567	657	701	730	3369
UK							
Commercial banks	68	76	84	85	88	85	486
Cooperative banks	0	0	0	0	0	0	0
Savings banks	0	0	0	0	0	0	0
Total	68	76	84	85	88	85	486
Listed banks							
Commercial banks	44	51	58	68	73	70	364

Source: Bankscope.

investment securities on total assets) for the bank i over the period t; $LR_{i,t}$ is the liquidity risk exposure (measured as the financing gap, that is, the difference between the average loans and the average amount of deposits[16]) for bank i over period t; $LEV_{i,t-h}$ is the financial leverage (measured as the ratio between the total amount of liabilities and equity capital) for bank i over period $t-j$ ($j=0$, 1, 2); $MS_{i,t-h}$ is the asset market share for bank i over period $t-j$ ($j=0$, 1, 2); $CONC_{i,t-h}$ are domestic banking industry concentration estimates over the period $t-j$ ($j=0$, 1, 2); Z_k ($k=1, \ldots, 9$) is a set of dummy variables capturing country effects (namely, France, Germany, Italy, and the UK) and specialization (for example, commercial, cooperative and savings banks),[17] $L_{i,t}$ is a dummy variable expressing if the bank i is publicly listed[18] at time t that has been included to assess if quoted banks are significantly different to non-listed banks in terms of profit and shareholder value creation.[19] It should also be noted that because many of the relationships being investigated are

Table 7.2   Descriptive statistics of variables used to analyse the sample of European listed and non-listed banks over the period 1999–2002 (6,714 observations)

	Minimum	Maximum	Mean	Dev. St
EVA on Invested capital	−0.13	0.14	−0.01	0.03
Cost efficiency	0.05	1.00	0.77	0.10
Profit efficiency	0.00	1.00	0.65	0.16
Credit risk provision	−136.50	1,608.00	10.17	51.01
Operational risk exposure	0.13	5,140.95	30.32	187.50
Investment securities	0.90	35,515.40	215.51	1,267.53
Financing gap (i.e. average loans – average deposits)	−235,487.00	33,191.40	−675.65	7,046.51
Financial leverage (i.e. total amount of liabilities and equity capital)	0.09	123.15	18.89	7.06
Asset market share	0.00	0.23	0.00	0.01
Concentration ratio (Herfindal Index)	20.80	3012.10	264.00	442.80

Source: Bankscope.

unlikely to be contemporaneous, we include up to two period (yearly) lags for all variables (except for liquidity and market risk).[20]

Our dataset consists of commercial, cooperative and savings banks from France, Germany, Italy and the UK between 1995 and 2002. The financial information was obtained from Bankscope and (to identify quoted banks) Datastream databases. Details of the number of banks in the sample are shown in Table 7.1.

The descriptive statistics of the sample are shown in the top half of Table 7.2 which illustrates that European banks destroyed shareholder value (by around 1.1 per cent) over the period analysed. Cost efficiency estimates display superior mean levels than profit estimates: this result is common in the bank efficiency literature.[21] European banks are found to have lost around one-third of their potential profits through inefficiency, whereas cost inefficiencies (although substantial at around 25 per cent) are lower. The equity capital required by regulators to cover bank's operational risk exposure is, on average, 0.01 per cent of total assets, while the mean credit risk exposure (measured by annual provisions to loan loss reserve) amounts to 0.4 per cent of total loans. Although not reported in the table, the German banking system has the lowest level of industry concentration, while the UK market is found to be the most concentrated of the four banking systems analysed.

7.4 Results

Table 7.3 reports the results obtained from estimating our model for bank profits (that is, using Return on Assets as the dependent variable). According to our results, bank efficiency is the most influential driver of bank's profits as the profit efficiency coefficients at time t and $t-1$ are positive and statistically significant at the 1% and 10% confidence levels, respectively, while the cost efficiency coefficient at time t is positive and statistically significant at the 1% level. A surprising result is that the estimated cost efficiency coefficients are larger than the profit efficiency coefficients, which suggests that cost efficiency improvements will have a larger (positive) impact on bank's accounting profits. Intuitively, one would expect profit efficiency to have a larger influence on accounting profits compared to cost efficiency; however, our result shows that if a bank is able to reduce its distance from the cost efficient frontier (for example, by 10 per cent), this will have a larger impact on the bank's ROA in the same year than those that could be achieved by reducing its distance from the profit efficient frontier in a similar dimension (that is, 10 per cent). We explain this unusual finding by considering that cost reductions are likely to improve the bank's profits in the same year. However, in the short term improvements in cost efficiency may be offset by a decline in revenues. For example, by reducing the number of employees, a bank likely improves its cost efficiency in the short term, but this may produce customer dissatisfaction and workforce disincentives.

We find that market risk exposure is positively related (and statistically significant at the 1% confidence level) to bank's ROA. Banks that have assumed more market risk over the period improved their performance. The other sources of risk in banking (credit, operational and liquidity risk) do not display a statistically significant relationship (at least, at the 10% significance level) with bank's ROA and this result may be interpreted as meaning that there are no substantial differences in the way in which these risks were managed by banks so that these did not have any statistically significant impact on bank's profits. We also find that banks with different ownership features have statistically significant different levels of profits. In addition, in contrast to the previous literature, market structure features (such as industry concentration and bank market share) do not display a statistically significant influence on bank's profits. Listed banks are also found not to have a statistically significant relationship with bank's ROA.

The influence of the performance drivers mentioned above appears to have a contrasting impact on shareholder value creation. Table 7.4

Table 7.3 The multiple-variable relationship between profits and its determinants in European banking ([the dependent variable (ψ) is the return on assets])

Variable		Observed coefficient	Bootstrap Std. err.
(Constant)	∂	0.00618	0.00345
Dummy variable for the year 2000 (T1)	$\alpha1$	−0.00028	0.00018
Dummy variable for the year 2001 (T2)	$\alpha2$	−0.00025	0.00021
Dummy variable for the year 2002 (T3)	$\alpha3$	−0.00103***	0.00034
Cost efficiency estimates at time t (x-eff$_t$)	$\beta0$	0.00511***	0.00128
Cost efficiency estimates at time t − 1 (x-efff$_{t-1}$)	$\beta1$	−0.00113	0.00118
Cost efficiency estimates at time t − 2 (x-eff$_{t-2}$)	$\beta2$	−0.00028	0.00140
Profit efficiency estimates at time t (π-eff$_t$)	$\chi0$	0.00275***	0.00080
Profit efficiency estimates at time t − 1 (π-efff$_{t-1}$)	$\chi1$	0.00156*	0.00086
Profit efficiency estimates at time t − 2 (π-eff$_{t-2}$)	$\chi2$	−0.00047	0.00080
Credit risk exposure at time t (CR$_t$)	$\delta0$	−0.00054	0.00063
Credit risk exposure at time t − 1 (CRf$_{t-1}$)	$\delta1$	0.00078	0.00069
Credit risk exposure at time t − 2 (CR$_{t-2}$)	$\delta2$	−0.00011	0.00062
Operational risk exposure at time t (OR$_t$)	$\phi0$	0.05274	0.03367
Operational risk exposure at time t − 1 (ORf$_{t-1}$)	$\phi1$	−0.01793	0.02944
Operational risk exposure at time t − 2 (OR$_{t-2}$)	$\phi2$	−0.02529	0.01730
Market risk exposure at time t (OR$_t$)	$\varphi0$	0.00023***	0.00008
Liquidity risk exposure at time t (LR $_t$)	γ	0.00000	0.00000
Bank's financial leverage at time t (LEV$_t$)	$\omega0$	−0.00004	0.00006
Bank's financial leverage at time t − 1 (LEV$_{t-1}$)	$\omega1$	−0.00001	0.00003
Bank's financial leverage at time t − 2 (LEV$_{t-2}$)	$\omega2$	−0.00005	0.00004
Bank's market share at time t (MS$_t$)	$\iota0$	−0.03950	0.05226
Bank's market share at time t − 1 (MS$_{t-1}$)	$\iota1$	−0.09192	0.11726
Bank's market share at time t − 2 (MS$_{t-2}$)	$\iota2$	0.11684	0.11612
Domestic market concentration at time t (CONC$_t$)	$\kappa0$	0.00000	0.00000
Domestic market concentration at time t − 1 (CONC$_{t-1}$)	$\kappa1$	0.00000	0.00000
Domestic market concentration at time t − 2 (CONC$_{t-2}$)	$\kappa2$	0.00000	0.00000
Dummy variable for Italian commercial banks (Z1)	$\lambda1$	−0.00299	0.00194
Dummy variable for Italian cooperative banks (Z2)	$\lambda2$	−0.00039	0.00186
Dummy variable for Italian savings banks (Z3)	$\lambda3$	−0.00241	0.00185
Dummy variable for French commercial banks (Z4)	$\lambda4$	−0.00613***	0.00122
Dummy variable for French cooperative banks (Z5)	$\lambda5$	−0.00698***	0.00113
Dummy variable for French savings banks (Z6)	$\lambda6$	−0.00847***	0.00115
Dummy variable for German commercial banks (Z7)	$\lambda7$	0.00064	0.00295
Dummy variable for German cooperative banks (Z8)	$\lambda8$	−0.00242	0.00288
Dummy variable for German savings banks (Z9)	$\lambda9$	−0.00224	0.00288
Dummy variable for publicly listed banks (L)	μ	0.00084	0.00062

Log likelihood = 27314.73159
AIC = −7.444796
BIC = −64885.7

where:

*/**/***indicate that estimated coefficients are statistically significance at the 10%, 5%, and 1% significance level, respectively.

The combined dummy effects for 1999 and UK commercial banks are incorporated in the constant term. Because of the two period lag, only dummy variables for 2000 to 2002 are included in the reported estimates.

Table 7.4 The multiple-variable relationship between shareholder value and its determinants in European banking (the dependent variable (ψ) is the ratio between EVAbkg, and the invested capital at time $t-1$)

Variable		Observed coefficient	Bootstrap std. err.
(Constant)	∂	0.00559	0.03109
Dummy variable for the year 2000 (T1)	$\alpha1$	0.01175***	0.00302
Dummy variable for the year 2001 (T2)	$\alpha2$	0.01823***	0.00294
Dummy variable for the year 2002 (T3)	$\alpha3$	0.00651**	0.00306
Cost efficiency estimates at time t (x-eff$_t$)	$\beta0$	−0.02373	0.01898
Cost efficiency estimates at time $t-1$ (x-efff$_{t-1}$)	$\beta1$	0.01755	0.01458
Cost efficiency estimates at time $t-2$ (x-eff$_{t-2}$)	$\beta2$	0.01946	0.01585
Profit efficiency estimates at time t (π-efft)	$\chi0$	0.04251***	0.01052
Profit efficiency estimates at time $t-1$ (π-efff$_{t-1}$)	$\chi1$	0.00267	0.00964
Profit efficiency estimates at time $t-2$ (π-eff$_{t-2}$)	$\chi2$	0.00461	0.00879
Credit risk exposure at time t (CR$_t$)	$\delta0$	0.00117	0.00455
Credit risk exposure at time $t-1$ (CRf$_{t-1}$)	$\delta1$	−0.00094	0.00508
Credit risk exposure at time $t-2$ (CR$_{t-2}$)	$\delta2$	−0.00003	0.00518
Operational risk exposure at time t (OR$_t$)	$\phi0$	0.32407**	0.13826
Operational risk exposure at time $t-1$ (ORf$_{t-1}$)	$\phi1$	−0.01742	0.25792
Operational risk exposure at time $t-2$ (OR$_{t-2}$)	$\phi2$	−0.29028	0.25535
Market risk exposure at time t (OR$_t$)	$\varphi0$	0.00083	0.00113
Liquidity risk exposure at time t (LR$_t$)	γ	0.00000	0.00000
Bank's financial leverage at time t (LEV$_t$)	$\omega0$	0.00000	0.00077
Bank's financial leverage at time $t-1$ (LEV$_{t-1}$)	$\omega1$	0.00005	0.00069
Bank's financial leverage at time $t-2$ (LEV$_{t-2}$)	$\omega2$	−0.00034	0.00055
Bank's market share at time t (MS$_t$)	$\iota0$	−0.59985	0.51438
Bank's market share at time $t-1$ (MS$_{t-1}$)	$\iota1$	1.23750**	0.63918
Bank's market share at time $t-2$ (MS$_{t-2}$)	$\iota2$	−0.71445	0.56908
Domestic market concentration at time t (CONC$_t$)	$\kappa0$	−0.00007**	0.00003
Domestic market concentration at time $t-1$ (CONC$_{t-1}$)	$\kappa1$	−0.00012**	0.00006
Domestic market concentration at time $t-2$ (CONC$_{t-2}$)	$\kappa2$	−0.00011***	0.00003
Dummy variable for Italian commercial banks (Z1)	$\lambda1$	−0.05836***	0.01327
Dummy variable for Italian cooperative banks (Z2)	$\lambda2$	−0.03124**	0.01280
Dummy variable for Italian savings banks (Z3)	$\lambda3$	−0.05567***	0.01357
Dummy variable for French commercial banks (Z4)	$\lambda4$	0.00032	0.01298
Dummy variable for French cooperative banks (Z5)	$\lambda5$	−0.00833	0.01036
Dummy variable for French savings banks (Z6)	$\lambda6$	−0.00471	0.01157
Dummy variable for German commercial banks (Z7)	$\lambda7$	−0.05263**	0.02163
Dummy variable for German cooperative banks (Z8)	$\lambda8$	−0.04514**	0.01982
Dummy variable for German savings banks (Z9)	$\lambda9$	−0.03601*	0.01954
Dummy variable for publicly listed banks (L)	μ	0.01780***	0.00600

Log likelihood = 8271.830345
AIC = −2.245659
BIC = −64900.32

where:

*/**/*** indicate that estimated coefficients are statistically significance at the 10%, 5%, and 1% significance level, respectively.

The combined dummy effects for 1999 and UK commercial banks are incorporated in the constant term. Because of the two period lag, only dummy variables for 2000 to 2002 are included in the reported estimates.

reports the results obtained from estimating our model for bank shareholder value (that is, using EVAbkg as the dependent variable). According to our results, profit efficiency at time t is found to be a statistically significant (at the 1% confidence level) driver of bank's EVA, while cost efficiency has no influence value creation. At first sight, this result may appear surprising, since they provide evidence that cost reductions will lead banks to increase profits over the same period, but not necessarily shareholder value since, for example, cost reduction strategies may increase bank risks and this may also raise the opportunity cost of capital. The estimated profit efficiency coefficient is larger than those estimated through the analysis of the bank's profits (Table 7.3), showing that a profit efficiency improvement will produce a larger effect on bank's EVA than on ROA: this may perhaps occur because shareholders are likely to judge a profit-efficient bank as less risky, thereby requiring a smaller opportunity cost for invested capital.

Regarding the relationship between banking risks and shareholder value, only the estimated coefficients for operational risk exposure at time t is positive and statistically significant. The positive relationship between operational risk exposure and bank's EVA is not really surprising since the 'simple' Basle approach for measuring operational risk exposure is based on bank's gross income.

In contrast to the analysis of the determinants of bank's profits, market structure features display a statistically significant role in influencing the bank's EVA. According to our results, banks with a larger market share at time $t - 1$ have a substantial advantage in creating shareholder value, especially if these banks operate in less concentrated banking industries. In addition, we found that listed banks display a statistically significant (at the 1% confidence level) advantage in creating shareholder value. In final, we find that some of control variables for country (namely, Germany and Italy) and bank ownership type are statistically significant (at least at the 5% confidence level).

Since we identify that the determinants of bank's profits and shareholder value may differ in terms of either countries or types of bank ownership, we estimated model (1) for various sub-samples according to the bank's nationality.[22] Regarding accounting profits, we found that cost and profit efficiency are statistically significant (at the 1% confidence level and with cost efficiency coefficients larger than profit efficiency coefficients) in France and Germany, but not in Italy and the UK. Bank's ownership types is found to be statistically significant in Germany where commercial banks appear to have an advantage in generating profits and whereas cooperative banks are less profitable. In

Table 7.5 The multiple-variable relationship between profits and its determinants in domestic European banking industries (the dependent variable (ψ) is the return on assets)

Variable		Observed coefficients			
		France	Germany	Italy	U.K.
(Constant)	∂	−0.04***	−0.00*	−0.01	−0.01
Cost efficiency estimates at time t (x-eff$_t$)	β_0	0.04***	0.01***	0.00	−0.00
Cost efficiency estimates at time t − 1 (x-efff$_{t-1}$)	β_1	0.00	0.00	−0.00	−0.00
Cost efficiency estimates at time t − 2 (x-eff$_{t-2}$)	β_2	−0.00	0.00	−0.00**	0.00
Profit efficiency estimates at time t (π-eff$_t$)	χ_0	0.02**	0.00***	−0.00	−0.00
Profit efficiency estimates at time t − 1 (π-efff$_{t-1}$)	χ_1	−0.01	0.00**	−0.00	−0.00
Profit efficiency estimates at time t − 2 (π-eff$_{t-2}$)	χ_2	0.01*	−0.00	−0.00	−0.00
Credit risk exposure at time t (CR$_t$)	δ_0	0.00	−0.00	0.00	−0.00**
Credit risk exposure at time t − 1 (CR$_{t-1}$)	δ_1	−0.00	0.01	−0.00	−0.01*
Credit risk exposure at time t − 2 (CR$_{t-2}$)	δ_2	0.00	0.00	0.00	0.00
Operational risk exposure at time t (OR$_t$)	ϕ_0	0.46	0.16	0.85*	0.05*
Operational risk exposure at time t − 1 (ORf$_{t-1}$)	ϕ_1	0.31	0.28	−0.25	−0.02
Operational risk exposure at time t − 2 (OR$_{t-2}$)	ϕ_2	0.21	0.02	−0.13	−0.01
Market risk exposure at time t (OR$_t$)	φ_0	0.00	0.00	0.00**	0.00***
Liquidity risk exposure at time t (LR$_t$)	γ	0.00	0.00	0.00	0.00
Bank's financial leverage at time t (LEV$_t$)	ω_0	0.00	−0.00	−0.00***	0.00
Bank's financial leverage at time t − 1 (LEV$_{t-1}$)	ω_1	0.00	0.00	−0.00**	−0.00
Bank's financial leverage at time t − 2 (LEV$_{t-2}$)	ω_2	−0.00	−0.00	0.00	−0.00
Bank's market share at time t (MS$_t$)	ι_0	0.03	−0.31	−0.00	−0.20
Bank's market share at time t − 1 (MS$_{t-1}$)	ι_1	−0.33	0.70	−0.01	0.05

(Continued)

Table 7.5 (Continued)

Variable		Observed coefficients			
		France	Germany	Italy	U.K.
Bank's market share at time $t-2$ (MS_{t-2})	ι_2	0.27	-0.47	0.01	0.02
Domestic market concentration at time t ($CONC_t$)	κ_0	0.00	0.00	0.00	-0.00
Domestic market concentration at time $t-1$ ($CONC_{t-1}$)	κ_1	0.00	-0.00	0.00	0.00
Domestic market concentration at time $t-2$ ($CONC_{t-2}$)	κ_2	0.00	-0.00	0.00	-0.00
Dummy variable for commercial banks (Z1)	λ_1	-0.00	0.00***	0.00***	N/A
Dummy variable for cooperative banks (Z2)	λ_3	0.00	-0.00***	0.00	N/A
Dummy variable for publicly listed banks (L)	μ	0.00	-0.00	0.00	0.01***
Log Likelihood =		2057.80	23966.50	3516.60	1100.90
AIC =		-5.90	-8.90	-7.40	-6.10
BIC =		-4258.80	-45773.70	-62263.80	-1924.10

Where:
*/**/***indicate that estimated coefficients are statistically significance at the 10%, 5%, and 1% significance level, respectively.
The combined dummy effects for 1999 and UK commercial banks are incorporated in the constant term. Because of the two period lag, only dummy variables for 2000 to 2002 are included in the reported estimates.

Italian banking, we find that the operational risk exposure has a positive relationship with bank's ROA, while bank's financial leverage at time t and t − 1 has a negative impact on ROA, suggesting that banks with lower levels of capital (that is, risky banks) are no more profitable than other banks. Commercial banks seem to have a slight advantage in generating profits. In the UK, few of the determinants of bank's ROA are found to be statistically significant.

The relationship between the set of determinants analysed and shareholder value is again substantially different to the one discussed above in the case of bank's profits. Profit efficiency seems to be the main driver in the shareholder value creation (in France, Germany and Italy), while cost efficiency is statistically significant only in France. With regard to the relationship between banking risks and shareholder value, only the estimated coefficients for operational risk exposure at time t is positive

Table 7.6   The multiple-variable relationship between shareholder value and its determinants in domestic European banking industries (the dependent variable (ψ) is the ratio between EVAbkg and the capital invested at time $t-1$)

Variable		France	Germany	Italy	U.K.
		Observed coefficients			
(Constant)	∂	0.25*	0.00	−0.18	0.23
Cost efficiency estimates at time t (x-eff$_t$)	β_0	0.29***	−0.02	−0.01	−0.01
Cost efficiency estimates at time $t-1$ (x-efff$_{t-1}$)	β_1	0.08	0.01	−0.02	0.01
Cost efficiency estimates at time $t-2$ (x-eff$_{t-2}$)	β_2	−0.04	0.01	0.06***	0.01
Profit efficiency estimates at time t (π-eff$_t$)	χ_0	0.18***	0.05***	−0.00	0.10***
Profit efficiency estimates at time $t-1$ (π-efff$_{t-1}$)	χ_1	−0.04	0.01	−0.00	0.07**
Profit efficiency estimates at time $t-2$ (π-eff$_{t-2}$)	χ_2	−0.05	−0.01	−0.00	0.08***
Credit risk exposure at time t (CR$_t$)	δ_0	−0.04	−0.01	−0.04	−0.01
Credit risk exposure at time $t-1$ (CR$_{t-1}$)	δ_1	0.21	0.01	0.05	0.01
Credit risk exposure at time $t-2$ (CR$_{t-2}$)	δ_2	−0.03	0.00	0.01	0.00
Operational risk exposure at time t (OR$_t$)	ϕ_0	−1.65	1.17	−9.26**	−0.12**
Operational risk exposure at time $t-1$ (ORf$_{t-1}$)	ϕ_1	−3.58	−5.54	2.25	−0.07
Operational risk exposure at time $t-2$ (OR$_{t-2}$)	ϕ_2	0.79	2.21	1.95	0.23
Market risk exposure at time t (OR$_t$)	φ_0	−0.00	0.00	−0.00	−0.00
Liquidity risk exposure at time t (LR$_t$)	γ	0.00	0.00	0.00	0.00**
Bank's financial leverage at time t (LEV$_t$)	ω_0	−0.00	0.00	−0.01*	−0.01***
Bank's financial leverage at time $t-1$ (LEV$_{t-1}$)	ω_1	0.00	−0.01	−0.01**	0.00
Bank's financial leverage at time $t-2$ (LEV$_{t-2}$)	ω_2	−0.00	0.00	−0.00	0.00
Bank's market share at time t (MS$_t$)	ι_0	−0.78	0.11	−0.54	0.37
Bank's market share at time $t-1$ (MS$_{t-1}$)	ι_1	1.74	5.14	0.78	0.09

(Continued)

Table 7.6 (Continued)

Variable		Observed coefficients			
		France	Germany	Italy	U.K.
Bank's market share at time t − 2 (MS_{t-2})	ι_2	−0.99	−4.31	−0.40	−0.01
Domestic market concentration at time t ($CONC_t$)	κ_0	−0.00	−0.00	−0.00	0.00**
Domestic market concentration at time t − 1 ($CONC_{t-1}$)	κ_1	0.00	0.01**	0.00**	−0.00**
Domestic market concentration at time t − 2 ($CONC_{t-2}$)	κ_2	−0.00	0.02***	0.00	0.00*
Dummy variable for commercial banks (Z1)	λ_1	0.02*	−0.01	0.00	N/A
Dummy variable for cooperative banks (Z2)	λ_3	0.01	−0.01***	−0.02**	N/A
Dummy variable for publicly listed banks (L)	μ	0.02*	0.01	0.02**	0.022
Log Likelihood =		463.30	6840.60	1204.40	385.40
AIC=		−1.30	−2.50	−2.51	−2.04
BIC=		−4293.40	−45749.40	−6222.60	−1921.90

where:
*/**/***indicate that estimated coefficients are statistically significance at the 10%, 5%, and 1% significance level, respectively
The combined dummy effects for 1999 and UK commercial banks are incorporated in the constant term. Because of the two period lag, only dummy variables for 2000 to 2002 are included in the reported estimates.

and statistically significant in Italy and the UK. We also found that the bank's financial leverage at time t and t − 1 has a negative impact on EVA in Italy and the UK supporting the view that banks with higher levels of capital have an advantage in creating shareholder value. In contrast to the previous European estimates, market structure features in domestic banking markets do not display a clear statistically significant role in influencing bank's EVA. We also find that quoted banks do better at creating shareholder value than their non-quoted counterparts in all countries analysed, especially France and Italy.

7.5 Conclusions

This chapter examines the determinants of profits and shareholder value creation in European banking between 1997 and 2002. It extends the established literature by examining whether or not various factors (for example, market structure, bank efficiency, financial structure and the main banking risks) impact on profits and shareholder value creation in banking. We also investigate whether there are differences in the performance generation between publicly quoted and unlisted banks, and also between banks of different ownership type (commercial, savings and co-operative banks), both across countries and over time.

Overall, we find that bank's cost and profit efficiency have a positive influence on bank's profits, while only profit efficiency displays a positive impact on the creation of shareholder value. Liquidity and credit risk do not seem to influence bank's profits and shareholder value. Instead, we found a larger market risk exposure (measured by the ratio of investment securities to total assets) creates a positive contribution to bank's profit, while operational exposure is positively linked to shareholder value. Nevertheless, it is surprising that the operational risk exposure is statistically significantly linked to EVA and not to ROA, suggesting that the relationship between bank's operational risk and bank's performance needs further investigation. Leverage is also found to be inversely related to shareholder value creation (especially in the Italy and the UK), suggesting that highly capitalized banks are more likely to generate profits and value for their owners compared with lowly capitalized counterparts. We also found that banks with a larger market share at time $t-1$ have a substantial advantage in creating shareholder value, especially if these banks operate in less concentrated banking industries. We also find that quoted banks do better at creating shareholder value than their non-quoted counterparts, especially in France and Italy.

Notes

1. Berger and Mester (1997) develop an 'alternative' profit efficiency concept referring to the bank's ability of producing at the maximum possible profit given a particular level of output levels, rather than its output prices.
2. Some studies (for example, Beccalli et al., 2006) note that stock returns may be influenced by efficiency changes across two consecutive periods (e.g. bank j improved its cost or profit efficiency by 40 per cent between period $t-1$ and t), rather than its efficiency levels (e.g. 30 per cent cost efficiency in $t-1$ and 70 per cent in t). As such, we run model (2) considering cost and profit efficiency changes (obtained comparing efficiency estimates in two different periods) as independent variables: results are very similar to these discussed for cost and profit efficiency levels in the papers.
3. Basel Committee on Banking Supervision (2000).
4. Basel Committee on Banking Supervision (2003).

5. See Berger et al. (2004), Berger (1995), Berger and Hannan (1989, 1998), Goldberg and Rai (1996), Berger and Hannan (1997, 1998), Maudos (1998), Goddard et al. (2001), Mendes and Rebelo (2003) and Fu and Heffernan (2005) who have all investigated the relationship between bank performance (but not focussing on shareholder value) and market structure – usually finding a positive relationship.
6. Note that one can only test for Berger's (1995) Relative market Power Hypothesis if the influence of bank level efficiency is controlled for.
7. For example, DeYoung et al. (2004)
8. For example, Barth et al. (2004), La Porta et al. (2002) and Berger et al. (2004).
9. For example, DeYoung and Nolle (1996) and Berger et al. (2000).
10. For example, Keeley (1990).
11. Considering the large size of our sample, model 1 is estimated using the Maximum Likelihood (Newton-Raphson) optimization procedure and the standard error of estimated coefficients is obtained using a bootstrapping procedure (with 200 replications). For further detail on MLE properties, see Greene (1997).
12. EVA is a trademarked variant of residual income developed by the consulting firm of Stern Stewart & Company. Several studies (for example, Easton, 1998 and Easton and Sommers, 2003) empirically demonstrate the distortion generated by 'scale effects' (which refers to the undue influence of large firms in the regression analysis) in studying the relationship between company's market returns and accounting data. While the independent variables in models (1) do not suffer from scale effects, it is necessary to standardize the dependent variable (that is, EVAbkg) to minimize heteroscedasticity and scale effect problems. Of the various solutions adopted in previous studies (see Brown et al. 1999, and Akbar and Stark, 2003), we use the capital invested (obtained following the EVAbkg calculation procedure as a deflator for EVA): this measure seems preferable to other accounting measures because it faces less accounting distortions and provides a meaningful shareholder value indicator (i.e. the shareholder value created for any one euro of capital invested by shareholders). We lag the capital invested term by one period assuming that it will take at least a year for capital investments to feed through into additional EVA.
13. The cost profit efficiency estimates are obtained using the stochastic frontier approach (details are outlined in the Annex).
14. We estimated the alternative profit efficiency (following Berger and Mester, 1997) using the stochastic frontier approach (details are outlined in the Annex).
15. As a proxy for these unexpected losses, we focus on the annual provision to loan loss reserves, i.e. the reserve that covers future unexpected loan losses Expected loan losses are measured by write-downs on loan, but these do not really express the bank's risk exposure being 'expected' losses.
16. Casu et al. (2006) support that the financing gap is one the most useful indicator of a bank's liquidity.
17. It is worthwhile to note that we have already considered these dummy variables to control for the influence of a specific bank specialization (namely, commercial, cooperative and savings banks) on bank's efficiency estimates. However, since Altunbas et al. (2001) and Goddard et al. (2004) highlight

differences in both efficiency and profits performance for various types of European banks, we prefer to include a broader set of dummy variable to control for the influence of country (namely, France, Germany, Italy, and the UK) and specialization (for example, commercial, cooperative and savings banks) on shareholder value created over a period.

18. Namely, Li is 1 if bank i is publicly listed and 0 otherwise.
19. Quoted banks may have some advantages in creating shareholder value since these banks can finance their size-growth by external sources 'more economically and easily' than non-quoted banks (see Goddard et al., 2004).
20. Since the liquidity and the market risk exposures may produce losses over the short-term, we expect that these risks may influence the bank performance 'only' over the same time period.
21. See Goddard et al. (2001) and Berger and Mester (1997).
22. Namely (a) French, (b) German, (c) Italian and (d) British banks.

References

Ahmed, A.S., R.M. Morton and T.F. Schaefer (2000) 'Accounting Conservatism and the Valuation of Accounting Numbers: Evidence on the Felthman–Ohlson (1996) Model', *Journal of Accounting, Auditing and Finance*, 15: 271–92.

Altumbas, Y. and S. Chakravarty (2001) 'Frontier Cost Functions and Bank Efficiency', *Economic Letters*, 72: 233–40.

Aly, H.Y., R. Grabowski, C. Pasurka and N. Rangan (1990) 'Technical, Scale and Allocative Efficiencies in US Banking: an Empirical Investigation', *Review of Economics and Statistics*, 72: 211–18.

Barnhill, T., P. Papapanagiotou and L.B. Schumacher (2000) *Measuring Integrated Market and Credit Risks in Bank Portfolios: An Application to a Set of Hypothetical Banks Operating in South Africa*, IMF Working Paper No. 00/212, Washington.

Barth, M.E. and W.H. Beaver (2001) 'The Relevance of the Value Relevance Literature for Financial Accounting Standard Setting: Another View', *Journal of Accounting and Economics*, 31: 3–75.

Barth, M.E., W.H. Beaver and W. Landsman (1998) 'Relative Valuation Roles of Equity Book Value and Net Income as a Function of Financial Health', *Journal of Accounting and Economics*, 25: 1–34.

Bartram, S. (2000) 'Corporate Risk Management as a Lever for Shareholder Value Creation', *Financial Markets, Institutions and Instruments*, 9: 279–324.

Bartram, S. (2002) 'Enhancing Shareholder Value with Corporate Risk Management', *Corporate Finance Review*, 7: 7–12.

Basel Committee on Banking Supervision (2000) *Principles for the Management of Credit Risk*, September.

Basel Committee on Banking Supervision (2003) *Sound Practices for the Management and Supervision of Operational Risk*, February.

Basel Committee on Banking Supervision (2005) *International Convergence of Capital Measurement and Capital Standards: a Revised Framework*.

Battese, G.E. and T.J. Coelli (1995) 'A Model for Technical Inefficiency Effects in a Stochastic Frontier Production Function for Panel Data', *Empirical Economics* 20: 325–32.

Bauer, P.W., A.N. Berger, G.D. Ferrier and D.B. Humphrey (1997) *Consistency Conditions for Regulatory Analysis of Financial Institutions: A Comparison of Frontier Efficiency Methods*, Federal Reserve Board of Cleveland – Finance and Economics Discussion Series no. 297, Cleveland.

Beccalli, E. (2004) 'Cross-country Comparisons of Efficiency: Evidence from the UK and Italian Investment Firms', *Journal of Banking and Finance*, 28: 1363–83.

Beccalli, E., B. Casu, and C. Girardone (2006) 'Efficiency and Stock Performance in European Banking', *Journal of Business Finance and Accounting*, 33: 245–62.

Beck, T., A. Demirgüç-Kunt and R. Levine (2003) *Small and Medium Enterprises, Economic Growth and Development*, World Bank research paper, Washington: World Bank.

Berger, A.N. (1993) 'Distribution-free Estimates of Efficiency in the US Banking System and Tests of the Standard Distributional Assumptions', *Journal of Productivity Analysis*, 4: 261–83.

Berger, A.N. (1995) 'The Profit–Structure Relationship in Banking – Test of Market Power and Efficient Structure Hypothesis', *Journal of Money, Credit and Banking*, 27: 404–31.

Berger, A.N., D. Bonaccorsi and E. Patti (2006) 'Capital Structure and Firm Performance: a New Approach to Testing Agency Theory and an Application to the Banking Industry', *Journal of Banking and Finance*, 30: 1065–102.

Berger, A.N. and R. De Young (2001) 'The Effect of Geographic Expansion on Bank Efficiency', *Journal of Financial Service Research*, 19: 163–84.

Berger, A.N., A. Demirgüç-Kunt, R. Levine and J.C. Haubrich (2004) 'Bank Concentration and Competition: an Evolution in the Making', *Journal of Money, Credit and Banking*, 36: 433–52.

Berger, A.N. and T.H. Hannan (1989) 'The Price–Concentration Relationship in Banking', *Review of Economics and Statistics*, 71: 291–9.

Berger, A.N. and T.H. Hannan (1997) 'Using Efficiency Measures to Distinguish among Alternative Explanations of the Structure–Performance Relationship in Banking', *Managerial Finance*, 23: 6–31.

Berger, A.N. and T.H. Hannan (1998) 'The Efficiency Cost of Market Power in the Banking Industry: a Test of the "Quiet Life" and Related Hypotheses', *Review of Economics and Statistics*, 80: 454–65.

Berger, A.N., I. Hasan and L.F. Klapper (2004) 'Further Evidence on the Link Between Finance and Growth: an International Analysis of Community Banking and Economic Performance', *Journal of Financial Services Research*, 25: 169–202.

Berger, A.N. and D.B. Humphrey (1992) 'Measurement and Efficiency Issues in Commercial Banking', in Z. Griliches (ed.), *Output Measurement in the Service Sectors*, Chicago: The University of Chicago Press.

Berger, A.N. and L.J. Mester (1997) 'Inside the Black Box: What Explains Differences in the Efficiency of Financial Institutions', *Journal of Banking and Finance*, 21: 895–947.

Berger, A.N. and L.J. Mester (2003) 'Explaining the Dramatic Changes in the Performance of US Banks: Technological Change, Deregulation, and Dynamic Changes in Competition', *Journal of Financial Intermediation*, 12: 57–95.

Berkowitz, J. and J. O'Brien (2002) 'How Accurate are the Value-at-Risk Models at Commercial Banks?', *Journal of Finance*, 57: 1093–111.

Biddle, G.C., P. Chen and G. Zhang (2001) 'When Capital Follows Profitability: Non Linear Residual Income Dynamics', *Review of Accounting Studies*, 6: 229–65.

Carbó Valverde, S., D.B. Humphrey and R. López del Paso (2007) 'Opening the Black Box: Finding the Source of Cost Inefficiency', *Journal of Productivity Analysis*, 27: 209–20.

Casu, B., C. Girardone and P. Molyneux (2006) *Introduction to Banking*, London: FT Prentice Hall.

Chaffai, M.E., M. Dietsch and A. Lozano-Vives (2001) 'Technological and Environmental Differences in the European Banking Industries', *Journal of Financial Services Research*, 19: 147–62.

Chu, S.F. and G.H. Lim (1998) 'Share Performance and Profit Efficiency of Banks in an Oligopolistic Market: Evidence from Singapore', *Journal of Multinational Financial Management*, 8: 155–68.

Community Banker (2001) 'What Drives Employee Satisfaction?', *America's Community Banker*, 10: 42–3.

Cummings, J.D., C.M. Lewis and R. Wei (2004) *The Market Value impact of Operational Risk Events for US Banks and Insurers*, paper presented at the Conference 'Implementing an AMA for Operational Risk', Federal Reserve Bank of Boston, Boston.

De Fontnouvelle, P., J. Jordan and E. Rosengren (2005) *Implications of Alternative Operational Risk Modeling Techniques*, NBER Working Paper no. 11103, Cambridge.

Dechow, P.M., A.P. Hutton and R.G. Sloan (1999) 'An Empirical Assessment of the Residual Income Valuation Model', *Journal of Accounting and Economics*, 26: 1–34.

Dietsch, M. and A. Lozano-Vives (2000) 'How the Environment Determines Banking Efficiency: a Comparison Between the French and Spanish Industries', *Journal of Banking and Finance*, 24: 985–1004.

Duffie, D. (2005) 'Credit Risk Modelling with Affine Processes', *Journal of Banking & Finance*, 29: 2751–802.

Eisenbeis, R.A., G.D. Ferrier and S.H. Kwan (1999) *The Informativeness of Stochastic Frontier and Programming Frontier Efficiency Scores: Cost Efficiency and Other Measures of Bank Holding Company Performance*, Federal Reserve Bank of Atlanta Working Paper no. 99–23.

Eskildsen, J.K. and J.J. Dahlgaard (2000) 'A Causal Model for Employee Satisfaction', *Total Quality Management*, 11: 1081–94.

Felthman, G. and J.A. Ohlson (1995) 'Valuation and Clean Surplus Accounting for Operating and Financial Activities', *Contemporary Accounting Research*, 11: 689–731.

Fernández, A.I., F. Gascón and E. González (2002) *Economic Efficiency and Value Maximization in the Banking Firms*, paper presented to the 7th European workshop on Efficiency and Productivity Analysis, Oviedo, Spain.

Fernández, P. (2002) *EVA, Economic Profit and Cash Value Added do not measure shareholder value creation*, University of Navarra research paper no. 453, Navarra.

Fiordelisi, F. and P. Molyneux (2006) *Shareholder Value in European Banking*. Basingstoke: Palgrave Macmillan.

Focarelli, D. and F. Panetta (2003) 'Are Mergers Beneficial to Consumers? Evidence from the Market for Bank Deposits', *American Economic Review*, 93: 1152–71.

Fu, X. and S.A. Heffernan (2005) *The Effects of Reform on China's Bank Structure and Performance*, Cass Business School Working Paper, London.

Galluccio, S. and A. Roncoroni (2006) 'A New Measure of Cross-sectional Risk and its Empirical Implications for Portfolio Risk Management', *Journal of Banking & Finance*, 30: 2387–408.

Garvey, G.T. and T.T. Milbourn (2000) 'EVA versus Earnings: Does it Matter Which is More Highly Correlated with Stock Returns?', *Journal of Accounting Research*, 38: 209–45.

Goddard, J.A., P. Molyneux and J. Wilson (2001) *European Banking: Efficiency, Technology and Growth*, Chichester: John Wiley and Sons.

Goldberg, L.G. and A. Rai (1996) 'The Structure–Performance Relationship for European Banking', *Journal of Banking and Finance*, 20: 745–71.

Greene, W.H. and D. Segal (2004) 'Profitability and Efficiency in the US Life Insurance Industry', *Journal of Productivity Analysis*, 21: 229–47.

Greene, W.H. (1997) *Econometric Analysis*. London: Prentice-Hall.

Hancock, D. (1986) 'A Model of the Financial Firm with Imperfect Asset and Deposit Elasticities', *Journal of Banking and Finance*, 10 (1986) 37–54.

Hicks, J.R. (1935) 'Annual Survey of Economic Theory: the Theory of Monopoly', *Econometrica*, 3: 1–20.

Holthausen, R.W. and R.L. Watts (2001) 'The Relevance of the Value-relevance Literature for Financial Accounting Standard Setting', *Journal of Accounting and Economics*, 31: 3–75.

Jacobson, T., J. Lindé and K. Roszbach (2006) *Credit Risk versus Capital Requirements under Basel II: Are SME Loans and Retail Credit Really Different?*, Central Bank of Sweden Working Paper.

Jobst, N.J., G. Mitra and S.A. Zenios (2006) 'Integrating Market and Credit Risk: a Simulation and Optimisation Perspective', *Journal of Banking & Finance*, 30: 717–42.

Kupiec, P. and J. O'Brien (1995) *Recent Developments in Bank Capital Regulation of Market Risks*, Finance and Economics Discussion Series, Board of Governors of the Federal Reserve System, no. 95–51.

La Porta, R., F. Lopez-de-Silanes and A. Shleifer (2002) 'Government Ownership of Banks', *Journal of Finance*, 57: 265–301.

Liu, J. and J.A. Ohlson (2000) 'The Feltham–Ohlson (1995) Model: Empirical Implications', *Journal of Accounting, Auditing and Finance*, 15: 321–31.

Lo, K. and T. Lys (2000) 'The Ohlson Model: Contribution to Valuation Theory, Limitations and Empirical Applications', *Journal of Accounting, Auditing and Finance*, 15: 337–67.

Lopez, J.A. (1999) 'Methods for Evaluating Value-at-Risk Estimates', *Federal Reserve Bank of New York Economic Policy Review*, 4: 119–24.

Lucas, A. and P. Klaassen (2006) 'Discrete versus Continuous State Switching Models for Portfolio Credit Risk', *Journal of Banking & Finance*, 30: 23–35.

Marshall, D.A. and S. Venkataraman (1998) *Bank Capital Standards for Market Risk: a Welfare Analysis*, FRB Chicago Working Paper.

Maudos, J. (1998) 'Market Structure and Performance in Spanish Banking Using a Direct Measure of Efficiency', *Applied Financial Economics*, 8: 191–201.

Mendes, V. and J. Rebelo (2003) 'Structure and Performance in the Portuguese Banking Industry in the Nineties', *Portuguese Economic Journal*, 2: 53–68.

Molyneux, P. and J. Thornton (1992) 'Determinants of European Bank Profitability – a Note', *Journal of Banking and Finance*, 16: 1173–8.

Morel, M. (1999) 'Multi-lagged Specification of the Ohlson Model', *Journal of Accounting, Auditing and Finance*, 12: 147–61.

O'Hanlon, J. and K. Peasnell (1998) 'Wall Street's Contribution to Management Accounting: the Stern Stewart EVA Financial Management System', *Management Accounting Research*, 9: 421–44.

Ohlson, J.A. (1995) 'Earnings, Book Values, and Dividends in Equity Valuation', *Contemporary Accounting Research*, 11: 661–87.

Ota, K. (2002) 'A Test of the Ohlson (1995) Model: Empirical Evidence from Japan', *International Journal of Accounting*, 37: 157–82.

Sathye, M. (2001) 'X-efficiency in Australian Banking: an Empirical Investigation', *Journal of Banking and Finance*, 25: 613–30.

Scandizzo, S. (2005) 'Risk Mapping and Key Risk Indicators in Operational Risk Management', *Economic Notes*, 34: 231–56.

Tan Lu Pheng, R. and J. Wirtz (2000) 'The Current State and Recent Advances in Customer Satisfaction Research', in S.B. Dahiya (ed.), *The Current State of Business Disciplines*, 6, Rothak, India: Spellbound Publications, pp. 2699–725.

Zheng, H. (2006) 'Interaction of Credit and Liquidity Risks: Modelling and Valuation', *Journal of Banking & Finance*, 30: 391–407.

8
The Impact of Mergers and Acquisitions on Shareholder Wealth in European Banking

Marcello Pallotta

8.1 Introduction

In recent years a substantial body of literature has emerged to investigate the effects produced by Merger and Acquisitions (M&A) operations in the banking industry. In the past decade, the financial markets in most industrialized nations have undergone an intense process of consolidation. While in the 1980s the growth of M&A operations was seen primarily in North America and the United Kingdom, since 1990 this phenomenon has been undertaken by all major industrialized nations and an even greater percentage of operations conducted have had an international dimension.

Focusing our attention on the banking industry, ECB (2005) show that there was a rising trend of M&A activity (in terms of both the number and the value of the operations undertaken) in the 1990s, but that this trend has declined in recent years (Figure 8.1). Despite the fall in the level of M&A activity that was observed at the beginning of 2003, it is perhaps premature to consider the phenomenon of accumulation of banks as being exhausted for at least two reasons: first, the number of banks per 1,000 inhabitants in Europe is still double that with respect to the US. Secondly, the degree of concentration of the domestic banking market in Europe appears still to be heterogeneous and a large part of the determining factors of completed M&A activity (for example, the globalization of financial systems and the creations of a European Banking System) are still active (Figure 8.1).

In the past decade, the M&A process has been the subject of numerous empirical studies, with the primary focus being on the situation in the US banking sector. This stream of research usually applies three

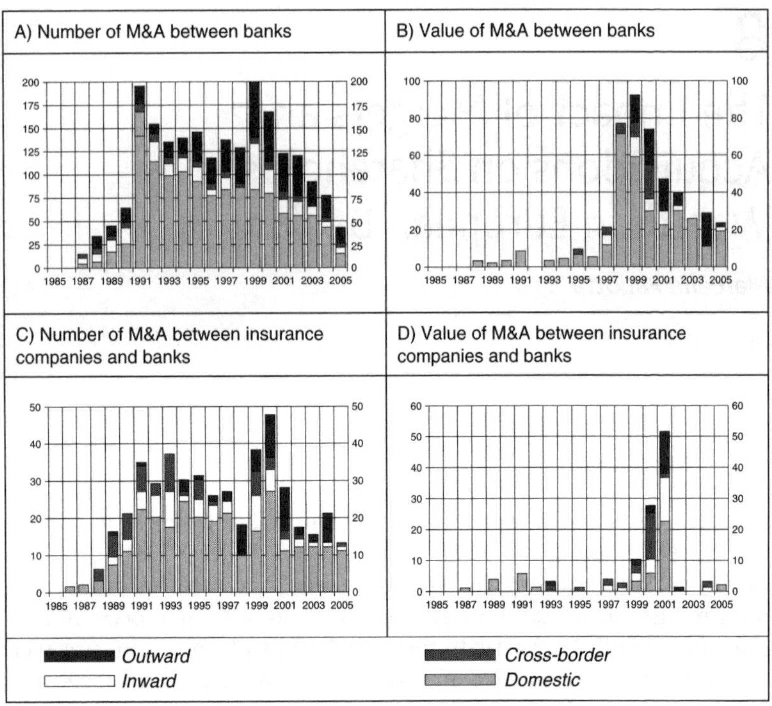

Figure 8.1 Merger and Acquisitions between European banks between 1985 and 2005

approaches: event studies, dynamic efficiency studies and performance studies (Beitel and Schiereck, 2001; Beitel et al., 2004). While dynamic efficiency studies and performance studies aim to assess the impact generated by M&A on a bank's efficiency or performance over the longer period, the event study methodology (applied in this chapter) enables us to assess if a M&A created or destroyed value (measured by abnormal returns, such as the total variation of the wealth of shareholders) over a short time period. Although over the past decade numerous studies have applied this methodology, there have only been a small number of contributions focusing on the European market. Among the most recent of these studies have been Cybo-Ottone and Murgia (1996, 2000), Beitel and Schiereck (2001) and Beitel et al. (2004).

Cybo-Ottone and Murgia (1996) conducted an analysis of 26 mergers between financial institutions in 13 European nations for the period 1988 and 1995, which result in a transfer of wealth from the acquiring firm to the target firm. Subsequently, Cybo-Ottone and Murgia (2000) analyse a larger sample size of 73 M&A operations of European banks with a market value greater than US$100 million during the period 1988–97. The results show that the markets' reaction, at the moment that the M&A activity is announced, determines a combined performance for both the target and acquiring firm that is both statistically significant and economically relevant. These results are influenced by positive abnormal returns both for domestic bank mergers and also for bank and insurance mergers (from the point of view of product diversification). By contrast, according to the authors, the announcement of M&A activity of different country banks does not give rise to a positive response from the markets. Beitel and Schiereck (2001) analyse 98 mergers that took place between European banks in the period 1985 and 2000. They identify significant positive abnormal returns for both the target firm and also the combined firm (resulting from the accounting collection of both the acquiring and the acquired bank) and nonsignificant abnormal returns for the shareholders of the acquiring bank. Given this finding, Beitel and Schiereck (2001) conclude that 'the operations of M&A conducted in Europe in the last 16 years can mildly be considered a success in an economic point of view'. Using the same sample, Beitel et al. (2004) propose a regression analysis to study the factors that explained the abnormal returns. From the given results, it would appear that M&A operations create value for the acquiring firm when the target firm involved is medium-sized and has a lower level of efficiency than that of the acquiring firm. It is much easier to verify the creation of value for the target bank: strong synergies are created and there is a greater potential to increase efficiency and, therefore, profits.

This chapter offers a further analysis of the effects produced by M&A operations within the European banking industry, and is able to new insights for a number of reasons. First, the number of studies investigating European banking markets is still limited – especially when two or more countries are considered. Secondly, our sample is one of the largest adopted in European banking; thirdly, we apply a new standardized measure of the Cumulative Abnormal Return and we test its statistical significance.

8.2   Sample description

The sample involved in our study considers M&A activity that has taken place in the European banking market between 2000 and 2004. The data on M&A operations have been extracted from the Zephyr database and the transactions have been chosen according to the following criteria: (1) the transaction must have been announced between 1 January 2000 and 31 December 2004; (2) the acquiring firm should be classified as a European bank (where European refers to an institution that is based within the EU-25); (3) the target firm should be classified as a European bank, insurance company or related financial services company; (4) the value of the transaction is not below €100 million; (5) the transaction must effectively have happened – that is, the sale is completed; (6) in all of the transactions there must have effectively been a change of control of the target firm, after the transaction, the acquiring firm must be able to exercise complete control (>50 per cent) on the target firm; (7) both the target firm and the acquiring firm must have been publicly quoted on a stock exchange for at least 252 days (an entire year) prior to an announcement, and at least 20 days after the day of the announcement.

Based on these criteria, 40 operations of M&A activity, with an average value of €3.1 billion, have been identified in the European banking markets. The sample shows two notable features: (1) contrary to what has been found in other studies (such as Beitel and Schiereck, 2001), the number of transactions seems to have remained relatively constant over time; and (2) the average annual value is in no way proportional to the number of transactions (Table 8.1). In 2003, 14 M&A operations have been identified, with an average annual value of €522 million, while in 2004 the number of M&A operations fell to five with the average annual value increasing to €3,241 million (Table 8.1).

More than half (that is, 52.5 per cent) of the M&A operations found in the sample have been carried out within national borders. With regard

Table 8.1   M&A operations in Europe between 1999 and 2004

Year	Banks	Insurance companies	Other financial institutions	Domestic M&A	EU cross-border M&A	Non-EU cross-border M&A	Mean value (euro million)
2000	5	1	1	3	3	1	8,622
2001	–	–	1	0	1	0	280
2002	10	–	3	8	1	4	3,083
2003	11	1	2	7	4	3	522
2004	4	–	1	3	1	1	3,241
Total	30	2	8	21	10	9	3,106
%	75	5	15	52.5	25	22.5	

Note: Diversification only pertains to the target firm: acquiring firms are only European banks.

to the cross-border operations, only half of these have been carried out within the confines of Europe. 75 per cent of the transactions (30 per cent in terms of absolute value) have occurred between banks, 5 per cent between banks and insurance companies, and 15 per cent of the transactions occurred with the target firm representing a financial services company. For each of the banks involved in an M&A transaction, the following data have been collected: (1) the share price of the securities of each of the firms involved, comprised within a period of 273 days before and 20 days after the announcement of such M&A activity; (2) the national sector index is used as a proxy of performance of the market (RMt); (3) Various accounting information (for example, net worth, total activity) of the firms within the sample.

8.3 Methods

The methods applied attempt to analyse if the price of the shares of the banks involved in an M&A transaction have undergone an abnormal trend in relationship to the announcement of such a transaction. This type of analysis requires the use of a model with the ability to determine the normal yield of such shares, and subsequently be able to calculate the abnormal yield (Brown and Warner, 1980, p. 207). With regard to the normal yield of a stock, this is normally estimated using the Capital Asset Pricing Model framework (ex. Brown and Warner, 1980; Beitel and Schiereck, 2001; Patell, 1976; Pilloff and Santomero, 1997; Resti and Galbiati, 2004; Scholes and Williams, 1977) or the Market Model of Sharpe (1963) (ex. Resti and Galbiati, 2004, p. 213), where the returns of the underlying securities are assumed to be jointly multivariate normal and independently and identically-distributed through time. Using this approach, the expected return of bank j at time t is estimated using the following model:

$$R_{jt} = \alpha_j + \beta_j RM_t + \varepsilon_{jt} \tag{8.1}$$

where R_{jt} is the actual dividend-adjusted return on security j on day t, calculated as $R_{jt} = \mathrm{Log}\,[(P_t + D_t)/P_{t-1}]$, where P_t is the market price of security j at time t and D_t is the daily flow dividend of security j at time t; RM_t is the rate of return index of the domestic market for that sector in which pertains to the target bank/bidder on day t, calculated as $RMt = \mathrm{Log}\,[(I_t/I_{t-1})]$, where I_t is the value of the market index at time t; α_j is the idiosyncratic component of bank j; β_j is the beta coefficient of security j and ε_{jt} is the error term in the regression. Under the assumption of joint normality, and independently and identically distributed

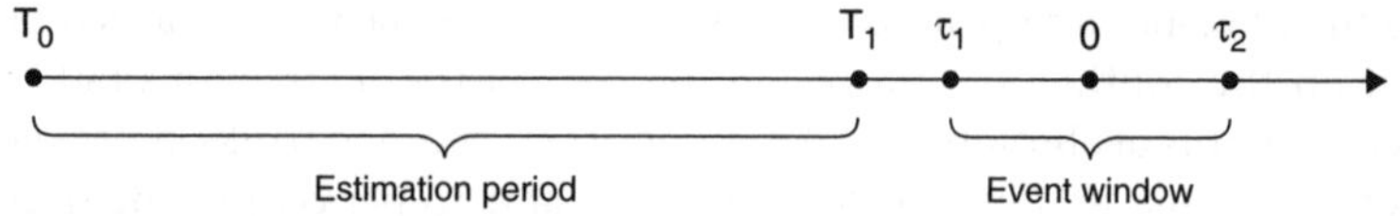

Figure 8.2 Estimation period and event window

returns, the error of regression with respect to our assumption assume the following characteristics: $E(\varepsilon_{jt}) = 0$ and $Var(\varepsilon_{jt}) = \sigma^2_{\varepsilon j}$

The time span considered in estimating our two market parameters α_j and β_j for banks chosen within our sample are based on 252 days of securities returns prior to the event window (Figure 8.2).

Our two estimated parameters ($\hat{\alpha}$ and $\hat{\beta}$) are used to determine the expected rate of return across the following model (Beitel and Schiereck, 2001; Cummins and Weiss, 2004):

$$R_{jt} = \hat{\alpha}_j + \hat{\beta}_j RM_t \tag{8.2}$$

8.3.1 Influence of the nonsynchronous exchange of securities as an estimation of the parameters

The application of CAPM over a continuous time span implies that the shares of the considered firm have prices distributed like random variables infinitely divisible log-normal (Scholes and Williams, 1977). From this assumption, the following considerations arise: (1) the rate of return of the securities is normally distributed with constant mean, variance and covariance; (2) the rate of return of the market indexes is normally distributed with constant mean, variance and covariance; and (3) it follows that the residual ε is also normally distributed with constant mean, variance and covariance (Scholes and Williams, 1977).

However, the market model taken into consideration is not observable in continuous time (Scholes and Williams, 1977). Since some quoted securities are traded only very infrequently, they will be priced at random – making it almost impossible to arrive at an accurate calculation of a given performance in a pre-fixed period, particularly if they are measured on a daily basis (Scholes and Williams, 1977). Indeed, this different synchrony in the buying and selling of securities means that the closing price of many traded shares with a low level of volatility reflects a value that is derived from the buying and selling that occurred in a much earlier time period, and therefore is quite different to the closing market price of the day (Scholes and Williams 1977). The main consequence of the nonsynchronous buying and selling is that, assuming a normal distribution the real (observed) instantaneous returns of the shares, their variance and covariance differ from the returns estimated with the Market Model (Scholes and Williams, 1977). All of this leads Scholes and Williams to assert that the estimates of alpha and beta obtained with the Ordinary Least Squares are for the greater part biased and inconsistent for the securities, defining the outcome of the estimates as nonbiased and consistent (Scholes and Williams, 1977).

Beginning with the conclusions of Scholes and Williams (1977), Brown and Warner (1985) observe that, for infrequently traded securities, the beta estimator has a downward bias, while the contrary happens for frequently traded securities. However, the authors think that the possible bias of beta does not necessarily bring us to an errant specification in an event study (Brown and Warner, 1985, p. 16). By construction, the sum of the residuals (model 2) sum to zero in the estimation period, so it is clear that a bias of the beta estimate is perfectly compensated by the bias of the alpha estimator (Brown and Warner, 1985, p. 16). In order to fulfil the stationarity condition (that is the case in which the average, variance and covariance of the process are constant, finite and independent with respect to time), the event period excess returns for an individual security can be shown to have a mean equal to zero, unconditional of the market returns (Brown and Warner, 1985, p. 16). By contrast, the excess return of a single security conditional on the market is biased (Brown and Warner, 1985, p. 17). However, no misspecification in an event study is implied if the average bias in the conditional excess returns of the sample securities is zero (Brown and Warner, 1985, p. 17). This final condition must be respected if the sample of the securities chosen was drawn in a way which mirrors a representative range of trading frequencies, or if there is a non-clustering of event dates (Brown and Warner 1985, p. 17). From what has been learned from Brown and Warner, procedures other than OLS for estimating the Market Model in the presence of nonsynchronous trading convey no clear-cut benefit in detecting abnormal performance (for example, the methodologies suggested by Scholes and Williams give rise to other problems) (Brown and Warner, 1985, p. 26). For this reason, in this chapter the estimates of the $\hat{\alpha}$ and $\hat{\beta}$ parameters have not been adjusted according to the suggestions of Scholes and Williams (1977); instead, we have followed the OLS regression procedure (Beitel and Schiereck, 2001).

8.3.2 The calculation of abnormal returns

Once defined, the size of the event window (which consists of $-t$ days before and $+t$ days after the date of the announcement, and the announcement date defined as day zero), the abnormal return on stock j on day t in the event window are estimated by the following:

$$AR_{jt} = R_{jt} - \hat{R}_{jt} \tag{8.3}$$

according to the calculations of Beitel and Schiereck (2001); or, according to the equivalent version of Cummins and Weiss (2004):

$$AR_{jt} = R_{jt} - \alpha_j - \beta_{j,RM_t} \tag{8.4}$$

The distributions of the abnormal return, conditional on the market return, is jointly normal with a zero conditional mean and a conditional variance equal to the following:

$$\sigma^2_{AR_{jt}} = \sigma^2_{\varepsilon j} + \frac{1}{L}\left[1 + \frac{\left(R_{Mt} - \bar{R}_m\right)}{\hat{\sigma}^2_m}\right] \tag{8.5}$$

where $\hat{\sigma}^2_{\varepsilon j}$ represents the sum of the squared residuals from the market model estimation divided by $(L_1 - 2)$, calculated using the following equation:

$$\sigma^2_{\varepsilon j} = \frac{1}{L_1 - 2}\sum_{t=t0+1}^{t1}\hat{\varepsilon}^2_{jt} \tag{8.6}$$

where L_1 represents the number of non-missing daily periods over which the Market Model was estimated for firm j, RMt represents the market return on day t pertaining to the event period of security j, $\bar{R}_t$ represents the average return on the market during the estimation period of security j, and $\hat{\sigma}^2_m$ represents the variance of the market return during the estimation period. Note that the variance $\hat{\sigma}^2$ (ARjt) of daily abnormal returns has two components: a disturbance term estimated from the market model residuals and a sampling error term (Cummins and Weiss, 2004). Since the sample error is common in all of the observations in the event period, this brings us to a correlation in the series of abnormal returns, in spite of the fact that the real disturbance is independent in time (MacKinlay, 1997). However, if the number of days in the estimation period turns out to be high, the second term of the equation $\hat{\sigma}^2$ (ARjt) tends to zero (MacKinlay, 1997). In this way the conditional variance of the abnormal returns converges at $\sigma^2_{\varepsilon j}$, and the abnormal returns become independent in time (Mackinlay, 1997; Cummins and Weiss,

2004). Since the estimation period considered in this study is sufficiently large, abnormal returns are normally distributed with a mean of zero and variance $\sigma^2_{\varepsilon j}$ $AR_{jt} \sim N(0, \sigma^2_{\varepsilon j})$, where $\sigma^2_{\varepsilon j}$ represents the variation estimate of the regression of security j. Because the conditional abnormal returns for all n securities are assumed to be independent and normally distributed, we can aggregate the abnormal returns across securities within any given time period. The average abnormal return for any given day in the event period is estimated as follows:

$$\overline{AR}_t = \frac{1}{n}\sum_{j=1}^{n} AR_{jt} \tag{8.7}$$

where n is the number of securities observed, and t is the day within the event window. At the same time, the variance of abnormal returns is estimated as follows:

$$\sigma^2\left(\overline{AR}_t\right) = \frac{1}{n^2}\sum_{j=1}^{n}\sigma^2_{\varepsilon j} \tag{8.8}$$

Where $\hat{\sigma}^2_{\varepsilon j}$ represents the variance of the estimated residuals across the regression of the market model of security j. Even the average abnormal returns within a given period are normally distributed with a zero conditional mean and a conditional variance of $\hat{\sigma}^2(\overline{AR}_t)$. Summing all of the AR_{jt} for each t contained in the event period [$\tau 1$, $\tau 2$], we obtain the cumulative abnormal returns (CAR = Calculated Abnormal Return) for each security:

$$CAR_j(T1, T2) = \sum_{\tau 1, \tau 2} AR_{jt} \tag{8.9}$$

Where $\tau 1$ represents the first day of the event period and $\tau 2$ represents the last day of the event period. Summing the various CARj ($\tau 1$, $\tau 2$) with respect to the security, and dividing by the n securities, we obtain the average CAR for the event period [$\tau 1$, $\tau 2$]:

$$\overline{CAR}_{(T1, T2)} = \frac{1}{n}\sum_{j=1}^{n} CAR_j(T1, T2) \tag{8.10}$$

with variance equal to:

$$Var\left[\overline{CAR}_{(T1, T2)}\right] = \frac{1}{n^2}\sum_{j=1}^{n}\sigma^2_{j(T1, T2)} \tag{8.11}$$

where:

$$\hat{\sigma}_j^2{}_{(T1,T2)} = (T2 - T1 + 1)\hat{\sigma}_{\varepsilon j}^2 \tag{8.12}$$

In the absence of abnormal performance, the expected value of $\overline{CAR}$ is equal to zero (Dodd and Warner, 1983). Therefore, under the null hypothesis with no market impact, we can draw inferences on $\overline{CAR}$, utilizing a standard Z-score statistic, calculated as the relationship between $\overline{CAR}(\tau1, \tau2)$ and its standard deviation (MacKinlay, 1997). It follows:

$$z = \frac{\overline{CAR}(\tau_1, \tau_2)}{Var\left[\overline{CAR}(\tau_1, \tau_2)\right]^{\frac{1}{2}}} \approx N(0, 1) \tag{8.13}$$

8.3.3   Analysis of the combined effects

The effects are analysed for both the shareholders of the target firm as well as the shareholders of the acquiring firm, both separately and in combination. The combined analysis enables us to pass a judgement on the entire transaction as a whole (Beitel and Schiereck, 2001). Using this method, it is possible to verify if the operations of banking M&A create or destroy value or, vice versa, imply if wealth is only transferred from the shareholders of the bidders to the shareholders of the targets. To calculate the abnormal returns for the combined entity of the target and acquiring firm we weight the AR for both the acquiring and target firm with respect to their market capitalization, realized the day prior to the event period:

$$AR_{jt} = \frac{AR_{A,t} + AR_{T,t} \times MV_{T,t}}{MV_{A,t} + MV_{T,t}} \tag{8.14}$$

where $AR_{i,t}$ represents the abnormal return on day t of the event period for the merged entity; $AR_{A,t}$ represents the abnormal return on day t of the event period of the acquiring firm; $AR_{T,t}$ represents the abnormal return on day t of the event period of the target firm; $MV_{A,t}$ represents the market value of the acquiring firm the day prior to the event period and $MV_{T,t}$ represents the market value of the target firm the day prior to the event period (Houston and Ryngaert, 1994). Once the $AR_{i,t}$ are determined from the various M&A operations, $\overline{CAR}$ is estimated using model (8.10), and the significance test of the results obtained for the combination of the target and acquiring firm are estimated using model (8.13), applying an adjustment to the calculation of standard deviation as suggested in Beitel and Schiereck (2001) and Houston and Ryngaert

(1994). For calculating the standard deviation, the starting point is the variance of $AR_{i,t}$ ($\hat{\sigma}^2_{i,t}$):

$$\sigma^2_{i,t} = \left(\frac{MV_{T,t}}{MV_{T,t} + MV_{A,t}}\right)^2 \times \hat{\sigma}^2_{T,t} + \left(\frac{MV_{A,t}}{MV_{T,t} + MV_{A,t}}\right)^2 \times \hat{\sigma}^2_{A,t}$$

$$+ 2\rho_{T,A}\left(\frac{MV_{T,t}}{MV_{T,t} + MV_{A,t}}\right)\left(\frac{MV_{A,t}}{MV_{T,t} + MV_{A,t}}\right) \times \sqrt{\hat{\sigma}^2_{T,t} \times \hat{\sigma}^2_{A,t}} \quad (8.15)$$

where $MV_{T,t}$ is the market value of the target firm, realized the day prior to the event period; $MV_{A,t}$ is the market value of the acquiring firm, realized the day prior to the event period; $\hat{\sigma}^2_{T,t}$ is the variance of abnormal returns of the target firm; $\hat{\sigma}^2_{A,t}$ is the variance of abnormal returns of the acquiring firm; and $\rho_{T,A}$ is the correlation coefficient between the residuals of the Market Model of the acquiring and target firm during the estimation period. At this point, we proceed to the summation of the variance $\hat{\sigma}^2_{i,t}$ obtained for each t belonging to the event period.

$$\hat{\sigma}^2_{i(T1,T2)} = T1 - T2 + 1\hat{\sigma}^2_{i,t} \quad (8.16)$$

Using this equation, we obtain the variance of $\overline{CAR}$, applying model (8.11) to the case of the combined analysis:

$$VAR\left[\overline{CAR}_{m(T1,T2)}\right] = \frac{1}{m^2}\sum_{i=1}^{m}\hat{\sigma}^2_i \quad (8.17)$$

where m represents the number of M&A operations taken into consideration. The square root of this value supplies the standard deviation that we can use to carry out our hypothesis test on $\overline{CAR}$ of the combined effect.

8.3.4 Verification of the independence condition between securities

The regression model assumes that the con-joint distribution of returns (of markets and securities) is stationary in time, and that:

$$E(\varepsilon jt) = 0;$$

$$Var(\varepsilon jt) = \sigma 2j = \sigma 2\varepsilon j;$$

$$Cov(\varepsilon j\gamma, \varepsilon jt) = \begin{cases} 0, & \gamma \neq t \\ \sigma^2_j, & \gamma = t; \end{cases}$$

$$Cov(\varepsilon jt, RMt) = 0; \quad \gamma, t = T0 \ldots \ldots T1; \quad j = 1 \ldots \ldots n;$$

In order to ensure the validity of described conditions even during the event period, the various ARjt results are distributed as follows:

$$E(ARjt) = 0$$

$$Cov(ARjs, ARjt) = \begin{cases} 0, & s \neq t \\ \sigma^2(AR_{j,t}), & s = t \end{cases}$$

$$Cov(ARjt, RMt) = 0; \quad s, t = \tau1 \ldots \ldots \tau2; \quad j = 1 \ldots \ldots n;$$

After applying a significance test on the given results, the distributions of the abnormal returns are considered normal with:

$$COV(AR_{it}, AR_{it}) = \begin{cases} 0 & i \neq j \\ \sigma^2(AR_{j,t}) & i = j \end{cases} \tag{8.18}$$

From this consideration, there follow two elements. The first is that the abnormal return distributions have a variance equal to:

$$\hat{\sigma}^2_{(AR_{it})} = \hat{\sigma}^2_{\varepsilon j} = \frac{1}{L_1 - 2} \sum_{t=T0+1}^{T1} \varepsilon^2_{it} \tag{8.19}$$

estimated by the means of the residuals of the regression carried out during the estimation period. In other words, the procedure in question estimates the variance of abnormal returns (residuals) calculated during the event window, through the residuals calculated with the regression on the estimation period. This presupposes that the variance of the securities in question remain constant during both the event period and also the estimation period. The studies conducted by Patell (1976), Cummins and Weiss (2004), MacKinlay (1997) and Brown and Warner (1985) show instead that the variance increases during the event period determining a bias in the estimator (Brown and Warner, 1985).

The second consequence is that the condition:

$$COV(AR_{it}, AR_{it}) = \begin{cases} 0 & i \neq j \\ \sigma^2(AR_{j,t}) & i = j \end{cases} \tag{8.20}$$

implies an independence of abnormal returns (residuals) and therefore of CAR, with respect to the securities (Patell, 1976; MacKinlay, 1997).

Finally, in order to reflect independence among the securities and to adjust for the estimation of the variance, it is necessary to apply the procedure of Standardized Cross Sectional (see also Cummins and Weiss, 2004; MacKinlay, 1997; Brown and Warner, 1985; Dodd and Warner, 1983).

For each given security j, we define the Standardized Cumulative Abnormal Return (SCAR):

$$SCAR_{j(T1,T2)} = \frac{CAR_j}{\sigma_j^2(\tau_1, \tau_2)} \tag{8.21}$$

where:

$$CARj(\tau 1, \tau 2) = \sum_{(\tau_1, \tau_2)} ARjt$$

$$\hat{\sigma}_j^2(\tau 1, \tau 2) = (\tau 2 - \tau 1 + 1)\hat{\sigma}_{\varepsilon j}^2$$

The standardization process ensures that no single firm (security) in the sample dominates the results of the analysis and helps improve the power of the test statistic. We can calculate average SCAR by summing the various SCARj and dividing by the number of securities:

$$SCAR_{(T1,T2)} = \frac{1}{n}\sum_{J=1}^{m} SCAR_{(T1,T2)} \tag{8.22}$$

and the adjusted variance is given as:

$$VAR[SCAR_{(T1,T2)}] = \frac{1}{n^2}\sum_{J-1}^{n} \left[SCAR_{(T1,T2)} - \overline{SCAR}_{(T1,T2)}\right]^2 \tag{8.23}$$

The new Z test statistic developed is:

$$Z = \frac{SCAR_{(\tau 1, \tau 2)}}{VAR\left[\overline{SCAR}(\tau_1, \tau_1)\right]^{1/2}} \tag{8.24}$$

8.4 Results

The calculations have been carried out for event windows of different sizes: from a maximum of 41 days (−20, +20), to a calculation carried out for a single announcement day (day zero). The different sizes of the event window were chosen in such a way that we can compare the results of our study with that of other studies. The values of SCAR are shown in

Table 8.2 SCAR target Firm[a]

Event window	SCAR medium[b]	SCAR positive (%)	Z Test	P-Value
$(-20, +20)$	47.0025*	75	1.3033	0.0968
$(-15, +15) =$	60.2788	67	1.2606	0.1038
$(-10, +10) =$	87.4353	75	1.2334	0.1073
$(-5, +5) =$	162.6458	75	1.2179	0.1112
$(-1, +1) =$	589.1119	75	1.1673	0.1423
$(0) =$	1662.6181	50	1.0921	0.1562
$(-1, 0) =$	857.5307	58	1.1303	0.1292
$(-5, 0) =$	300.0251	83	1.1985	0.1151
$(-10, 0) =$	170.3075	75	1.2288	0.1093
$(-15, 0) =$	118.2619	67	1.2583	0.1038
$(-20, 0) =$	85.3448	67	1.1930	0.1170

Notes: [a]The table shows the results of an event study analyzing data of 40 target firms, acquired by 40 European banks (EU 25) between 2000 and 2004. The abnormal return has been calculated using OLS regression. The OLS parameters have been estimated during a period of 252 days in which the markets were open prior to the event window, maximum $(-20, +20)$. As for market returns, the market sector index was applied. We applied the Standard Cross Sectional procedure to CAR. The significance test is reported in the below paragraph 8.4.2.4. [b]* = significance at 10%.

Tables 8.2–8.4 for the target bank, the acquiring bank and the combined bank respectively.

The application of the standardization procedure registers a positive effect on CAR. According to our results (Table 8.2), the shareholders of target banks experience positive effects from the M&A: the mean SCAR values for all event windows considered are positive and the majority of the M&A analysed achieved a positive SCAR. However, estimated SCAR are nonstatistically significant (at least at the 10 per cent significance level or less) whichever window is taken into consideration, except for the longest time window $(-20, +20)$.

With regarding to the acquiring banks (Table 8.3), the M&A analysed are found to have destroyed (on average) value for their shareholders, whichever window is taken into consideration. The estimated CAR are found to be nonstatistically significant even though, contrary to the CAR of the target firms, they have a strong negative sign. Considering the magnitude of estimated SCAR, we note that these are all negative, but tend to be zero over the longest event windows. We interpret these results as a signal that bidder banks are penalized around the M&A announcement, but the 'true' effect produced by these operations can be properly

Table 8.3 SCAR Bidder Firm[a]

Event Window	SCAR medium[b]	SCAR positive (%)	Z Test	P-Value
$(-20, +20) =$	−0.3265	57	−0.0956	0.4641
$(-15, +15) =$	−0.6842	53	−0.1593	0.4404
$(-10, +10) =$	−0.1882	47	−0.0289	0.4920
$(-5, +5) =$	−4.8271	40	−0.4442	0.3300
$(-1, +1) =$	−5.9911	47	−0.2263	0.4129
$(0) =$	−63.1903*	47	−1.5571	0.0606
$(-1, 0) =$	−40.2524	40	−0.9488	0.1736
$(-5, 0) =$	−21.0162	37	−1.0954	0.1379
$(-10, 0) =$	−11.5580	37	−1.1244	0.1314
$(-15, 0) =$	−6.0474	50	−0.7380	0.2300
$(-20, 0) =$	−0.3265	57	−0.0956	0.4641

Note: [a]The table shows the results of an event study analyzing the data of 40 European banks acquiring 40 target firms between 2000 and 2004. The abnormal return has been calculated using OLS regression. The OLS parameters have been estimated during a period of 252 days in which the markets were open prior to the event window, maximum (−20, +20). As for market returns, the market sector index was applied. We applied the Standard Cross Sectional procedure to CAR. The significance test is reported in the below paragraph 8.4.2.4. [b]* = significance at 10%.

Table 8.4 SCAR combined effect[a]

Event Window	SCAR medium[b]	SCAR positive (%)	Z Test	P-Value
$(-20, +20) =$	−3.0188	55	−0.5959	0.2743
$(-15, +15) =$	−2.3221	44	−0.3429	0.3669
$(-10, +10) =$	−2.0847	44	−0.3016	0.3821
$(-5, +5) =$	−18.3845*	20	−1.4216	0.0778
$(-1, +1) =$	−39.1104*	32	−1.4291	0.0764
$(0) =$	−1387.5948***	10	−3.5796	<0.00000
$(-1, 0) =$	−909.9919***	12	−3.5796	<0.00000
$(-5, 0) =$	−18.1589	28	−1.1121	0.1335
$(-10, 0) =$	−3.2968	40	−0.3620	0.3594
$(-15, 0) =$	−3.2444	30	−0.3915	0.3483
$(-20, 0) =$	−3.0188	55	−0.5959	0.2743

Note: [a]The table shows the results of an event study analysing the data of 40 European banks acquiring respectively 40 target firms between 2000 and 2004. The CAR of both the acquiring and target firm have been weighted for their market value obtained one day before the event window, maximum (−20, +20). The abnormal return has been calculated using OLS regression. The OLS parameters have been estimated during a period of 252 days in which the markets were open prior to the event window, maximum (−20, +20). As for market returns, the market sector index was applied. We applied the Standard Cross Sectional procedure to CAR. The significance test is reported in the below paragraph 8.4.2.4. [b]* = significance at 10%; ** = significance at 5%; *** = significance at 1%.

analysed only over the medium or the long term. This interpretation seems to be supported by the fact that we find a statistically significant negative SCAR only at the time window (0) (that is, the announcement date).

In respect of the combined entity, their mean values of SCAR are negative for all event windows considered and statistically significant only in the event window of very brief time spans (namely, around the announcement date) and assume negative values. This lends support to the notion that European banking operations do not bring about a simple transfer or wealth from the shareholders of the acquiring firm to the shareholders of the target firm; rather, on a net basis they destroy value more than they create it. These results provide new insights to develop the previous analyses in the European field (see, for example, Beitel and Schiereck 2001; Cybo-Ottone and Murgia, 2000).

8.5   Conclusions

Over the past decade or so M&A operations between financial institutions within the European Union have undergone an intense period of acceleration. Although a decreasing trend has been recorded during the most recent period, it is nonetheless unreasonable to believe that such mergers and acquisitions will cease to continue. This chapter has been written to conduct an empirical evaluation, by means of the event study methodology, to find out if the M&As taking place between banks in the European Union (the EU-25) have created or destroyed shareholder value. The model most frequently used in the literature is a general form of the Capital Asset Pricing Model (CAPM), the Market Model of Sharpe (1963), which, with respect to CAPM, foresees the addition of a single constant α that is not equal to zero. Using this model, we have estimated the two parameters of the market, αj and βj, for each firm interested in M&A operations. The two parameters have been estimated by use of regression over a period of 252 days of trading, prior to any event window.

The two estimated parameters, $\hat{\alpha}$ and $\hat{\beta}$, together with the observation of the market indexes during the event period, are used to calculate the expected returns during the event window. Once the size of the event window is determined, we can calculate the abnormal returns of security j on day t partaken on the event window. The M&A operations that have taken place between 2000 and 2004 have been obtained from the Zephyr database and the sample chosen is one of the largest ever selected for a study into the European banking system. The calculations have been carried out for event windows of different sizes: from a maximum of 41 days (−20, +20), to a calculation carried out for a single announcement day (day zero), in such a way that we can compare the results of our study with that of other studies. As far as the CAR of the target firm is concerned, the results are positive but nonsignificant, whatever event window is taken into consideration, except the (−20, +20) window. By contrast, the CAR of the acquiring firm produce negative results – however, these are also nonsignificant. The CAR of the combined entity produces negative and significant results for certain windows with very brief time spans. This lends support to the idea that European banking operations do not bring about a simple transfer or wealth from shareholders of the acquiring firm to the shareholders of the target firm, but indeed, on a net basis, that they destroy value more than they create it. The results observed are contrary to other studies in the European field, while they are in line with a large number of the studies that have focused on financial institutions in the USA.

References

Beitel, P. and D. Schiereck (2001) *Value Creation at the Ongoing Consolidation of the European Banking Market*, paper presented at the X International Conference of Banking and Finance, Tor Vergata University Rome.

Beitel, P., D. Schiereck and M. Wahrenburg (2004) 'Explaining M&A Success in European Banks', *European Financial Management*, 10: 109–39.

Brown, S.J. and J.B. Warner (1980) 'Measuring Security Price Performance', *Journal of Financial Economics*, 8: 205–58.

Brown, S.J and J.B. Warner (1985) 'Using Daily Stock Returns', *Journal of Financial Economics*, 14: 3–31.

Cummins, J D and M.A. Weiss (2004) 'Consolidation in the European Insurance Industry: Do Mergers and Acquisitions Create Value for Shareholders?', Wharton Working Paper 04-02 (2004).

Cybo-Ottone, A. and M. Murgia (1996) 'Mergers and Acquisitions in the European Banking Market', University of Pavia working paper, Pavia.

Cybo-Ottone, A. and M. Murgia (2000) 'Mergers and Shareholder Wealth in European Banking', *Journal of Banking and Finance*, 24: 831–59.

Dodd, P. and J.B. Warner (1983) 'On Corporate Governance: a Study of Proxy Contest', *Journal of Financial Economics*, 11: 401–38.

ECB (2004) *Structural Analysis of the EU Banking Sector – Year 2003*, November.

ECB (2005) *Financial Stability Review*, December.

Houston, J.F. and M.D. Ryngaert (1994) 'The Overall Gains from Large Bank Mergers', *Journal of Banking and Finance*, 18: 1155–76.

MacKinlay, A.C. (1997) 'Event Studies in Economics and Finance', *Journal of Economic Literature*, 35: 12–39.

Patell, J. (1976) 'Corporate Forecast of Earning Per Share and Stock Price Behaviour: Empirical Tests', *Journal of Accounting Research*, 14: 251–66.

Pilloff, S.J. and A.M. Santomero (1997) *The Value Effect of Bank Mergers and Acquisitions*. Wharton Working Paper 97-07, Philadelphia.

Resti, A. and L. Galbiati (1998) 'Regulation Can Foster Mergers, Can Mergers Foster Efficiency? The Italian Case', *Journal of Economics and Business*, 50: 157–69.

Ruozi, R. (1968) 'Le economia di scala nelle aziende di credito italiane', *Il Risparmio*, 16: 1124–97.

Scholes, M. and J. Williams (1977) 'Estimating Betas from Nonsynchronous Data', *Journal of Financial Economics*, 5: 309–27.

9
Does Corporate Culture Affect Shareholder Value? Evidence from European Banking

Alessandro Carretta, Vincenzo Farina, Franco Fiordelisi and Paola Schwizer[1]

9.1   Introduction

This chapter presents an empirical investigation of the relationship between bank performance and corporate culture in European banking using a sample of quoted banks over the period 2001–03. There is a substantial literature dealing with bank performance and shareholder value,[2] but few studies have attempted to conduct an empirical analysis of the relationship with business conditions that may lead to create shareholder value.

A number of studies (Beccalli, Casu and Girardone, 2006; Fernández, Gascón and González, 2002; Eisenbeis, Ferrier and Kwan, 1999; Chu and Lim, 1998) have sought to link measures of the productive efficiency of banks to stock returns, and have generally found there to be a positive relationship between the two measures. However, these studies really tell us little about the determinants of shareholder value creation as the costs of capital considerations are typically ignored. A second shareholder value determinant is the level of customer satisfaction: the link between customer satisfaction and shareholder value creation has also been identified in the theoretical literature (Bauer and Hammerschimidt, 2005) and empirically investigated for non-financial companies (Van der Wiele, Boselie and Hesselink, 2001), yet only one study (Loveman, 1998) provides evidence about how employee satisfaction and customer loyalty positively influence bank performance (using data from the branches of a large regional bank in the United States). Others have investigated the relationship between operational risk and bank stock price reactions (Cummings et al., 2005) and the role played by corporate risk management in the process of shareholder value creation (Bartram, 2000, 2002).

Overall, however, it can be seen that the existing empirical literature on the determinants of shareholder value creation in banking is somewhat esoteric and limited.

Following Schein (1985), the corporate culture is defined as a set of shared norms and values expressed in terms of common language, shared coding procedures and shared knowledge. The hypothesis that corporate culture is a predictor of firm performance, allowing organizations to adapt to the environment's constantly changing conditions, is investigated by many different studies, including Barney (1986), Siehl and Martin (1990), Gordon and Di Tomaso (1992), Alvesson (1993), O'Reilly and Chatman, (1996); Wilderom and Van den Berg (2000); Sorensen (2002); Van den Steen (2004).

Despite the importance of the link between corporate culture and bank's performance, a small number of studies investigate this relationship in banking and most of them focus on cross-cultural management and/or emerging markets (Davis, 2004; Moussetis, Rahma and Nakos, 2005). This contribution presents a novel insight since it is the first (as far as we are aware) to focus on shareholder value and to assume (and empirically investigate) that bank profitability and shareholder value may have a different link with different corporate culture orientations. In detail, our study introduces a new instrument for assessing corporate culture since the corporate cultural orientation of European commercial banking is measured using three different dimensions[3] according to a possible orientation towards results (labelled as result-oriented culture), their own power development (labelled as power-oriented culture) or the human aspect (labelled as human-oriented culture). For each of these three set of corporate culture estimates, we measure their ability to explain variations in both bank profitability and shareholder value.

9.2 The relationship between shareholder value and corporate culture

Corporate culture can be considered to be the set of values and decisions that represent the manner in which individuals can perform their activities within the organization, and defines which behaviours may be considered to be appropriate (Schein, 1985).

Kaplan and Norton (2004), in a discussion of the 'organizational capital' of firms, examine culture, as the first of its four components; among the other components considered are leadership, alignment, and teamwork.

Hansen and Wernerfelt (1989) provide evidence to show how organizational factors explain almost twice as much variance in profit rates as economic factors, concluding in their study that intangible attributes of firms are crucial for its performance.

If it is true that firm's growth and value creation are a matter of the broad organizational features and routines, unique to a firm, then corporate culture allows it to adapt to the constantly changing conditions of the environment.

The idea that culture is a predictor of firm performance and firm's overall value is emerged in response to the need to understand more of firm's dynamics than can be explained through financial measures alone and is investigated by different studies following different perspectives (Burns and Stalker, 1961; Lawrence and Lorsch, 1967). In fact, while some academics consider attempts to measure corporate culture and its effects on firm performance as highly problematic (Alvesson, 1993; Siehl and Martin, 1990), other studies see culture as a measurable characteristic with some effects in terms of organizational behavior and processess (Barney 1986; Gordon and Di Tomaso, 1992; O'Reilly and Chatman, 1996; Wilderom and Van den Berg, 2000; Sorensen, 2002; Van den Steen, 2004).

According to Burns and Stalker (1961) and Lawrence and Lorsch (1967), the linkage between corporate culture and firm performance could be the expression of a contingency approach: firms that show a fit among culture and strategy could be able to reach improved performances.

Based upon this assumption, good strategies would not be a sufficient condition for achieving good results: it is also necessary for them to be implemented correctly. In fact, implementation requires organizational behaviours that are functional to a firm's goals and to the adaptability with environmental changes.

Kotter and Heskett (1992) argue that culture should be coherent with firm strategies in order to enhance the adaptability to external changes and in order to constantly discover critical factors for competition. In addition, Quinn and McGrath (1985) argue that it should be possible to obtain an improved definition of goals and firm performance through a fit between culture and pursued strategies.

As a consequence of this view, corporate culture could be a source of competitive advantage mainly if environment is characterized by high levels of competition and the ability to formulate and to implement strategies is very important (Burt, Gabbay, Holt and Moran, 1994).

Consistent with these assumptions, Sorensen (2002) argues that the link between culture and performance depends upon the ability to affect organizational learning in response to both internal and external changes. In fact, he shows how in stable environments firms with a strong corporate culture have a less variable performance. However, the relationship between what he defines as a strong culture and performance in the competitive environment is less evident. This phenomenon could be due to the consideration that in some instances a strong culture is an obstacle to organizational changes because of the limited ability to renew its contents. This is also consistent with Schein (1985), when he states that corporate culture can (or not) enhance the acquisition of new values and norms required by changed competitive contexts, and with Hodgson (1996), when he says that culture supplies the basis for the development of new competencies.

Generally, when changes occur, firms still use cognitive models already in their possess in order to respond to new rules of competition but in many cases these models could be inadequate.

Moreover as a result of the previous considerations, it has been observed that strong cultures determine good performance only in the short term while in the longer term the performance of business that do not change becomes negative (Denison, 1990).

According to this evidence, a corporate culture can be defined as strong only if, as a result of its flexibility and willingness to adapt to changes, also generates superior performance over the long term (Kotter and Heskett, 1992). In strong cultures, norms and values are highly diffused within organization and the consequences deriving from them can be summarized as follows (Gordon and Di Tomaso, 1992; Kotter and Heskett, 1992; O'Reilly and Chatman, 1996):

- enhanced coordination and control of resources within firms;
- improved goal alignment between a firm and its members;
- increased individual efforts and motivation.

In general, referring to the improved coordination and control of resources within firms and goal alignment between a firm and its members, culture could enhance coordination and decision-making processes through its capacity to influence organizational mechanisms.

Following this perspective, Gordon and Di Tomaso (1992) argue that different performance levels in financial intermediation could be explained by different forms of organizational cultures and by the combination of different key characteristics of culture.

In their study of the more frequent characteristics of successful firms, Peters and Waterman (1982) found that the sharing of basic values is a condition for performance improvement because it implies lesser coordination efforts.

Wilkin and Ouchi (1983) argue that the presence of 'clans' and a high degree of the involvement of people in the execution of different tasks could be at the basis of superior results compared with bureaucratic and power-based organizations.

In addition, Denison (1990) observes that the development of shared cooperative values within organizations could improve a firm's return on investments and, in general, firm performance.

These effects of culture can be explained in terms of the minimization of transaction costs and the maximization of the motivation of people deriving from the sharing of strong values and norms. Moreover, culture can be considered an informal tool, based on social mechanisms, for the control (Berger and Luckmann, 1967): while formal control requires behavioural rules and codified procedures and organizational routines, informal control is based on the respect of some types of norms and values and for this it is considered less expansive and more effective (Van Maanen, 1991).

Corporate culture could make more effective the allocation of firm resources because of some key elements that are able to address individual efforts towards common goals (Carretta, 2001).

In synthesis, Van den Steen (2004) observes that cooperative culture involves: (i) increasing delegation mechanisms; (ii) improving control mechanisms; and (iii) improving coordination mechanisms.

Moreover, referring to increased individual efforts and motivation, it is necessary to specify that a same culture could have different meanings for different people and at the same time it could generate commitment and efforts but also resistance and opposition to changes with negative effects on performance (Weick, 1979).

Following this, it is important to analyse the type of involvement deriving from culture within organizations. From one side there is a formalized involvement that, because it is based on formal rules and mechanisms, could not reflect collective values. From the other side there is a spontaneous involvement that, based on shared norms and rules, is the real expression of corporate culture.

Another perspective, based on the resource based view of the firms, considers the indirect linkage between culture and firm performance (Wilderom and Van den Berg, 2000).

Surveying the personnel of 58 locally banking firms owned by one of the largest financial institutions in Netherlands they find that leadership is one of the elements that, influenced by culture, could explain performance.

Also Pennings, Lee and van Witteloostuijn (1998) argue that firm culture is indirectly related to firm performance and assume the existence of a relationships among human and social capital and differences in firm performance.

Siehl and Martin (1990) suggest that culture might impact financial performance through variables such as productivity, quality control, turnover or absenteeism and they recognize implicitly that culture does not provide a direct explanation of performance.

In this regard, Pettigrew (1979) observes that culture is only one component of a much more complex system of relationships that sees human agents in a central role in the explanation of firm performance.

However, the development of a real theory on the effects of culture is hindered by different problems: in the current literature there is still no generally accepted definition of culture and the absence of widely accepted measurement methodologies of corporate culture makes it difficult to study the linkages with firm performance.

In this sense, Van den Steen (2004) argues that could be superior performances to generate cohesion around an homogeneous cultural context rather than the contrary.

Moreover, Barney (1986), studying the effects of corporate culture, argues that it is possible to have some forms of linkages with performance only if culture is rare, imperfectly imitable, non substitutable and valuable. The main limit implicit in these conditions is that they are very difficult to operationalize.

Aware of these limits, we focus on some dimensions reflecting particular attitudes of corporate culture: power orientation (Hofstede, 1980; Denison and Mishra, 1995; Carretta, Farina and Schwizer, 2005); result orientation (Hofstede, Neuijen, Ohayv and Sanders, 1990) and human resource orientation (Wilderom and Van den Berg, 2000). The power-orientation of corporate culture pertains the modalities of the organization, in terms of the propensity to share and cooperate, or in terms of importance of the hierarchy and according to an individualistic criteria (Harrison, 1975). The result-orientation represents the importance given by the organization to the achievement of results. The human orientation views the human resource content as an explicit part of the organizational culture construct (Quinn, 1988; Gordon and Di Tomaso, 1992).

Moreover, in this analysis we refer the concept of culture to some important aspects of the banking industry. Consistent with the findings of Carretta, Farina and Schwizer (2005) and Martin (1992), some firm's aspects and themes such as human resources policies, existing competencies, competition ways, risk, disclosure and innovation are related to firm performance. We define each of these representative concepts as 'key concept' and our study of corporate culture is based upon them.

In assessing the relationship between corporate culture and bank's performance, we measure bank performance by focusing on both profitability and shareholder value. We expect that shareholder value creation or profit making may be fostered by different corporate culture orientations. The shareholder value creation requires that the opportunity cost of invested capital is taken into consideration in any management decision, while profit making may be achieved regardless of the risk involved in the bank's activity. For example, banks may increase their profits by increasing the risk of their activities (for example, providing poor quality loans or having a more aggressive policy of security trading), while value-oriented banks would be concerned with the higher risk involved in these operations since shareholders may require a higher return so that the overall result may be a destruction of shareholder value.

The power-oriented corporate culture is based on the hierarchy and individualistic criteria. A high level of firm's power orientation means that there is an absence of shared cooperative values (Wilderom and Van den Berg, 2000) and involvement within organizations and is expected to be negatively related to bank profits and shareholder value. The result-oriented corporate culture represents the importance given by the organization to the achievement of results. In this case, a high level of this orientation is assumed to be positively related to bank profits, which may be not related to shareholder value since a result-oriented corporate culture may lead a manager to increase revenues regardless of the risks involved in the bank's activities. The human-oriented corporate culture considers human resources to be a fundamental part of the organizational culture construct (Quinn, 1988; Gordon and Di Tomaso, 1992). According to this culture orientation, Pettigrew (1979) argues that human agents are central to the achievement of high performance. As such, we expect that bank human resources play a key role in achieving performance and it is assumed to be positively related to bank profits and, especially, to shareholder value creation.

Based on our theoretical, we conduct an empirical investigation of the following hypotheses:

- Hypothesis 1 (H1): There is a negative link between power-orientated bank corporate culture and profits.
- Hypothesis 2 (H2): There is a positive link between result-orientated bank corporate culture and profits.
- Hypothesis 3 (H3): There is a negative link between human-orientated bank corporate culture and profits.
- Hypothesis 4 (H4): There is a negative link between power-orientated bank corporate culture and shareholder value.
- Hypothesis 5 (H5): There is a weakly positive link between result-orientated bank corporate culture and shareholder value.
- Hypothesis 6 (H6): There is a negative link between human-orientated bank corporate culture and shareholder value.

9.3 Methodology

This section outlines the methodology approaches used in this chapter. First, it is illustrated how we measure corporate culture, secondly, we explain how we measure bank's profits and the shareholder value created over a period and, next, we discuss the model for linking bank performance and culture.

9.3.1 Measuring bank's corporate culture

Corporate culture is measured focussing on language as its particular artifact and developing a cultural survey based on the application of a text-analysis approach in order to obtain its profiles and orientations. The study of corporate culture through language is a relatively new approach in economic literature that belongs to cultural anthropology, the study of human behaviours based on the interpretation of symbols and artifacts, and has never been applied in the case financial institutions. Language may be considered a particular symbol and artifact of culture and, in consideration of the linguistic-textual differences when examining diverse cultural contexts, is a useful tool for understanding them.

- Geertz (1973) analyses culture in 'semiotic' terms and suggests that 'is not an experimental science in search of laws, but an interpretational science in search of meanings'. He asserts the possibility of analysing social phenomena and organizational processes and behaviours by considering them as the symbols and artifacts typical of a cultural system.

- Schein (1985) identifies language as an artifact of the corporate culture and claims that it is possible to analyse the different cultures through the vocabularies expressed.
- Wuthnow (1989) claims that some linguistic categories and lexical expressions typical of a certain context allow the analysis of different corporate cultures, because their definition is closely related to the vocabulary developed within them.
- Finally, DiMaggio (1997 and 2002) considers language to be the result of both social interaction and individual cognition. He maintains that, through the empirical analysis of written texts it is possible to determine the cultural aspects of language. This means that when the members of an organization use a term drawn from the vocabulary of their organization, what they are really doing is making reference to an individual cognitive representation transformed into organizational behaviours shared by and common to the organization to which they belong (Rosa and Porac, 2002). As regards the role of vocabularies (Berger and Luckmann, 1967) of linguistic categories, it is further specified that - although in certain contexts it is (theoretically) possible to develop cultural categories even without a language – vocabularies play a very important role in their development and sharing (Levinson, 2003).

All of this implies that the analysis of culture is closely connected to the analysis of the type of vocabulary used by the members of an organization, which vocabulary is used in all the forms of communication, both oral and written, produced internally by that organization The distinctive characteristics of every organization, therefore, are reflected in the documents it produces and the language used may represent a key for their interpretation.

In other words, if the organization leaves traces of its particular characteristics in the documents it produces, then it is possible to use text analysis to observe and 'measure' these traces and determine their cultural implications.

Based on this assumption, various surveys have been carried out in literature aimed at comprehending a series of issues concerning corporate culture, among which the research on the leadership characteristics within organizations (D'Aveni and MacMillan, 1990), the determinants of corporate reputation (Fombrun and Shanley, 1990), the measurement of the intensity of orientation to 'corporate social responsibility'

(Wolfe, 1991), the classification of the types of organization based upon the existence and intensity of certain cultural values (Kabanoff and Holt, 1996). These studies have two common objectives: (i) to provide representations of the content of the corpus of texts; (ii) to extract information, i.e. several properties, from the corpus of texts through quantity-based measurements.

Compared with the previous studies, this chapter focuses on an evolutionary aspect of text analysis – concerning standardization in the treatment of data – combined with the use of standard vocabularies. This allows a greater comparability of the output of the various studies, enabling us to further refine the analysis methodology. The analysis model includes the definition of several key concepts, at the base of the development of banking culture (Carretta, 2001).

The study of corporate culture, in terms of power orientation, result orientation and human resource orientation, is based on some linguistic categories drawn from the Harvard IV Psychosocial Dictionary (Zuell, Weber and Mohler, 1989) and the Lasswell Value Dictionary (Lasswell and Namenwirth, 1969). The different intensity of these categories, expressed in terms of 'orientations', characterizes each concept and allows us to compare the corporate culture against the various benchmark contests.

For the text analysis, we used the Wordsmith 4 software developed by Oxford University (Scott 1999) and the empirical assessment has been carried out in the phases as follows (Figure 9.1)

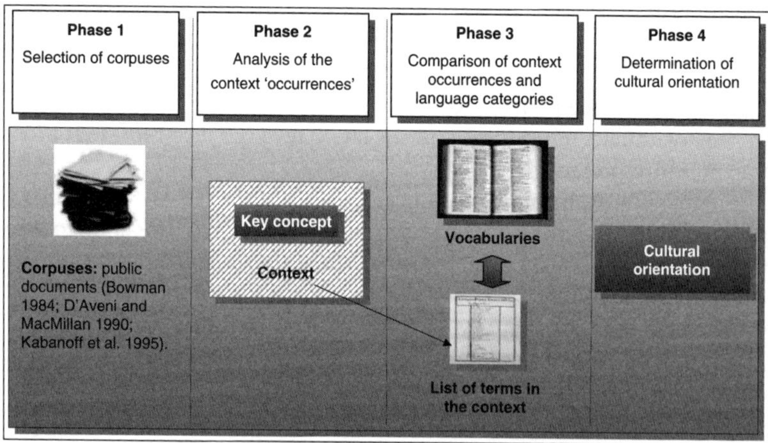

Figure 9.1   The four phases of our text-analysis method

- definition of the sample of banks to be analysed and selection of the corpus to be analysed;
- analysis of the context 'occurrences', in respect of the key concepts of the culture of banks (this analysis allows to obtain of lists of words making up a text, accompanied by the number of times in which they occur);
- comparison of the context occurrences and the language categories extracted from the Harvard IV Psycho-Social Dictionary and the Lasswell Value Dictionary;
- determination of the predominant cultural orientation and of the relevant intensity.

9.3.2   Shareholder value

We measure the shareholder value created by European banks using the Economic Value Added (EVA) measure, EVA expresses the surplus value created by a company in a given period, i.e. the firm's profit net of the cost of all capital. This measure is computed as the product of the difference between the return on invested capital (ROIC) and its composite financing cost (i.e. cost of capital – CC) and the capital invested (CI) at the beginning of the period (t − 1).

$$EVA_{t-1} = NOPAT_{t-1} - (CI_{t-1} * CC_{t-1,t}) \tag{9.1}$$

In order to move the book values closer to their economic values, various accounting adjustments are made. The first adjustment is standard for all kind of companies and concerns Research and Development (R&D) costs and training costs: these expenses are designed to generate future growth and, therefore, representing intangible investments. Current assets do not benefit from these expenses and it would be incorrect to reduce operating income by the amount of these expenses. However, accounting standards require companies to treat all outlays for R&D as operating expenses in the income statement. As a consequence, this accounting distortion can be corrected by: (a) adding back these expenses in calculating NOPAT; (b) capitalising all R&D expenses and training costs in capital invested; (c) amortising these capitalised expenses over an appropriate period: for example, according to Stern Stewart's statistics,[4] five years is the average useful life of R&D expenses. As such, investments in intangibles are treated in the same manner as investments in tangible assets.

Also the second adjustment is standard for all kind of companies and it concerns operating lease expenses. These costs are usually considered as operating costs in companies' cost-income statement. However, operating leases are disguised financial expenses since companies acquire a productive asset (and, therefore, finance their future production) by paying periodic rent (i.e. operating leases expenses). In order to face this conservative accounting practise, it is opportune to: (d) capitalise any operating lease expenses in calculating NOPAT; (e) treat the present value of expected lease commitments over time as capital invested in the firm; (f) amortise these capitalised expenses over an appropriate period.[5]

The other adjustments made accounts for banking peculiarities and therefore these are specific for banks.[6] The third adjustment concerns loan loss provisions and loan loss reserves. The loan loss reserve is a reserve that aims to cover any future loan losses and for this reason it should be equal to the net present value of all future loan losses. In any single period, this reserve is reduced by net charge-offs (that is, the current period losses due to credit risk) and replenished by loan loss provisions (that is, the provision made in the current period to adjust the reserves both for pre-existing loans and for estimated future loan losses related to newly originated loans). This convention is certainly commendable from a management perspective since it implies that all loan losses are pre-funded out of current earnings. However, loan loss provisions are commonly used to manage earnings: if a bank achieves high operating returns, bank managers tend to overestimate this provision, while they are inclined to underestimate it if operating earnings are poor. This accounting practice introduces an important distortion in analysing bank performance since it smoothes earnings. Business is risky, and the volatility of profits is a manifestation of this risk: for purposes of economic performance evaluation, smoothing earnings is inappropriate. In order to face this conservative accounting practice, it is opportune to: (g) add back loan loss provisions and deduct the net charge-offs in calculating NOPAT; (h) capitalize the net loan loss reserve as capital invested. These adjustments are intended to reduce the opportunities open to management to smooth accounting profits.

The fourth adjustment regards taxes. Many banks show significant and persistent differences between book tax provisions and cash tax payments. Since these differences are quasi-permanent, deferred taxes should be considered as capital and, similarly to situation with loan loss provisions, taxes need to be considered as current period expenses for purposes of economic performance evaluation. This accounting conservatism can be faced by: (i) adding back loan book tax provisions and deducting the cash operating tax; (j) capitalizing the deferred tax credits (net of the deferred tax debits) as capital invested. Similarly to the adjustments for loan loss provisions, taxation adjustments are intended to reduce the opportunities open to management to smooth accounting profits.

The fifth adjustment concerns restructuring charges. Over the last decade or so, many banks have carried out restructuring plans in order to improve their operating efficiency. To the extent that such restructuring charges represent disinvestments, these costs should be treated as a capital reduction rather than costs (and therefore reduce NOPAT). Data availability limitations do not allow us to evaluate the extent of real disinvestments due to restructuring charges; these costs are omitted when adjusting NOPAT and capital invested.

The sixth adjustment concerns banks' general risk reserve. This adjustment aims to correct for distortions derived from the 'general risk reserve', a standard feature in Italian banking. This provision is a reserve that covers a bank's future generic loan losses: in any single period, this reserve is reduced by net charge-offs (that is, the current period losses) and replenished by general risk provisions (that is, the provision made in the current period to adjust the reserve according to the bank's risks). Similarly to the loan loss reserve, this convention is certainly commendable from a management prospective, but it is used in an opportunistic manner. This accounting practice introduces an important distortion in analysing banks' performance since it smoothes earnings. In order to face this conservative accounting practice, it is opportune to: (k) add back general risk provisions and deduct the net charge-offs in calculating NOPAT; (l) capitalize the general risk reserve as capital invested. These adjustments aim to reduce the opportunities open to management to smooth accounting profits.

Regarding the definition of capital invested, this cannot be measured using total assets (as for a non-financial company) and, consequently, the cost of invested capital is not estimated as Weighted Average Cost of Capital (WACC). While this solution is certainly accurate for non-banking companies, this procedure would be misleading for commercial banks. Since financial intermediation is the core business for banks, debts should be considered as a productive input in banking rather than a financing source (as for other companies). As such, interest expenses represent the cost for acquiring this input and, consequently, should be considered as an operating cost rather than a financial cost (as for other companies). As a consequence, if the capital charge is calculated following a standard procedure (that is, applying WACC on total assets), EVA will be biased since it will double-count the charge on debt. As such, the charge on debt should be firstly subtracted from NOPAT (the capital charge is calculated on the overall capital – that is, equity and debt – invested in the bank and, consequently, it includes the charge on debt) and, secondly, it would be subtracted from operating proceeds in calculating NOPAT: interest expenses (that is, the charge on debt capital) are in fact subtracted from operating revenues. In the case of banks, it seems reasonable to calculate the capital invested (and, consequently, the capital charge) focussing on equity capital[7] and measure the capital invested in the bank as the book value of shareholder equity. Regarding the cost of capital, the capital charge cannot be obtained applying the bank's WACC on the capital invested because the latter is given by the equity capital and not by the overall capital (debt and equity). Consequently, a commercial bank's cost of capital invested should be measured by the cost of equity.[8] To support this view, Sironi (1999) identifies four differences (labelled as 'the separation principle', 'banks as providers of liquidity services', 'capital ratios', 'off-balance sheet pro') between a bank's cost of capital and that of a non-financial company, and observes 'with a capital structure exogenously determined by regulators, a marginal cost of debt close to that obtainable from the interbank market, and relatively similar to that of all other major banks, and an array of products that do not need any debt financing, banks should look at their cost of equity capital as a key variable'.[9] The cost of equity (ke) is estimated using the Capital Asset Pricing Model (CAPM) looking at investors' expected return. In this framework, there are three inputs for estimating the cost of equity: (1) Risk Free Rate: following a standard procedure,[10] this has estimated taking the annual rate of return of a long term Government Bond; (2) Equity risk premium: the modified historical approach proposed by Damodaran (1998) has been applied.[11] Equity Risk Premium is obtained by adding up a country premium to the case premium for mature equity markets, such as the US.[12] The country premium is obtained by adjusting[13] the country bond spreads: this latter spread has been obtained by comparing European government bond rates[14] with the US MORGAN Government Bond return indices over the period analysed (January 1995–June 2003); (3) Beta: these coefficients have been estimated using daily data on an annual basis by regressing the bank's share returns against stock market returns.[15] These regression Betas have been successively adjusted following the Bloomberg procedure.[16] Figure 9.2 summarize our EVA calculation procedure.

9.3.3   Model

To assess the relationship between banks corporate culture and bank performance, we examine which of our three bank's culture measures

<table>
<tr><td colspan="2">$EVA_{t-1,t} = NOPAT_{t-1,t} - (IC_{t-1} * Ke_{t-1,t})$</td></tr>
<tr><td>Where:</td><td>$NOPAT_{t-1,t}$ = EBIT $(1 - \text{tax rate}) +$
+ R&D Expenses
+ Training expenses
+ Operating Lease Expenses
+ Loan loss provisions − Net charge-off
+ Book tax provisions − Cash operating tax
+ General risk provisions − Net charge-off
IC_{t-1} = Book value of equity</td></tr>
<tr><td></td><td>+ Capitalised R&D expenses
+ Training expenses
− Proxy for amortised R&D expenses
− Proxy for amortised training expenses
+ Proxy for the present value of expected lease commitments over time
− Proxy for amortised operating lease commitments
+ Net Loan loss reserve
+ Deferred tax credits
− Deferred tax debits
+ General Risk Reserve</td></tr>
</table>

Figure 9.2   Economic Value Added (EVA) for European commercial banks: our calculation procedure

(namely, power-orientated culture, results-oriented culture and human-oriented culture) best explains variations in bank profitability and shareholder value created over the study period. We use the following two multivariate regression model estimated using the Full Feasible Generalized Least-Squares (FGLS)[17] approach:

$$\pi_i = \sum_{i=1}^{n} \alpha_i T_i + \sum_{k=0}^{m} \beta_k Z_k + \delta R_i + \chi TA_i + \phi C_i + e_i \tag{9.2}$$

$$\psi_i = \sum_{i=1}^{n} \alpha_i T_i + \sum_{k=0}^{m} \beta_k Z_k + \delta R_i + \chi TA_i + \phi C_i + e_i \tag{9.3}$$

where π_i is the variable representing bank profitability over the period t (measured by the ratio of net income and total assets at time $t - 1$[18]), ψ_i is the variable representing shareholder value created over the period t (measured by the ratio of Economic Value Added (EVA_{bkg}) and capital invested at time $t - 1$[19]), Ti are time effects capturing the effect of period t which is common across individual bank observations, Z is a set of dummy variables capturing country effects (namely, France, Germany, Italy, and the UK), R is bank net income at time $t - 1$ standardized by total asset at time t − 2 for bank i and TA is bank total assets at time t − 1 (these terms are included to control for the problem of self-selection bias, i.e. banks of good performance in the previous year and/or large banks are more likely to invest in projects that aim to improve their performance); C is our measure for the bank's culture and $e_{i,t}$ is the random error term and sub-indices i and t refer to the individual bank and the time period, respectively. Both models 2 and 3 are repeated three times according to the different orientations of bank's corporate cultures: namely, power-oriented, results-oriented and human-oriented corporate culture.

The analysis of estimated regression coefficients in models 2 and 3 enable us to test our hypotheses about the relationship between different attitudes of corporate culture and shareholder value and namely: In detail, the following hypotheses are verified if:

> H1 (i.e. There is a negative link between power-orientated bank corporate culture and profits): ϕ is negative and statistically significant.
> H2 (i.e. There is a positive link between result-orientated bank corporate culture and profits): ϕ is positive and statistically significant.
> H3 (i.e. There is a negative link between human-orientated bank corporate culture and profits): ϕ is positive and statistically significant.
> H4 (i.e. There is a negative link between power-orientated bank corporate culture and shareholder value): ϕ is negative and statistically significant.
> H5 (i.e. There is a weakly positive link between result-orientated bank corporate culture and shareholder value): ϕ may be positive and weakly statistically significant.
> H6 (There is a negative link between human-orientated bank corporate culture and shareholder value): ϕ is positive and statistically significant.

9.4 Data and results

Our dataset consists of the largest 35 commercial banks from France, Germany, Italy and the UK between 2001 and 2003 with financial information obtained from Bankscope and (to identify quoted banks) Datastream databases. We focuses on large commercial banks since we wanted to focus on a homogenous set of comparable banks in Europe in order to attempt to reduce biases resulting from other business conditions. Descriptive statistics of banks in the sample are shown in Table 9.1.

Consistent with the other text analysis applications,[20] the selection of the corpuses concerned public documents, such as financial reports and presentations.

Table 9.1 Sample descriptive statistics (102 European commercial banks between 2001 and 2003)*

	Total loans	Total deposit	Total assets	ROE (%)	ROA	EVA/CI
Mean	17,695.56	32,100.81	52,597.92	7.51	0.52	−1.10
Median	3,216.90	4,281.40	5,876.20	5.81	0.46	−1.42
Dev. St.	31,144.07	68,556.34	115,751.67	5.80	0.41	3.44
Min	21.00	36.00	44.00	0.06	0.00	−10.05
Max	175,187.00	335,348.00	565,367.00	27.88	2.53	8.63
Sum	1,804,947.00	3,274,283.00	5,364,988.00	765.71	53.41	−112.41

	Corporate culture		
	Power oriented (%)	Results oriented (%)	Human oriented (%)
Mean	22.93	35.37	41.70
Median	23.21	35.15	41.70
Dev. St.	8.97	7.13	7.36
Min	0.00	17.65	20.00
Max	47.06	55.56	60.00
Sum	2338.73	3607.40	4250.00

Note: * 30 British, 11 French, 30 German and 31 Italian commercial banks.

Table 9.2 reports our findings investigating the relationship between bank profitability and the corporate culture. According to these results, none of our hypotheses about the relationship between bank's profitability and corporate culture is verified: estimated regression coefficients for power oriented and result-oriented corporate culture are not statistically significant (even at the 10% confidence level) showing that there is not a statistically significant link between these two culture orientations and bank's profits. The third hypothesis is also not verified; while we expected positive and statistically significant regression coefficients for the human-oriented culture, we find a negative and statistically significant at the 5% confidence level. The results contrast theoretical expectations and so provide a substantial contribution to the existing literature since provide evidence that large European commercial banks cannot influence their profitability by strengthen/weaken their hierarchy and individualistic criteria (that is, changing their power orientation is not related to profit making) and by strengthen/weaken the importance given to the achievement of results (that is, changing their result orientation). Our finding about a human-oriented corporate culture are even more surprising: while one would expect that banks may increase

Table 9.2 The relationship between profits and corporate culture for European banks, respectively

Coefficients	Independent variables	Dependent variable net income/total assets t − 1		
		(1) Power-oriented bank's culture	(2) Results-oriented bank's culture	(3) Human-oriented bank's culture
(Constant)	(Constant)	0.008*** (5.048)	0.007*** (3.446)	0.014*** (5.907)
$\alpha 1$	Dummy variable for the year 2002 (T1)	−0.003 (−0.107)	−0.013 (−0.116)	−0.004 (−0.144)
$\alpha 2$	Dummy variable for the year 2003(T2)	−0.051 (0.388)	−0.042 (0.372)	-0.061 (0.404)
$\beta 0$	Dummy variable for French commercial banks (Z1)	−0.194 (0.084)	−0.216 (0.103)	−0.193 (−0.229)
$\beta 1$	Dummy variable for Italian commercial banks(Z2)	−0.460 (0.005)	−0.478 (0.005)	−0.440 (−0.005)
$\beta 2$	Dummy variable for German commercial banks (Z3)	−0.231* (−1.979)	−0.276** (−2.494)	−0.174 (−1.526)
δ	Net income at time t on Total Assets at time t − 1	0.388*** (4.066)	0.372*** (3.943)	0.404*** (4.348)
χ	Total Assets at time t	−0.107 (−0.854)	−0.116 (−0.922)	−0.144 (−1.164)
ϕ	Bank's corporate culture	0.084 (0.863)	0.103 (1.131)	−0.229** (−2.364)
Adjusted R-square		0.197	0.202	0.236

Note: * ** *** indicate that estimated coefficients are statistically significant at the 10%, 5% and 1% significance levels, respectively.
In model (1), ϕ refer to Power oriented bank's culture at time t
In model (2), ϕ refer to Result oriented bank's culture at time t
In model (3), ϕ refer to Human oriented bank's culture at time t
The combined dummy effects for 2001 and UK commercial banks are incorporated in the constant term.

profits by considering their workforce as a fundamental part of the organizational culture construct, we find that bank profitability is in fact negatively influenced by this culture orientation. This result may signal that a bank's investment in human resources is costly in the short term (reducing profitability over the same period) and/or profits may achieved in other ways than empowering human resources (for example, by increasing risks in banking activities). In all models, the estimated regression

Table 9.3 The relationship between shareholder value creation and corporate culture for European banks, respectively

	Independent variables	Dependent variable net (Ψ) income/total assets t − 1		
		(1) Power- oriented bank's culture	(2) Results- oriented bank's culture	(3) Human- oriented bank's culture
(Constant)	(Constant)	−0.035**	−0.045**	−0.097***
		(−2.398)	(−2.555)	(−4.328)
$\alpha 1$	Dummy variable for the year 2002 (T1)	−0.059 (−0.565)	−0.053 (−0.498)	−0.052 (−0.507)
$\alpha 2$	Dummy variable for the year 2003(T2)	0.073 (0.681)	0.065 (0.604)	0.080 (0.763)
$\beta 0$	Dummy variable for French commercial banks (Z1)	0.209 (1.334)	0.236 (1.490)	0.217 (1.411)
$\beta 1$	Dummy variable for Italian commercial banks(Z2)	0.333*** (2.729)	0.367*** (2.999)	0.335*** (2.811)
$\beta 2$	Dummy variable for German commercial banks (Z3)	0.371*** (3.071)	0.455)*** (4.106)	0.330*** (2.778)
δ	Net income at time t on Total Assets at time t − 1	0.379*** (3.730)	0.380*** (3.676)	0.411*** (4.071)
χ	Total Assets at time t	0.097 (0.634)	0.097 (0.627)	0.150 (0.985)
ϕ	Bank's corporate culture	−0.149* (−1.673)	−0.033 (−0.347)	0.244** (2.325)
Adjusted R-square		0.196	0.167	0.212

Note: * ** *** indicate that estimated coefficients are statistically significant at the 10%, 5% and 1% significance levels, respectively.
In model (1). ϕ refer to Power oriented bank's culture at time t
In model (2). ϕ refer to Result oriented bank's culture at time t
In model (3). ϕ refer to Human oriented bank's culture at time t
The combined dummy effects for 2001 and UK commercial banks are incorporated in the constant term.

coefficients for net income at time t − 1 are found to be positive and statistically significant, showing that most profitable banks have an advantage in achieving profits in the following year (and that there would be a self-selection bias omitting to considering this variable in analysing the relationship between bank's profitability and corporate culture).

Table 9.3 reports our findings investigating the relationship between shareholder value and corporate culture. According to these results, hypotheses 4 and 6 are verified. We find that there is a statistically significant (at the 10% confidence level) negative link between a power-oriented corporate culture and the shareholder value created over a given time period (H1). Namely, if a bank would increase the power orientation of their corporate culture by 10 per cent (from example, from 20 per cent to 30 per cent), the ratio between EVA and invested capital would decline by 1.49 per cent in the following year. We find that the estimated regression coefficient for the human-oriented corporate culture is positive and statistically significant (at the 5% confidence level), providing evidence that banks with a human-oriented capital have an advantage in creating EVA (H6): namely, if a bank would be able to increase the human orientation of their corporate culture by 10 per cent (for example, from 10 per cent to 20 per cent), the ratio between EVA and invested capital would rise by 2.44 per cent. Regarding hypothesis 5, the estimated regression coefficient for the results-oriented corporate culture is slightly negative and non-statistically significant (even at the 10% confidence level): this result supports our expectation that banks with a result-oriented culture have no advantage in creating shareholder value, providing evidence that when a bank forces its workforce to achieve high results in the short term, this would lead it to take higher risks and the overall result is a decline in shareholder value. In all models, the estimated regression coefficients for net income at time $t-1$ are found to be positive and statistically significant, showing that most profitable banks have an advantage in creating shareholder value in the following year (and that there would be a self-selection bias omitting to considering this variable in analysing the relationship between shareholder value and corporate culture).

9.5   Conclusions

Does banking culture affect shareholder value? The answer is positive, although only selectively. Banking strategies are giving increased attention to the use of culture as a potential for leading change and enhancing innovation. In order to promote strategic change and match short-term with long-term goals, organizational restructuring involves both hard and soft value drivers. A flexible and eclectic culture, built on such values as human resources' motivation and satisfaction, broad communication flows and information sharing, and widespread through an open leadership style, can support integration needs following growth processes and diversification strategies and create competitive advantage.

Nevertheless, the link between culture, profitability and value creation in the banking sector has been only poorly investigated in previous studies. This chapter represents a first attempt to assess the impact of some cultural dimensions of European banks and their performance, measured in terms of both bank profitability and shareholder value. The three dimension of corporate culture are operationalized through a text analysis model, which has only occasionally been applied in the existing economic literature.

The contribution of this chapter focuses on three aspects – two relating to content, with important implications for banking management, and one to method, fostering further research on the topic.

First, the results show a link between culture and shareholder value, while it is clear that, at least in the short run, cultural orientation does not influence the profitability of the panel banks. Corporate culture is therefore a value driver which banks have to control in order to achieve a strategic change. The link also seems to be consistent over short time periods, even if the cultural changes could require several years to become effective.

Secondly, in the light of the achieved results, the 'old' banking culture, driven by bureaucratic and mechanical organizational models, can represent a barrier to change that must be replaced by a culture which is both people-centred and based on cooperation. A results-oriented corporate culture is instead negatively affecting shareholder value, giving support to the idea that applying considerable pressure to short-term performance can lead to higher risk and thereby to a destruction of shareholder value.

Thirdly, from a methodological point of view, the study confirms the importance of text analysis as a technique for formalizing some aspects of culture in order to introduce that dimension in statistical models and to assess its contribution to firm strategy and performance. Therefore, it is expedient to develop this line of study, which can be done by testing the former hypothesis on different cultural dimensions and by applying the model in question to increasingly 'internal' corpuses of texts and firm-specific documents, such as circular letters and internal service orders, organizational regulations and other materials reflecting the day-to-day performance of the corporate activities, in order to bring the survey method closer to the characteristics typical of ethnographical studies of culture.

Notes

1. This chapter is the result of close cooperation between the authors. However, all authors have contributed to section 9.2, Vincenzo Farina also

contributed sections 9.3.1, Franco Fiordelisi sections 9.1, 9.3.2, 9.3.3 and 9.4, and Alessandro Carretta and Paola Schwizer to section 9.5.

2. Studies analysing shareholder value usually focus on developing and comparing new performance measures (O'Hanlon and Peasnell, 1998; Garvey and Milbourn, 2000; Fernández, 2002), assessing the value-relevance of different company items such as performance measures, accounting information, and so on (Barth and Beaver, 2001; Holthausen and Watts, 2001), modelling the link between market value with accounting values (Ohlson, 1995; Felthman and Ohlson, 1995; Morel, 1999; Dechow, Hutton and Sloan, 1999; Lo and Lys, 2000; Ahmed, Morton and Schaefer, 2000; Liu and Ohlson, 2000; Biddle, Chen and Zhang, 2001; Ota, 2002).

3. In order to have a greater comparability of results, these culture dimensions are consistent with those used in other studies (Hofstede, 1980; Hofstede, Neuijen, Ohayv and Sanders, 1990; Denison and Mishra, 1995; Wilderom and Van den Berg, 2000; Carretta, Farina and Schwizer, 2005).

4. Every year Stern Stewart publishes a performance report for the 1,000 largest companies (see Stewart, 1991). In this chapter, these capitalized expenses are amortized every year (that is, from 1995 to 1999) using a proxy defined by dividing the overall amount of R&D expenses over the period 1995–99 for five years.

5. Since the limited availability of data does not allow us to evaluate the present value of expected lease commitments over time, the present value of expected future lease commitments capitalized (for every year between 1995 and 1999) is assumed to be equal to the overall amount of operating leases expenses over the period 1995-99. The amount amortized every year (that is, from 1995 to 1999) is near to the overall amount of R&D expenses over the entire period 1995–99.

6. These adjustments were originally suggested by Uyemura, Kantor and Pettit (1996).

7. Otherwise, it would be necessary to distinguish between borrowed funds assigned to finance banking operations and those representing a productive input.

8. This point is also supported by Uyemura et al. (1996) and Di Antonio (2002).

9. Sironi (1999).

10. See, for example, Damodaran (1999).

11. Fama and French (2002) propose a different model using dividend and earnings growth rates to measure the expected rate of capital gain and estimate the equity risk premium: this model was labelled Earnings growth model.

12. Regarding the US risk premium, the estimation provided by Damodaran (1998) has been adopted: 6.10 per cent

13. Since one would expect the country equity risk premium to be larger than the country default risk spread, the country equity spread is obtained by adjusting the country bond spreads as follows:

$$\text{Country Equity Risk Premium} = \text{Country Bond Spread} \times \frac{\sigma_{equity}}{\sigma_{bond}}$$

Where: (1) the volatility of the equity market (σ equity) has been estimated by focussing on CAC 40, DAX 30, MIBTEL storico, FTSE 100; and (2) the volatility of the bond market (σ bond) has been estimated by focussing on the French, Italian, German, British and J.P. Morgan Government Bond return indices.

14. Namely, the French, Italian, German, British and J.P. Morgan Government Bond return indices.
15. Namely, CAC 40 for France, DAX 30 for Germany, MIBTEL storico for Italy and FTSE100 for UK.
16. Namely: Beta = Regression Beta $(0.67) + 1.00 \ (0.33)$.
17. We employ the Full Feasible Generalized Least-Squares (FGLS), estimated using the Prais-Winsten estimator, since we observe a first-order autoregressive process in the OLS estimation (see Greene, 1997). In addition, independent variables do not suffer from scale effects and, consequently, it is not necessary to deflate independent variables.
18. We lag the capital invested term by one period assuming that it will take at least a year for capital investments to feed through into additional net income.
19. We lag the capital invested term by one period assuming that it will take at least a year for capital investments to feed through into additional EVA.
20. For example, Bowman, (1984); D'Aveni and MacMillan (1990); Kabanoff, Waldersee and Cohen (1995); Carretta, Farina and Schwizer (2005).

References

Ahmed, A.S., R.M. Morton and T.F. Schaefer (2000) 'Accounting Conservatism and the Valuation of Accounting Numbers: Evidence on the Felthman–Ohlson (1996) Model', *Journal of Accounting, Auditing and Finance*, 15: 271–92.

Alvesson, M. (1993) *Cultural Perspectives on Organizations*, New York: Cambridge University Press.

Barney, J. (1986) 'Organizational Culture', *Academy of Management Review*, 11: 656–65.

Barth, M.E. and W.H. Beaver (2001) 'The Relevance of the Value Relevance Literature for Financial Accounting Standard Setting: Another View', *Journal of Accounting and Economics*, 31: 3–75.

Bartram, S. (2000) 'Corporate Risk Management as a Lever for Shareholder Value Creation', *Financial Markets, Institutions and Instruments*, 9: 279–324.

Bartram, S. (2002) 'Enhancing Shareholder Value with Corporate Risk Management', *Corporate Finance Review*, 7: 7–12.

Bauer, H.H. and M. Hammerschmidt (2005) 'Customer-based Corporate Valuation', *Management Decision*, 43: 331–48.

Beccalli, E., B. Casu and C. Girardone (2006) 'Efficiency and Stock Performance in European Banking', *Journal of Business, Accounting and Finance*, 33: 218–35.

Berger, P.L. and T. Luckmann, (1967) *The Social Construction of Reality: a Treatise in the Sociology of Knowledge*, Garden City: Anchor Books.

Biddle, G.C., P. Chen and G. Zhang (2001) 'When Capital Follows Profitability: Non Linear Residual Income Dynamics', *Review of Accounting Studies*, 6: 229–65.

Bowman, E.H. (1984) 'Content Analysis of Annual Reports for Corporate Strategy and Risk', *Interfaces*, 14: 61–71.

Burns, T. and G. Stalker (1961) *The Management of Innovation*, London: Tavistock.

Burt, R.S., S.M. Gabbay, G. Holt and R. Moran (1994) 'Contingent Organization as a Network Theory: the Culture Performance Contingency Function', *Acta Sociologica*, 37: 346–70.

Carretta, A. (2001) *Il governo del cambiamento culturale in banca. Modelli di analisi, strumenti operativi, valori individuali*, Rome: Bancaria Editrice.

Carretta, A., V. Farina and P. Schwizer (2005) *Banking Regulation Towards Advisory: the 'Culture Compliance' of Banks and Supervisory Authorities*, paper presented at the 5rd annual conference of European Academy of Management, Munich.

Chu, S.F. and G.H. Lim (1998) 'Share Performance and Profit Efficiency of Banks in an Oligopolistic Market: Evidence from Singapore', *Journal of Multinational Financial Management*, 8: 155–68.

Cummings, J.D., C.M. Lewis and R. Wei (2005) 'The Market Value Impact of Operational Risk Events for US Banks and Insurers', paper presented at the Conference 'Implementing an AMA for Operational Risk', Federal Reserve Bank of Boston, Boston.

Damodaran, A. (1998) *Applied Corporate Finance*, New York: John Wiley & Sons.

D'Aveni, R. and I.C. MacMillan (1990) 'Crisis and the Content of Managerial Communication: a Study at the Focus of Attention of Top Managers in Surviving and Failing Firms', *Administrative Science Quarterly*, 35: 634–57.

Davis, S. (2004) *Excellence in Banking Revisited*, Basingstoke: Palgrave Macmillan.

Dechow, P.M., A.P. Hutton and R.G. Sloan (1999) 'An Empirical Assessment of the Residual Income Valuation Model', *Journal of Accounting and Economics*, 26: 1–34.

Denison, D.R. (1990) *Corporate Culture and Organizational Effectiveness*, New York: Wiley.

Denison, D.R. and A.K. Mishra (1995) 'Toward a Theory of Organizational Culture and Effectiveness', *Organization Science*, 6: 204–23.

Di Antonio, M. (2002) *Creazione di valore e controllo strategico nella banca*, Rome: Bancaria Editrice.

DiMaggio, P. (1997) 'Culture and Cognition', *Annual Review of Sociology*, 23: 263–88.

DiMaggio, P. (2002) 'Why Cognitive (and Cultural) Sociology Needs Cognitive Psychology', in K.A. Cerulo (ed.), *Culture in Mind: Toward a Sociology of Culture and Cognition*, New York: Routledge.

Eisenbeis, R.A., G.D. Ferrier and S.H. Kwan (1999) *The Informativeness of Stochastic Frontier and Programming Frontier Efficiency Scores: Cost Efficiency and Other Measures of Bank Holding Company Performance*, Federal Reserve Bank of Atlanta working paper no. 99–23, Atlanta.

Fama, E.F. and R.K. French (2002) 'The Equity Premium', *Journal of Finance*, 57: 637–59.

Felthman, G. and J.A. Ohlson (1995) 'Valuation and Clean Surplus Accounting for Operating and Financial Activities', *Contemporary Accounting Research*, 11: 689–731.

Fernández, A.I., F. Gascón and E. González (2002) *Economic Efficiency and Value Maximization in the Banking Firms*, paper presented to the 7th European workshop on efficiency and productivity analysis, Oviedo, Spain.

Fernández, P. (2002) *EVA, Economic Profit and Cash Value Added Do Not Measure Shareholder Value Creation*, University of Navarra research paper no. 453, Navarra.

Fiordelisi, F. and P. Molyneux (2006) *Shareholder Value in European Banking*. Basingstoke: Palgrave Macmillan.

Fombrun, C. and M. Shanley (1990) 'What's in a Name? Reputation Building and Corporate Strategy', *Academy of Management Journal*, 33: 233–58.

Garvey, G.T. and T.T. Milbourn (2000) 'EVA versus Earnings: Does it Matter Which is More Highly Correlated with Stock Returns?', *Journal of Accounting Research*, 38: 209–45.

Geertz, C. (1973) *The Interpretation of Cultures*, New York: Basic Books.

Gordon, G.G. and N. Di Tomaso (1992) 'Predicting Corporate Performance from Organizational Culture', *Journal of Management Studies*, 29: 783–98.

Hansen, G.S. and B. Wernerfelt (1989) 'Determinants of Firm Performance: the Relative Importance of Economic and Organizational Factors', *Strategic Management Journal* 10: 193–206.

Harrison, R. (1972) 'Understanding Your Organization's Character', *Harvard Business Review*, 50: 119–28.

Herskovits, M.J. (1955) *Cultural Anthropology*, New York: Knopf.

Hodgson, G.M. (1996) 'Corporate Culture and the Nature of the Firm', in J. Groenewegen (ed.), *Transaction Cost Economics and Beyond*, Boston: Kluwer Academic Press.

Hofstede, G. (1980) *Culture's Consequences: International Differences in Work-Related Values*, Beverly Hills, CA: Sage Publications.

Hofstede, G., B. Neuijen, D.D. Ohavy and G. Sanders (1990) 'Measuring Organizational Cultures: a Qualitative and Quantitative Study Across Twenty Cases', *Administrative Science Quarterly*, 35: 286–316.

Holthausen, R.W. and R.L. Watts (2001) 'The Relevance of the Value-relevance Literature for Financial Accounting Standard Setting', *Journal of Accounting and Economics*, 31: 3–75.

Kabanoff, B. and J. Holt (1996) 'Changes in the Espoused Values of Australian Organizations 1986–1990', *Journal of Organizational Behavior*, 17: 201–19.

Kabanoff, B., R. Waldersee and M. Cohen (1995) 'Espoused Values and Organizational Change Themes', *Academy of Management Journal*, 38: 1075–104.

Kaplan, R.S. and D.P. Norton (2004) *Organizational Capital: Leadership, Alignment, and Teamwork*, Balanced Scorecard Report, Cambridge, MA: Harvard University Press.

Kotter, J.R. and J.L. Heskett (1992) *Corporate Culture and Performance*, New York: Free Press.

Lasswell, H.D. and Z.J. Namenwirth (1969) *The Lasswell Value Dictionary*, New Haven: Yale University Press.

Lawrence, P. and J. Lorsch (1967) *Organisation and Environment: Managing Differentiation and Integration*, Cambridge, MA: Harvard University Press.

Levinson, S. (2003) 'Language and Mind: Let's Get the Issues Straight!', in D. Gentner and S. Goldin-Meadow (eds), *Language in Mind*, Cambridge, MA; MIT Press.

Liu, J. and J.A. Ohlson (2000) 'The Feltham–Ohlson (1995) Model: Empirical Implications', *Journal of Accounting, Auditing and Finance*, 15: 321–31.

Lo, K. and T. Lys (2000) 'The Ohlson Model: Contribution to Valuation Theory, Limitations, and Empirical Applications', *Journal of Accounting, Auditing and Finance*, 15: 337–67.

Loveman, G.W. (1998) 'Employee Satisfaction, Customer Loyalty and Financial Performance: an Empirical Examination of the Service Profit Chain in Retail Banking', *Journal of Service Research*, 1: 18–31.

Martin, J. (1992) *Cultures in Organizations: Three Perspectives*, New York: Oxford University Press.

Morel, M. (1999) 'Multi-lagged Specification of the Ohlson Model', *Journal of Accounting, Auditing and Finance*, 12: 147–61.

Moussetis, R.C., A.A. Rahma and G. Nakos (2005) 'Strategic Behavior and National Culture: the Case of the Banking Industry in Jordan', *Competitiveness Review*, May: 101–15.

O'Hanlon, J. and K. Peasnell (1998) 'Wall Street's Contribution to Management Accounting: the Stern Stewart EVA Financial Management System', *Management Accounting Research*, 9: 421–44.

Ohlson, J.A. (1995) 'Earnings, Book Values and Dividends in Equity Valuation', *Contemporary Accounting Research*, 11: 661–87.

O'Reilly, C.A. and J.A. Chatman (1996) 'Culture as Social Control: Corporations, Cults, and Commitment', *Research in Organizational Behavior*, 18: 157–200.

Ota, K. (2002) 'A Test of the Ohlson (1995) Model: Empirical Evidence from Japan',*International Journal of Accounting*, 37: 157–82.

Pennings, J.M., K. Lee and A. Van Witteloostuijn (1998) 'Human Capital, Social Capital and Firm Dissolution', *Academy of Management Journal*, 41: 425–40.

Peters, T. and R. Waterman (1982) *In Search of Excellence*, New York: Harper & Row.

Pettigrew, A. (1979) 'On Studying Organizational Culture', *Administrative Science Quarterly*, 24: 570–81.

Quinn, R.E. (1988) 'Beyond Rational Management: Mastering the Paradoxes and Competing Demands of High Performance', San Francisco: Jossey-Bass.

Quinn, R.E. and M. McGrath (1985) 'Transformation of Organizational Cultures: a Competing Values Perspective', in P. Frost (ed.), *Organizational Culture*, Beverly Hills: Sage Publications.

Rosa, J. and J. Porac (2002) 'Categorization Bases and Their Influence on Product Category Knowledge Structures', *Psychology & Marketing*, 19: 503–32.

Schein, E.H. (1985) *Organizational Culture and Leadership*, San Francisco: Jossey-Bass.

Scott, M. (1999) *WordSmith Tools*, Oxford: Oxford University Press.

Siehl, C. and J. Martin (1990) 'Organizational Culture: a Key to Financial Performance?', in B. Schneider (ed.), *Organizational Climate and Culture*, New York: John Wiley & Sons.

Sironi, A. (1999) *Estimating Banks' Cost of Equity Capital: Evidence from an International Comparison*, Milan: Quaderno NEWFIN, Università L. Bocconi.

Sorensen, J.B. (2002) 'The Strength of Corporate Culture and the Reliability of Firm Performance', *Administrative Science Quarterly*, 77: 70–91.

Stewart, B.G. (1991) *The Quest for Value*, New York: Harper Business.

Uyemura, D.G., G.C. Kantor and J.M. Pettit (1996) 'EVA for Banks: Value Creation, Risk Management and Profitability Measurement', *Journal of Applied Corporate Finance*, 9: 94–105.

Van den Steen, E.J. (2004) *Culture Clash: the Costs and Benefits of Homogeneity*, MIT-Sloan School of Management Working Paper, Cambridge.

Van der Wiele, T., P. Boselie and M. Hesselink (2001) *Empirical Evidence for the Relation Between Customer Satisfaction and Business Performance*, Erasmus Research institute of Management report series, Rotterdam.

Van Maanen, J. (1991) 'The Smile Factory', in P.J. Frost, L.F. Moore, M.R. Louis, C.C. Lundberg and J. Martin (eds), *Reframing Organizational Culture*, London: Sage.

Weick, K.E. (1979) *The Social Psychology of Organizing*, Reading, MA: Addison-Wesley.

Wilderom, C. and P.T. Van den Berg (2000) *Firm Culture and Leadership as Firm Performance Predictors: a Resource Based Perspective*, Tilburg University Working Paper, Tilburg.

Wilkin, A.L. and W.G. Ouchi (1983) 'Efficient Cultures: Exploring the Relationship Between Culture and Organizational Performance', *Administrative Science Quarterly*, 28: 468–81.

Wolfe, R.A. 'The Use of Content Analysis to Assess Corporate Social Responsibility', in J. Post (ed.), *Research in Corporate Social Performance and Policy*, Greenwich, CT: JAI Press.

Wuthnow, R. (1989) *Communities of Discourse*, Cambridge, MA: Harvard University Press.

Zuell, C., R. Weber and P. Mohler (1989) *Computer Aided Text Classification for the Social Sciences: the General Enquirer III*, Mannheim: Zentrum für Methoden und Analysen.

Part III
Regulation and Change in Banks' and Customers' Behaviour

10
The Consumer's Financial Capability: a Regulatory Perspective

Gianni Nicolini

10.1 Introduction

At present, the development of consumers' self-evaluation of their own financial situation is still in its infancy. In the interests of consumers, it is important that there is a narrowing in the current gap in information and financial expertise between themselves and financial intermediaries. This could contribute to a reduction in the instances of over-indebtedness and bankruptcy. At the same time, it might make it easier for consumers to compare products and hence to increase the level of competition between lenders.

The need to support consumers by providing them with information instruments that are capable of facilitating the decision-making process thus takes the form of a request for an intervention based on a regulatory approach of fair play. Such a regulatory initiative would be intended to guarantee parity in relations between lenders and debtors through transparency rather than modifying relations between the parties through invasive activity involving sanctions.

The objective of this chapter is to evaluate whether or not it is advisable to introduce a regulatory initiative designed to stimulate debtors' awareness of their own financial capabilities. I propose the development of a financial capability index and also discuss how we would determine the appropriate information to be included in such an index. The present discussion is only an exploratory one. Further research is needed to address what information should be included in the index and also what procedures should be employed in constructing the index.

10.2 Financial capability as a problem with many solutions

By analysing the different contributions in the literature, it is possible to summarize the concept of 'financial capability' (or financial literacy) as the capacity of the consumer to implement a decision-making process given a specific set of information regarding his/her financial situation. Improving financial capability means improving the results of a decision-making process.

The objective of improving financial conduct requires an increase in the individual's capacity to be aware of issues and to work out appropriate actions. This objective is pursued by improving knowledge, skills and confidence. Everything which may help increase these three elements is valued in a positive way.[1] For example, holding training courses and putting into place less traditional solutions.[2] Although such responses have the potential to improve the financial capabilities of individuals, they are not the only way to improve financial capability.

The key concepts underlying the concept of 'financial capability' are know-how and expertise, with both of these being geared towards developing the capacity to understand financial affairs. Improving financial knowledge includes raising the consumers' level of knowledge, but also working on the inputs of the decision-making process (the information) in order to increase its suitability for their use.

The awareness of individuals can certainly be improved with regard to the increasing complexity of financial products. In particular, the information used by individuals in their decision-making process could be simplified in order to make its use more effective.

The topic of financial capability therefore presents itself as a problem with a number of solutions that, rather than being mutually exclusive alternatives, may be introduced simultaneously. Such an approach would amplify the effectiveness of each measure. The different solutions are distinguished from one another by the assumptions regarding the financial capabilities of the individuals. When training is used as a tool, it is assumed that there is room for improvement in the individual's capacity to work out appropriate actions. On the other hand, when efforts focus on the information the quality of the process of working out appropriate actions is taken as a given, while the quality of the information input is deemed to play a critical role. In the first case, any initiative designed to improve financial capability focuses on the individual and his or her capabilities, while the second approach focuses on the set of information available.

10.3 The role of legislation: 'invasive approach' vs 'information approach'

Before taking time to consider the topic of financial capability, it is best to examine the relationship between the creditor and the borrower. Specific consideration should be given to the status of the weaker contracting party – usually the borrower. There are two main arguments for this assumption. The first stresses the fact that the borrower's need to obtain credit is often greater than the lender's need to provide it.

The second is the relatively small amount of information possessed by the borrower when it comes to making decisions.[3] This asymmetry of information is often worsened by the borrower's inability to correctly interpret the information available – a condition that hampers his/her capacity to evaluate the lender's credit offer.

Having taken note of the different inherent conditions of the lender and the borrower, it must be determined whether, in order to place the relationship on a more balanced footing, it is necessary to: (1) intervene directly in the transaction with a third party limiting the range of action for the debtors; or (2) if there is a form of intervention that would preserve the decision-making autonomy of the borrower.

In the first case, intervention in the lender–borrower relationship would be justified by the acknowledgement that the borrower is structurally incapable of dealing on an equal footing with a lender. This means that, in order to improve the role of the weaker contracting party, the borrower would need an 'invasive intervention' geared towards safeguarding the interests of the debtor. The intervention in the financing relationship would take the form of a series of limitations that affect the decision-making freedom of both parties.

By contrast, the second scenario holds that the consumer possesses adequate decision-making capabilities, and identifies the different levels of information as the cause of the gap in the relationship between the lender and the borrower. By adjusting the level of information available to the debtor, therefore, the contractual relationship can be returned to a more balanced relationship without restricting the parties' freedom to negotiate.

Should it be deemed impossible for the debtor to deal with the lender on an equal footing, then the state would be called upon to safeguard the interests of the borrower. In contrast, should it be held that the debtor, when he is in possession of adequate information, is able to deal independently with the lender, then state intervention is not the only option. Nevertheless, the use of legislation to guarantee adequate information remains an advisable course of action.[4]

Given that, in both cases, legislative intervention is needed to offset the weakness of the debtor, under the first scenario state intervention is structural and inhibitory in nature while the approach taken in the second case is closer to the logic of 'fair-play regulation', meaning that it is based on the idea of transparency of information. Thus, in this circumstance the judgement as to whether or not the debtor is capable or incapable of acting in an independent and fully aware manner becomes crucial. The consequences of an approach stressing invasive intervention as opposed to one focusing on the transparency of information also becomes relevant with regard to the topic of financial capability.

The definition of financial capability as the capacity to evaluate the consequences of one's own financial decisions ties this concept directly to the capability to estimate one's own capacity for indebtedness. Viewed from a practical perspective, the level of financial capability can be defined as the degree of precision with which a subject is capable of evaluating its own level of sustainable indebtedness. The latter means the level of debt for which the borrower is still able to pay back the loan(s) without having to resort to extra financing. The invasive approach gives rise to a demand for regulations designed to inhibit any forms of conduct on the part of debtors held to be incompatible with their levels of sustainable indebtedness. The information approach, on the other hand, which is based on the assumption that consumers are capable of making decisions, is designed to improve the level of information. In this scenario, debtors, who draw upon an external information support, succeed in independently evaluating the consequences of their financial conduct and in interacting with the lender with a greater degree of freedom.

Considering the credit market as a whole, the first type of approach holds that the differences between the demand and the supply of credit are fundamental and prevent that this prevents the establishment of a situation of balance. The argument is that this will remain the case unless a corrective intervention is carried out on the basis of legislation that introduces remedial measures. In contrast, the second type of approach views the scope of application of any legislation as being limited to considerations of transparency. The market, in and of itself, is considered to be potentially efficient, and, following an adequate corrective intervention in the area of information, is viewed as being able to improve the levels of competition and efficiency. In fact, a higher level of information leads to increased competition among the creditors, driving out less efficient ones.

In other words, the topic of financial capability is not focussed on safeguarding the debtor in individual credit relations, but has macroeconomic implications in relation to the level of efficiency in the market. The proposal for an approach based on a 'fair-play' regulation emphasizes how an improved supply of information to consumers allows them to improve their financial capabilities and to arrive at more accurate estimates of their financial capacities.

This could reach a point where they are able to foresee situations of potential difficulty (excessive indebtedness, default and so on) and thus select from the credit options on offer in a more precise manner.

While the alternative stances regarding the decision-making autonomy of consumers are fundamental assumptions in any analysis of financial capability, the approach that this chapter adopts is the second one. It is the approach geared towards improving the level of information of consumers without compromising their decision-making independence.

10.4   The current regulatory framework in Europe

An analysis of the regulatory framework currently in force in European countries is of great help in identifying possible areas of intervention regarding financial capability. It is especially worthwhile examining how current legislation in Europe (at both the Community and national levels) addresses the issue.

In order to do this, I conducted an analysis of legislation in the main European countries (Belgium, France, Germany, Ireland, Italy, Holland, Portugal, Spain, Switzerland and the UK), paying particular attention to the legislation on consumer credit. This is an area in which safeguards for the debtor as the weaker party in the credit relationship have already been put in place. Consumer credit is an area in which the legislative intervention of the EU has contributed to placing the different national laws on a uniform footing, guaranteeing a minimum level of homogeneity.

The topic of financial capability is given explicit consideration only under Swiss legislation, while English laws contain measures which, although they do not deal with financial capability per se, pay close attention to the defence of consumers. In the other countries under consideration, the theme of financial capability was found to be dealt with only implicitly, with regard to the obligations of transparency that must be observed by creditors. In other words, the attention paid to the level of information and to the level of consumer understanding of the information is not especially high.

In all of the countries examined, the legislation appears to be designed to provide the consumer with an adequate level of information. This is pursued by placing the obligations to communicate on the creditor. Particular attention is focussed on the cost of credit. In the case of consumer credit, the European Community directive on the subject[5] can be credited with having introduced the annual percentage rate of interest (APR) as a simplified cost indicator. As part of an analysis meant to determine the procedures under which the level of information to the consumer is increased, the APR represents an example of how (by using an information tool) the legislation has made an improvement for the consumer's decision-making capabilities. The strengths of the APR are that it ensures standardization, simplification and comparability. The APR provides consumers with a measurement that makes possible immediate comparison of different credit offers. In addition to being a standardized information tool, the APR provides consumers with the benefit of information that has been subjected to a process of selection, focussing attention on one of the main decision-making variables – cost.

The attention paid to transparency in the creditor–borrower relationship is not limited to the APR; rather, it takes the form of a series of further procedures that must be fulfilled by the creditor. The assumption underlying the current European regulatory framework appears to be that – by increasing the quantity of information available to the client and standardizing the procedures through which this information must be communicated – the consumer is provided with the means to evaluate the characteristics of a credit offer. If the availability of information is an indispensable precondition for making an informed decision, then the question must be raised as to whether it really is sufficient for guaranteeing rational decisions on the part of the consumer. Another related question would be if the focus of attention must be expanded to include not only the quantity of the information supplied but also the manner in which the information was communicated.

However, there could be an error in the assumption that an increase in the information available to the client results automatically in an increase in the amount of information possessed by the client. In fact, the information collected by a borrower for decision making tends to change, depending upon the nature and importance of the financial product or service being purchased. In the case of higher amounts of credit such as mortgages, the decision-making process of the borrowers might follow non-compensatory rules.[6] This process demands a large quantity of information. In the case of loans of a smaller amount (that is, consumer credit), the use of compensatory rules means that the borrower bases his or her decision on a restricted set of what is considered to be the most meaningful information. In this second case, the assumption that an increased quantity of information leads to an improvement in the level of information (and thus an increase in the decision-making capability of the debtor) is not an absolute one.

In the case of consumer credit, it is highly likely that the decision-making process follows non-compensatory rules. However, a large quantity of information could be perceived as excessive information with the countermeasure being a process of selection designed to identify the most relevant information concerning a credit offer. A legislative measure that focuses on the quantity of information therefore guarantees neither an adequate level of safeguards for the consumer nor an increase in the transparency of the system as a whole, thus also compromising the levels of efficiency.

To return to the legislation, features commonly found at the European level include the need for a clear indication of the price agreed, plus the requirement that the client be presented with a copy of the contract at the moment that it is concluded.

Although the values described are common to the different legislative acts, there are also specific national measures that provide safeguards for the consumer. As is the case with Italian law, Belgian legislation[7] provides the consumer with the possibility of obtaining a copy of the contract even before it is signed. The reason is also to enable the consumer to evaluate the contents in detail, especially with regard to any vexatious clauses. Another positive side-effect is that it is an explicit reminder for creditors of the need for clarity and correctness in communications with their clientele.

Belgian legislators go even further by preventing the creditor from forwarding a credit application from a consumer which, in the opinion of the creditor, formulated on the basis of the available information, is not or will not be able to honour the obligations stipulated in the contract.[8] This measure, unmistakably consumer-oriented, is a clear example of the invasive approach.

The intention to safeguard the position of the consumer to such an extent can also be found in Portuguese legislation. In this case, under Law No. 24/1996 (31 July 1996), consumers are assigned the right to training and education as well as the right to information. Although the act makes reference to a general principle, it appears to acknowledge the need to move beyond mere measurement of the quantity of information supplied in line with the principle of shifting attention to the consumer rather than focusing exclusively on the creditors.

Although the underlying intentions are the same, Spanish legislation takes a different approach.[9] There is a possibility under Spanish law of bringing a class action suit – an option that backs up the role played by consumer associations in terms of consumer protection. Such associations are able to go into court either in the name of their members or in order to defend the public interest.

While the measures referred to are at risk of remaining nothing more than mere principles, English legislation appears to address the need to select the information, or at least to recognise that different types of information are of greater or lesser importance.[10] Of particular interest is the measure that requires the use of a differentiated layout in order to draw the attention of the contracting parties to the consequences of signing the contract. The following phrases are examples of warnings meant to alert the debtor:

> 'Your home may be repossessed if you do not keep up repayments on a mortgage or any other debt secured on it.'
> 'Think carefully before securing other debts. Think carefully before securing other debts against your home.'
> 'Check that this mortgage will meet your needs if you want to move or sell your home or you want your family to inherit it. If you are in any doubt, seek independent advice.'

The regulatory concern in question is part of a legislative framework (the British one) generally constructed around transparency criteria.

English legislation also provides an example of how, by establishing a system designed to guarantee an adequate level of attention to consumers, the level of external intervention by regulatory authorities can be reduced, to the point of implementing the principle of responsibility, under which consumers are obliged to take responsibility for the decisions they make.[11] The situations in the other countries of the EU do not present peculiarities that deserve particular reflection.[12] French, Italian and German legislation is in line with European Community standards, ensuring transparency but delegating responsibility for interpreting and processing the information to the consumer. In other words, there is no intervention in the decision-making process of the debtor.[13]

The Swiss FLCC (Federal Law on Consumer Credit),[14] on the other hand, is an example of a highly invasive measure. Art. 28, which contains provisions on the capability of consumers to obtain credit,[15] states that consumers are deemed to possess the financial capacity to enter into a credit relationship if they are able to repay the credit without drawing on the portion of their income meant to satisfy basic needs. The capacity to engage in a credit relationship is evaluated by assuming that the duration of the credit is longer than 36 months – even if the contract stipulates a longer duration. If the applicant has already been found in default in the past, then this information must be taken into consideration.

The objective of the law is made explicit in Art. 22, which states that 'the evaluation of the consumer's capacity to enter a credit agreement is aimed at preventing excessive indebtedness a credit agreement could cause'.[16] An analysis of the articles clearly points to the conclusion that, regardless of the level of information they possess, consumers are subjects whose conduct must be guided. The idea of legally establishing criteria to be used by consumers in evaluating their financial capability is definitely a positive development. However, the fact that this evaluation must be carried out by the creditor denies consumers the recognition of their capacity for self-evaluation, and, by asking the lender to safeguard the interests of the party being financed, creates a potential conflict of interest.

10.5   Legislative intervention: pros and cons

Given that the topic of consumer financial capability involves the supply of credit in the retail sector, it touches on a finely balanced relationship of noteworthy social relevance. This means that the prospect of legislative intervention risks creating situations of imbalance, making an attentive evaluation of the possible consequences necessary.

To support legislative intervention, there is, first and foremost, a need to establish a uniform set of rules capable of standardising the evaluation process. The results obtained with the APR in the consumer-credit sector are typical of this. Had nothing more than general principles been indicated rather than specific instructions on the calculation procedures, the effectiveness of the Index as an information tool would not have been the same. In the same way, a piece of legislative intervention would result in the definition of uniform criteria, thus guaranteeing, through standardisation, the effectiveness of the result.

Legislative intervention is also justified by the coercive nature of the measure in question. Standards for procedures used to calculate financial capability could also be established without legislative intervention. They could be allowed to develop through the progressive and spontaneous 'sedimentation' of operating practices, with the legislators providing varying levels of stimulus to move the operators in this direction. On the other hand, the coercive approach has the advantage of shortening the necessary period of time while guiding the process under which financial capability is adopted as information of use in evaluating financing proposals.

Legislative intervention is also advisable in those financial systems where the use of credit is part of a process of change whereby consumption patterns based on an advance accumulation of savings are being replaced with conduct geared towards financing purchase through the activation of financing arrangements, leading to repayment plans of varying length. In such systems, the risk that consumers will learn the correct procedures for the use of credit through negative experiences (excessive indebtedness, default, legal proceedings and so on) is high. Legislative intervention meant to manage the change would make it possible to avoid (or at least reduce) the associated social costs.

But there are also elements that give rise to potential confusion over the future use of the legislative instrument. An initial point which, though it may not be confusing, gives cause for concern all the same, is the possibility that consumers will view the estimate of their own financial capabilities, carried out using parameters and indexes introduced under the legislation, as a type of rating. They may then mistake positive evaluations generated by the indices for a right to financing that they can pressurise financial intermediaries for. In this context, it is of fundamental importance that the criteria set for the measurement of financial capability be clearly distinguishable from the scoring models used to arrive at credit ratings. Legislative intervention that gives rise to erroneous interpretations of the concept of financial capability, linking it to a 'right to obtain credit', would run the risk of damaging the fundamental principle of contractual independence as well as the intermediaries' freedom of choice in terms of the subjects they wish to finance.

We have noted the risk that subjects held to be unreliable by the credit system could demand that they be given credit 'under the law'. In addition, stipulating the use of financial capability indices might drive those borderline subjects away from official channels of credit who would indeed find intermediaries willing to finance them, but who, in the light of a less than positive evaluation of their capacity to make repayments, forgo applying for credit and do business with illegal credit providers. Apart from the importance of constructing an index that cannot be traced to an estimate of credit worth, there is no mistaking the need to implement an information campaign designed to create an underlying culture of interest in the topic of financial capability.

A third element to be taken into consideration is the cost of adjusting to the legislation. Should a cost–benefit analysis indicate that the benefit for the system is not sufficient to cover the costs of the change, then the measurement of financial capability would have to be left to the discretion of the more attentive consumers.

10.6   Guidelines for a legislative intervention

The use of legislation to attempt to reduce the differences that inherently keep the relationship between the lender and the borrower from developing on an equal footing creates a number of risks – although, at the same time, it creates a range of opportunities. We believe that the advantages that can be obtained through legislative intervention justify the attendant risks. In particular, it is held that the introduction through legislation of a parameter capable of improving the level of consumer information on financial products can make a concrete contribution to improving the relationship between lenders and the parties financed. This conviction is reinforced further by an analysis of European legislation, which points to a fairly heterogeneous framework that does not always represent the optimal situation.

Before drawing up an intervention proposal designed to modify the current regulatory framework, a number of guidelines for the formulation of the change must be identified.

Holding that the gap between the lender and the borrower can be traced primarily to the information gap that penalizes the borrower, the ideal legislative intervention on financial capability would be one that remains within the realm of transparency. The contribution of the measure should focus specifically on defining an index of financial capability. This index should be conceived of as an information tool available to the consumer and used by the latter to evaluate his/her financial capacity in a more informed manner. The decision to focus on transparency and to act on the demand side of credit (the consumer) is based on two sets of reasons.

Intervention meant that improving the cognitive capacity of the consumer has the primary advantage of avoiding intervention from outside the credit market, thus favouring competition between the operators. In fact, a better informed consumer is capable of distinguishing between different financing proposals and selecting the one closest to his/her needs. In this way, the decision-making independence of the consumer is protected, while the information tool both allows consumers to deal more effectively with intermediaries and also stimulates supply-side competition, given that lenders will be dealing with an average consumer who is better informed and thus better able to tell the more efficient operators from the less efficient ones. Legislative intervention aimed at market transparency also presents the advantage of streamlining the operating procedures for the supply of credit and avoiding regulatory costs that would otherwise be present. These costs would inevitably affect the cost of the financing service as well the efficiency of the market in general.

As has been noted already, in many cases the current regulatory framework regarding transparency already guarantees a large quantity of information. The introduction of a financial capability index would thus be in keeping with the approach followed to date in many European countries. The task of the index would be to select the information and organize it in such as way as to optimize its use by consumers.

The danger in the current regulatory framework is of a potential excess of information not being filtered efficiently by the consumer. This may undermine the consumers' level of understanding, thus limiting their capability to make decisions.

The decision to intervene on the supply side is supported by the need to avoid potential conflicts of interest. Were the lenders to be assigned the task of disclosing full information to the consumers, lenders would become stakeholders wearing two hats. While they operate as the main suppliers of information on the supply side, the demand side would also have to rely on them. To remedy this situation, a considerably more elaborate regulatory framework would have to be drawn up. This framework should be able to define in detail the information which the creditors are required to supply and, at the same time, establish a system of controls for and penalties against the creditors to act as incentives encouraging legal behaviour.

However, steps should be taken to avoid an increase in regulation, both by working on the level of transparency of the market and by stipulating various types of prohibition. It should be noted that, in modifying the legislation, the objectives of consumer protection and market efficiency are not necessarily mutually exclusive. An improvement in consumers' capacity to evaluate their own financial capabilities also leads to higher levels of consumer protection and improved market efficiency.

10.7   A preliminary approach to an index of financial capability

There are three different stages in the construction of a financial capability index. The first is to identify the information to be included in the financial capability index. The next stage is designed to evaluate the procedures used to group together and process the information considered. The final step consists of selecting the ways to communicate the result. There are two alternatives – a monetary index (for example, an amount in euros allocated to the monthly repayment of a loan) and a discrete index (that is, an index based on different levels, each of which identifies a greater or lesser financial capacity). The creation of a financial capability index must not be the same as a credit rating.

The idea of using a simplified financial capability index stems from the assumption that information overload, as well as the use of relatively inefficient methods of communication, drastically reduces the information content for the consumer. The use of technical language with frequent references to legislative articles or the use of small print are only some examples of the communication barriers that can emerge in terms of the content of the information. In order to overcome these barriers, specific skills must be supported, such as learning the technical terms or studying the legislative article cited. An index that includes relevant information and maximizes the information content for the consumer would be advantageous. It would remove the obstacles that separate the consumer from the information needed for wise financial decisions.

The purpose of a parametric measurement is to simplify the content and to make it easily understandable to less educated consumers. However, in the simplification process carried out to produce the index, a wealth of information is lost. The risk of oversimplification is that it will make the input for a parameter used in a decision-making process insignificant where, in reality, that input is very significant.

In addition to the risk of reducing the quality of the information content, the use of a simplified index might also act as a distortion. Consumers who are incapable of evaluating the structure of the model in depth are at risk of interpreting the index erroneously.

In proposing an index which is difficult for its users to understand, the risk is that the decision-making process will be distorted, leading to decisions that would not otherwise be made. The use of a simplified index to make decisions means choosing not to analyse the information in depth, but rather to place trust in the choices made by the creators of the index. In proposing an index, there is a risk of replacing the user in the decision-making process, causing them to bear the consequences of the choices implicit in the structure of the index.

The pitfalls in the process of creating a simplified index are not, therefore, reason enough not to present a proposal for a financial capability index. The latter can be understood as the capability to repay loans.

It is now time to turn to the first phase of the construction of the index (the analysis of the information considered) by contemplating a number of preliminary considerations that lead to a proposal for an index that estimates financial capability.

In terms of the selection of the information to be included in the index, it should be remembered that the objective of the index is to increase the consumer's perception of his or her repayment capacity. The index must enable the consumer to evaluate how taking out a given loan would affect his or her financial situation. In particular, the index must evaluate the consumer's repayment capacity in terms of a specific offer of credit.

In selecting what information to include and what to exclude, it is best to focus on the current financial flows of the consumer, given that income elements are more directly tied to the repayment of credit. Extraordinary events such as the sale of real estate or the sale of assets in general are factors that deserve only marginal consideration. Underlying this assumption is the fact that the repayment plan for a loan is usually a periodic repayment of predetermined instalments. If, therefore, taking out a loan leads to recurrent expenditure, the regular income of the consumer represent the immediate benchmark for comparison.

For the evaluation of a consumer's financial capability, it must be possible to identify the financial flows generated by wages and other periodic revenues (rents for real estate owned, royalties or other sources). The estimation of periodic revenues is the first step in the process of evaluation. After examining the periodic revenues, consideration must be given to the outlays that are also certain to occur and that reduce the amount of the income that can be allocated to the repayment of the debt. This would include expenses related to food, clothing and housing.

With regard to the expenditure to be included in the financial capability index, some doubts may arise. While it is plausible to include expenditure regarding food, clothing and housing, there is a question as to whether other outlays should be considered indispensable. Expenses for transport and communications are examples of cost items which some individuals cannot do without. The greater or lesser willingness of the consumer to modify his or her habits of consumption after taking out a loan is a factor to be taken into consideration in determining the relevant financial flows.

The financial capability index may not, therefore, consist of an exhaustive and detailed list of entries regarding current revenues and outlays. But it must cover the criteria under which the consumer would evaluate (taking into account his or her own preferences and habits) which financial flows to include and which to exclude from the calculation of his or her financial capability. The margin of discretion left to the consumer for the identification of the relevant financial flows is consistent with the assumption of the decision-making independence of the consumer.

The identification of the information to be included in the calculation of the index also calls for an evaluation of the potential role of the consumer's assets. The evaluation of the financial capability of an individual should be based primarily on income and on the capacity to have enough income over time to sustain repayment of the debt. However, some consideration should also be given to his or her assets. As a rule, the financial capability of an individual should be considered as adequate if the person can meet the loan commitments without having to take extraordinary steps to ensure the financing of debt. While the sale of the home would certainly be regarded as an example of an extraordinary operation, it is open to question whether or not one should exclude securities or real estate not used as the primary residence. If the consumer is willing to include such assets, they should be used in the calculation of the index. This means that a consumer with limited income and major real estate wealth should be evaluated in exactly the same way as somebody with limited funds, if the person is not willing to sell the estate. Likewise, somebody who is willing to sell securities in order to reimburse their debt should be evaluated just like an individual with high financial capability.

In addition to identifying the information to be included in the evaluation, there must also be an examination of the stability of the flows. For instance, in terms of income assessment, a worker's wage can be considered over the short term as being almost certain.

But if a worker's wage is not time-constant – because, for instance, it is based on commission – we cannot consider the actual level of wage as a perfect forecast of the level of future wages. If the worker has a variable wage, we have to estimate different possible wage values and, for each value, we have to calculate the probability to be reached.

If the income of the consumer is provisional in nature, then the evaluation of financial capability must estimate the future amount of the financial flow for that income source, taking into account the probability that, in the future, it shall remain at almost the same levels recorded in the past.

The question that must be addressed in establishing a financial capability index is whether or not the index needs to consider the fact that certain income flows cannot be precisely predetermined because they are unstable.

One further point is if there are any guarantees capable of expanding the credit capacity of the consumer. There are two reasons for excluding guarantees. These are that the purpose of such an index is that it is different from a credit rating and that the assumption that financial capability should estimate the 'individual' financial capacity of the consumer.

In addition to the analysis of the nature of the flows being evaluated, the establishment of the indicator also requires that a timeframe be set. This is necessary to identify the (future) financial flows being evaluated. In general, the financial capability to be evaluated should encompass the duration of the whole credit agreement timeframe.

The estimation of an individual's financial capability is not an absolute but an estimate of sustainability that depends on the duration and the commitments laid down in a credit contract. The evaluation of a subject's financial capability will thus be higher or lower depending on the consequences that the specific loan could have on his/her overall financial situation.

Once the criteria for the selection of the (financial) information have been identified, the income amounts have been identified and a timeframe has been set, it would then be possible to consider the procedures for pooling this information. By comparing financial capability with the commitments implicit in the repayment of the loan, it will thus be possible to express a judgment on the sustainability of the debt. A detailed analysis of the factors to be considered as well as the calculation method of the index, however, must be subject to further scrutiny.

10.8 Conclusions

Starting from possible approaches to the topic of consumer financial capability, we have analysed the current regulatory framework in order to evaluate the advisability of legislative intervention in the relationship between borrowers and lenders. The analysis demonstrated that legislative intervention would mean using information tools such as the financial capability index. This would represent an opportunity both to increase the protection of the consumer and also to improve the performance of the credit market. Reinforcing this position is the assumption that legislation capable of improving the level of information possessed by consumers would make it possible, on the demand side of credit, to avoid 'out-of-control' situations such as over-indebtedness. At the same time, in a market where the debtors are able to evaluate different offers of credit, the level of competition on the supply side would also rise – leading to an increased level of efficiency for the market as a whole.

In constructing a financial capability index, however, care must be taken to avoid the risk of the index being interpreted as a credit rating. Unlike a credit rating, the financial capability index should not abstractly evaluate the capacity of the borrower to repay the capital and the interest. Instead, the index should evaluate the borrower's capacity to meet his or her commitments without having to resort to extraordinary operations. Both the role of guarantees and also the question of the borrower's assets are considered to be of secondary importance, while the periodic financial flows (current income and outlays) play a leading role in the estimation of financial capability. The financial capability index is therefore meant to help consumers to estimate their financial situation, and specifically to evaluate the impact that a (new) loan would have on their situation.

This chapter is only a preliminary work. There is a need for further research on the subject of financial capability. Having evaluated the consequences of an approach based on a simplified index and having identified the guidelines to be followed in establishing such an index, further research must tackle both the selection and the pooling of the information.

Notes

1. For a detailed analysis of the factors influencing the conduct of consumers of financial products and services, see Kempson, Moore and Collard (2005).
2. The reference is to the use of training tools not based on an explicit teaching process, but which draw on alternative learning processes, such as television shows where common financial situations are analysed in order to provide the audience with knowledge based upon indirect experience.
3. In carrying out their professional activities, lenders gain skills and have greater information at their disposal regarding the conditions – current and future – of the credit market, for instance.
4. The arguments that lead to the conclusion that a legislative intervention is necessary are presented in the subsequent paragraphs of this chapter.
5. European Communities (Consumer Credit) Regulations, 2000.
6. 'Non-compensatory rules' refers to a decision-making process under which a subject tends to analyse every single piece of information available, establishing an especially accurate decision-making process. In contrast, a process follows 'compensatory rules' when it includes an initial phase of information selection designed to simplify the decision-making procedure, with the end goal of reducing the time needed for its performance. For a more in-depth consideration of the topic, see M. Caratelli, 'Information Needs and Public

Role in Transparency of Bank–Client Relationships ('Fabbisogni informativi ed intervento pubblico nella trasparenza dei rapporti negoziali tra banca e clienti'), in 'The Behaviour of Financial Markets Operators' ('Il comportamento degli operatori nei mercati finanziari ed assicurativi – Atti del Convegno'), Ancona, 28 October 2005.

7. Loi relative au crédit à la consommation du 12 Juin 1991.
8. Loi relative au crédit à la consommation du 12 Juin 1991 art. 64 'L'intermédiaire de crédit ne peut introduire de demande de crédit pour un consommateur si, compte tenu des informations dont il dispose ou devrait disposer, notamment sur base des renseignements visés à l'article 10, il estime que le consommateur ne sera manifestement pas à même de respecter les obligations découlant du contrat de crédit'.
9. Law 26/1984, 19 July 1984 'General para la Defensa de Consumidores y Usuarios'.
10. The Consumer Credit (Advertisements) Regulations 2004.
11. Financial Services and Markets Act 2000, art.5 (2-d) 'the general principle that consumers should take responsibility for their decisions'.
12. For an analysis of the non-EU European countries, see Szpringer (2005).
13. An admirable proposal was made, however, by the Verbraucherzentrale Bundesverband e. V. (vzbv) (Federation of German Consumer Associations), which, in a proposal to the European Parliament for modification of the legislation on consumer credit, holds that a legislative effort should be made to prevent situations of excessive indebtedness: 'The Directive should at least uphold standards set by the previous Directive. It should incorporate consumer protection and the prevention of overindebtedness into its goals [see Article 1], reinsert the minimum harmonisation clause and the article concerning circumvention [see Article 30] applicable to legal constructs achieving the same economic goals as those regulated by the Directive.' – Verbraucherzentrale Bundesverband e. V. 'Reifner Proposal Consumer Credit Directive 2002 – Report', 2002.
14. Federal Law on Consumer Credit (FLCC) of 23 March 2001.
15. FLCC – art. 28 'Evaluation of the consumer's capacity to enter a credit agreement'.
16. FLCC – art. 22 'Capacity to enter a credit agreement'.

References

Belgium – Consumer credit law (12/06/1991) (1991).
Belgium – Mortgage credit law (4/08/1992 – modified in 2003), 2003.
Caratelli M. (2005) 'Information Needs and Public Role in Transparency of Bank–Client Relationships', in AA.VV., *The Behaviour of Financial Markets Operators*, Workshop papers, Ancona, Italy, 28 October.
European Union – Directive 98/7/EC (16/02/1991) 'Consumer credit'.
European Union – Directive 2002/65/CE.
European Union – Directive 87/102/EEC.
European Union – European Communities (consumer credit) regulations, 2000 S.I. No. 294 of 2000.
France – Finance and money law-code.

Germany – Verbraucherzentrale Bundesverband e. V. 'Reifner Proposal for Consumer Credit Directive 2002 – Report', 2002.
Ireland – Consumer Credit Act, 1995.
Italy – Bank of Italy, 'Governor's decision of 25/07/2003 on financial services' transparency', 2003.
Italy – CICR, 'Decision of 4th March 2003 on bank and financial services' transparency contract level', 2003.
Italy – Government law 58/98 (24/02/1998), 1998.
Italy – Government law. 358/93 (01/09/1993), 1993.
Italy – Government law 394/2000 (29/12/2000) 'Explanation of law 108/96 on usury', 2000.
Kempson, E., N. Moore and S. Collard, (2005) *Measuring Financial Capability: an Exploratory Study*, Financial Service Authority research paper, no. 37.
Portugal – Government law 143/2001 (26/04/2001), 2001.
Portugal – Government law 359/91 (21/09/1991) 'Contratos de crédito ao consumo', 1991.
Portugal – Law 24/96 (31/07/1996), 1996.
Spain – Internal communication number 3/2001 (24/09/2001), sent to banks, that modifies the internal communication 8/1990, of 7th September on transparency and consumer protection, 2001.
Spain – Internal communication 3/2001 (24/09/2001) sent to banks, which modifies the internal communication 8/1990 of 7 September, on transparency and consumer protection, 2001.
Spain – Law 11/2002 (02/12/2002), 2002.
Spain – Law 16/1984 (19/07/1984), 1984.
Spain – Law 26/1988 (29/07/1988), 1988.
Spain – Law 3/2003 (12/02/2003) of Canarias local community, 2003.
Spain – Law 39/2002 (28/10/2002) that introduced in Spain the EU directive on consumer protection, 2002.
Spain – Law 6/2001 (24/05/2001) of Extremadura community, 2001.
Spain – Law 7/95 (23/03/1995) 'Consumer credit', 1995.
Spain – Order PRE/1019/2003 (24/04/2003) on the price transparency of ATM bank services, 2003.
Spain – Royal law 303/2004 (20/02/(2004) about the regulation that protects the financial services' client 2004.
Spain – Royal law 3423/2000 (15/12/2000) on the price discovery of products sold to consumers, 2000.
Spain – Royal law 424/2005 (15/04/2005) about the regulation of e-mail communications in consumers' contracts, 2005.
Spain – Royal law 894/2005 (22/07/2005) that regulate the Consumer's Council, 2005.
Switzerland – Federal Law on Consumer Credit (FLCC) (23/03/2001), 2001.
Szpringer, W. (2006) 'An Institutional Perspective on Consumer Financial Capability', in ECRI, *Consumer Financial Capability: Empowering European Consumers*, ECRI Publications.
UK – Consumer Credit (Agreements) Regulations 1983.
UK – Consumer Protection (Distance Selling) Regulations 2000, 2000.
UK – Directive 2002/65/EC of the European Parliament and of the Council of 23 September 2002 concerning the distance marketing of consumer financial

services and amending Council Directive 90/619/EEC and Directives 97/7/EC and 98/27/EC, 2002.
UK – Electronic Commerce Directive (Financial Services and Markets) Regulations 2002.
UK – Financial Services and Markets Act 2000.
UK – The Bank Accounts Directive (Miscellaneous Banks) (Amendment) Regulations 2005.
UK – The Bank Accounts Directive Regulations 2005.
UK – The Consumer Credit (Advertisements) Regulations 2004.
UK – The Consumer Credit (Advertisements) Regulations 2004.
UK – The Consumer Credit (Agreements) (Amendment) Regulations 2004.
UK – The Consumer Credit (Miscellaneous Amendments) Regulations 2004.
UK – The Financial Services (Distance Marketing) Regulations 2004.
UK – The Unfair Terms in Consumer Contracts (Amendment) Regulations 2001.
UK – The Unfair Terms in Consumer Contracts Regulations 1994.

11
Transparency Between Banks and Their Customers: Information Needs and Public Intervention

Massimo Caratelli

11.1 Introduction

In recent decades, factors such as the spread of complex financial instruments, the broadening of available alternatives, the general interest in making sure that financial activities are conducted efficiently and effectively, and the opening up of markets to international competition, have fostered more decisive public intervention in support of greater transparency between banks and their customers.

The arguments in favour of greater disclosure are based essentially on the role played by transparency in the efficient allocation of resources and in the efficacy of the mechanisms for coordinating economic activities in a market system.

The regulations issued to this effect have concerned two groups of stakeholders: the banks, as the subjects of the regulations, on the one hand, and the consumers of financial services, who are the beneficiaries of the protection afforded by such conduct, on the other hand. In particular, the new transparency standards require that the conduct of financial intermediaries should be aimed at rebalancing the information asymmetry typical of relations between banks and their customers, by transferring to the latter information on the characteristics and the general conditions of purchase of the services provided.

The effectiveness of the public intervention measures, of course, depends upon the correctness of the underlying assumption that customers are interested in receiving the information contents transmitted to them; in short, it depends upon the actual information needs of consumers.

The aim of this chapter is to assess the extent and characteristics of the information needs, by analysing the decision-making processes and the manner in which knowledge is built up and used, with respect to the purchase of financial services.

Sections 11.2 and 11.3 discuss the reasons that a consumer may have for purchasing a financial service. Section 11.4 presents a description of the decision-making process and its constituent phases. Section 11.5 contains a classification of the purchasing processes, based on the time and effort required to make a choice. Section 11.6 sets out an estimate of the information needs when arranging a mortgage or taking out consumer credit. Finally, section 11.7 provides an overview of the main results achieved.

11.2   Individual needs and financial requirements

A need may be defined as a necessity, a request coming from within our body, the satisfaction of which is necessary to survive or to maintain a good psycho-physical balance. Of course, not all of the needs are strictly necessary to ensure survival – the satisfaction of some of them allows us to live better lives (Dalli and Romani, 2000).

Traditionally speaking, needs are classified according to type and, at times, can be hierarchically organized. The classifications with the greatest consensus in literature are those by Maslow (1943, 1954), Murray (1938, 1955) and McGuire (1974, 1976).

In the literature, there is a consensus of opinion that consumers make use of financial services primarily in order to:

- regulate trade;
- build up savings (intended here as a source for future consumption, by oneself or by one's nearest and dearest);
- finance expenditure beyond one's present means;
- manage one's financial assets and/or liabilities in an integrated manner, with a view to ensuring that the purposes set out above are pursued most effectively.

Therefore, the function of financial services becomes the efficient transfer of resources in space and time; which transfer is necessary to 'finance' the purchasing of products and services deemed appropriate to satisfy one's needs. According to this view, satisfying one's needs is the ultimate motive that justifies purchasing a financial service. It ensues that, generally speaking, a consumer's interest in a financial service is of a reflexive nature (Tagliavini, 1990).

Table 11.1 General needs and financial requirements based on Maslow's hierarchy of needs

Class of need (in growing order of importance)	Associated financial requirements
Physiological	availability of payment instruments indebtedness (for necessity)
Safety and belonging	paying back debts keeping up one's lifestyle protecting one's assets from inflation buying a first home paying into a supplementary pension scheme saving for unforeseen circumstances
Esteem	improving one's lifestyle early retirement paying less tax indebtedness (for convenience and comfort)
Self-actualization	financial planning for training objectives financial planning for setting up and managing an independent business

Table 11.1 displays the financial needs of a typical consumer. It is the result of the application of Maslow's hierarchy of needs to the individual life-cycle theory.

The application of Maslow's hierarchy of needs to the individual life-cycle theory makes it possible to appreciate how a consumer's scale of purchasing priorities may develop in time. Maslow's work is valuable for putting the matter in context. It is less useful, however, when making a detailed analysis of specific behaviours for forecasting purposes. There are, in fact, innumerable examples of behaviours that are inconsistent with the hierarchy of needs.

11.3 The relationship between need and motivation

The existence of an unsatisfied need is a prerequisite for motivation to manifest itself. Motivation, in fact, can be described as the drive to act in order to accomplish a certain objective – namely, that of adequately satisfying a perceived need.

Satisfying a need requires the implementation of a decision-making process, according to a series of sequentially ordered steps (Dalli and Romani, 2000; Engel, Blackwell and Miniard, 1993). Control over each step is proportional to the intensity of one's motivation (Rheinberg, 2003): intensity of motivation, in fact, can affect the time, commitment and financial resources an individual is willing to invest to satisfy a need (Dalli and Romani, 2000).

11.4   The decision-making process

Once a state of need has been perceived, step one of the decision-making process will take place. This concerns the search for alternatives capable of achieving satisfaction.

In order to overcome the state of stress, consumers start by searching among their own memories for any relevant information (internal search). When they realize that their own knowledge is insufficient to ensure a satisfactory outcome (Schmidt and Spreng, 1996), they turn to additional information from other sources (external search). These external sources may include information provided by the supplier or dealer or by independent organizations. Other information may be obtained through one's personal contacts or from a first-hand examination of the service (Olshavsky and Wymer, 1995).

In step two of the decision-making process, there is an assessment of the available alternatives. This operation is typically effected based on certain decision-making rules. The function of these rules is to help the consumer to sort the alternatives in an order of preference.

Once the assessment has been completed, the next step is the decision to purchase and use the service.

The final step in the decision-making process is the post-use phase: after having used the service, consumers evaluate whether or not it meets their expectations.

11.4.1   The decision-making rules

The rules generally adopted when making a choice can be grouped into two main categories: 'compensatory' and 'non-compensatory' rules. The principal difference between the two types of rules is whether or not the values assigned to the different attributes of the choice alternatives can be 'balanced' (Rumiati and Bonini, 2001).

'Compensatory rules' are so called because they help the consumer to conclude that the best option is the one in which one or more appreciable attributes trade off – or 'compensate' – against other less desirable attributes. The additive rule is an example of compensatory rule (formula 11.1).[1]

$$Va = \sum_{i=1}^{n} Wi \cdot V(Xa_i) \tag{11.1}$$

where:
V_a = value of alternative a
W_i = weight of the i-th attribute
X_{ai} = the i-th attribute of alternative a
$V(X_{ai})$ = assessment of the i-th attribute of alternative a

The advantage in applying compensatory rules lies in the systematic assessment of the entire set of available information (the accuracy of the decision-making process). The use of these rules, however, also has its disadvantages: first of all, they require complex judgements of value. In addition, the use of compensatory rules also requires a certain mental effort and a considerable amount of time to make a choice (Bettman, Luce and Payne, 1998).

Not all decision-making rules are compensatory in nature. 'Non-compensatory rules', in fact, are so called because their application does not provide for any compensation between one or more 'attractive' attributes and other less attractive ones. The satisfying rule is an example of non-compensatory rule, whereby consumers define a level of acceptance for each attribute (Simon, 1955). An alternative becomes unsatisfactory – and, therefore, to be discarded – when even only one of its attributes fails to exceed the assigned cutoff level.[2]

Non-compensatory rules are deemed to be easy to apply: it seems, in fact, that they require less mental effort, since it is unnecessary to weigh and compare the various features (Rumiati and Bonini, 2001); furthermore, the volume of data to be examined is typically smaller, compared to the compensatory rules (Rumiati and Bonini, 1996). The acknowledged simplicity of application of the non-compensatory rules, however, is set off by certain disadvantages: for example, these rules do not always ensure the invariance of the order of preference. It often occurs, in fact, that an alternative is discarded simply based on the order in which the options are examined.

The study of the selection processes has shown that consumers tend to select the decision-making rules on a case-by-case basis, based on factors such as the characteristics of the problem (complexity of the decision-making process and time pressure), their personal experience and skills, and their involvement with the product class (Bettman, Johnson and Payne, 1991).[3]

By studying selection processes it has also been possible to infer that the compensatory and non-compensatory rules may be used in a complementary manner, within the same decision-making process (Rumiati and Bonini, 2001). A typical combination of strategies comprises an initial phase, in which certain alternatives are discarded by applying non-compensatory rules, and a second phase in which the shortlisted alternatives are assessed with greater attention, by applying compensatory rules (Bettman, Luce and Payne, 1998). It can safely be assumed, when passing from one stage to another, that the analysed information increases in detail, while the strictness with which the consumer selects the significant attributes weakens.

It has been observed that the adoption of a multi-phase strategy of this kind is typical of particularly complex decision-making dilemmas, which feature a relatively high number of both alternatives and attributes (Rumiati and Bonini, 1996).

11.5   Types of decision making and the search for and processing of the information

Not all decision-making processes are as complex as described in the foregoing paragraph. If this were not the case, the whole of life would be spent in making decisions.

Howard (1994) has classified decision-making processes into extensive and limited processes, based on the time and the effort required to make a choice.

Extensive decision-making processes entail a complex and difficult phase of searching for alternatives and defining the selection criteria. In the case of extensive processes, one can reasonably assume that consumers apply compensatory decision-making rules. Most of the studies conducted to date seem to support this theory (see, for example, Bettman, Luce and Payne, 1998), which features some important consequences, with respect to significant information. In particular, the consumers' preference for compensatory rules entails that individuals search for and process a large number of attributes and alternatives. Generally speaking, the information taken into account features a high degree of detail.

Limited decision-making processes consist of repeating consolidated cognitive and behavioural patterns, which are applied with almost no variation. These processes require a limited effort and a short time frame and, in this case, one can reasonably assume that non-compensatory decision-making rules are applied. The preference accorded to non-compensatory rules implies that the consumer searches for and processes a limited number of attributes and alternatives, based on a selective analysis of the information. Typically, no detailed data are required.

In the case of limited processes, therefore, consumers do not appear to take account of the entire set of potentially available information, limiting themselves to a summary analysis of the data, which is likely to be principally related to the cost and quality of the service. It would also seem that special attention is given to those aspects deemed capable of producing or preventing large-scale negative effects on the consumer's assets and social status. With respect to these aspects, significant information might include early termination conditions, the reporting requirements of credit bureaus and credit registries,[4] the possibility of unilaterally amending the conditions of the relevant agreement, conditional insurance, and the risks related to the occurrence of catastrophic events.

The theory according to which customers pay special attention to the aspects deemed capable of producing or preventing large-scale negative effects on their assets and social status is consistent with the results obtained by Gollwitzer and Heckhausen (1987), who, especially in relation to their studies on the motivational states of conscience, have shown that, when purchasing financial services, most individuals tend to reflect essentially on the negative (social and other) effects of an originally appealing desire (Kahneman and Tversky, 1979; Goldberg and von Nitzsch, 2001; Lichtenstein, Slovic, Fischhoff, Layman and Combs, 1978; Wyer and Srull, 1980).

Analysing the decision-making processes, many studies – including Punj and Staelin (1983), Beatty, Smith (1987), Srinivasan and Ratchford (1991), Solomon (1996), Wells and Prensky (1996) and Schmidt and Spreng (1996) – have identified several of the factors capable of influencing the type of process applied, each time, by consumers, as follows:

- the required financial disbursements;
- the perceived risks (performance-related and of a social nature);
- any differences between the available alternatives on the market;
- their involvement, with respect to the class of product;
- their financial knowledge and experience;
- the complexity of the service;
- information accessibility;
- any time-related restrictions imposing constraints on the decision-making processes.

In particular, by analysing these factors it would seem possible to estimate the decision-making process implemented by consumers, when purchasing financial services.

What follows is a description of the effects that are apparently produced by the above mentioned factors on the motivation to search for and process information. The greater the motivation, the higher the chances of applying an extensive decision-making process.

The term disbursements, or 'perceived financial sacrifice', refers to the amount of interests and fees paid to the financial intermediary (Schmidt and Spreng, 1996). The maximum amount consumers are willing to spend depends upon their interest in the product they are purchasing (enduring/situational involvement with the product). The greater the financial sacrifice perceived by the individual, the greater is the fear to find, once the purchase has been made, that his or her money has been ill spent, having obtained only a modest benefit, compared to the resources invested and, generally speaking, compared to the opportunities offered by the environment in which he or she lives. One can reasonably assume that a significant financial sacrifice enhances the consumer's desire to accurately examine the available options, thus fostering the implementation of an extensive decision-making process.

Perceived risk is the term given to the uncertainty one may have with respect to the performance of the financial service, vis-à-vis the expected standards (Schmidt and Spreng, 1996). The perceived risk is especially high in the case of new services and is socially relevant when the expectations of loss are very high. A high level of perceived risk should enhance the consumer's desire to make an accurate consideration of the alternatives, thus fostering the adoption of an extensive process.

Faced with perceived differences in the financial services, one can reasonably assume that the consumer's fear of making a bad choice will increase (Schaninger and Sciglimpaglia, 1981). In this case also the customer would probably be committed to attentively searching for and assessing the alternatives.

The more or less lasting enduring/situational involvement for financial services identifies another factor that is capable of positively influencing the desire to make an accurate analysis of the selection alternatives (Schmidt and Spreng, 1996). Involvement may be partly justified by an enduring/situational involvement with product.

Experience and knowledge of financial services usually translate into a considerable amount of information for consumers, allowing them to reduce the amount of (cognitive and behavioural) resources needed in connection with the purchasing process (Srinivasan and Ratchford,

1991; Andersson, 2004). Experience and knowledge can also reduce the perceived risk, thus producing a further negative effect – this time indirectly – on the consumer's desire to examine the selection alternatives accurately (Srinivasan and Ratchford, 1991; Andersson, 2004). Experience and knowledge apparently foster the implementation of a limited decision-making process.

The level of satisfaction with previous purchases is also important: in particular, Punj and Staelin (1983) have shown how a satisfactory purchasing experience reduces both the perceived benefits of an accurate search for and the assessment of alternatives and the perceived risk.

The (monetary and other) costs for identifying and comparing alternatives diminish the consumers' desire to conduct an in-depth analysis of the alternatives. The perceived costs seem to be influenced by the complexity of the financial services, information accessibility and time pressure (Bettman, Luce and Payne, 1998). It can be assumed that a high perceived complexity, difficulty to access information and strong time pressure can foster the implementation of a limited decision-making process. One may reasonably expect that time pressure is more stringent in the case of enduring/situational involvement with product.

Figure 11.1 provides a graphical overview of the relation between the factors capable of influencing the decision-making process: the benefits, the costs and the motivation to search for and process the information. Motivation represents the consumers' desire to commit themselves to an in-depth search for and assessment of the options. It can be assumed that benefits enhance motivation, while costs diminish it. The greater the intensity of motivation, the more likely the implementation of an extensive decision-making process.

Based on the foregoing, it can be maintained that there are various types of decision-making processes that an individual can identify in connection with the perception of a need. These types of processes differ according to the intensity with which consumers search for information, the characteristics of the information for which they are searching (selectivity and detail), and the effort required to process the information. Factors such as a high level of financial sacrifice, a high perceived risk, significant differences between the alternatives, and a high level of involvement, seem to justify a committed search for – and processing of – the information. On the contrary, financial experience and knowledge, the perceived excessive complexity of the service, the difficulty to access information and a strong time pressure tend to diminish the accuracy with which information is searched for and the time employed to make a choice.

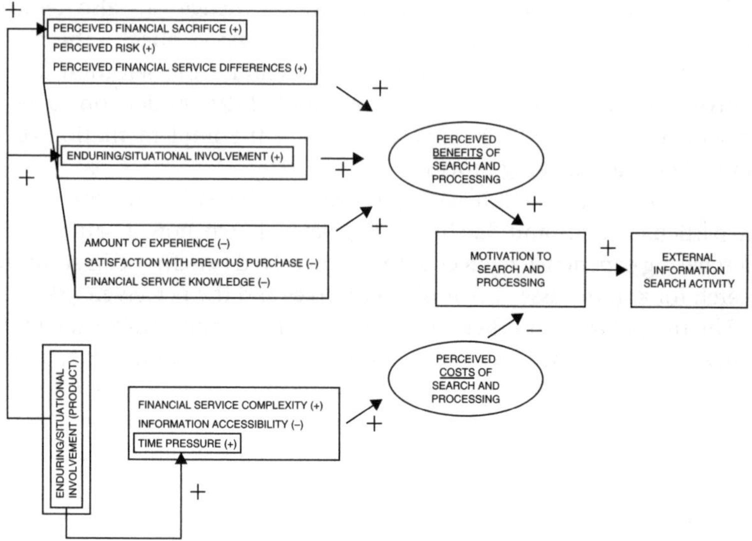

Figure 11.1   The search for and processing of information: benefits, costs and motivation

These considerations feature two important consequences, with respect to the significant information:

- the greater the commitment and perseverance consumers are ready to invest willingly in the search for and processing of information, the greater the interest they will show in disposing of a large set of data (large number of alternatives and attributes taken into account), with a high level of detail (contents of the information);
- in the case of particularly complex decisions (that is, characterized by a relatively high number of both alternatives and attributes), it is likely that consumers will adopt a multiphase strategy to assess the alternatives. In this case, they will take stock of the different degree of detail of the information they are interested in analysing, when passing from one phase to the other; moreover, the strictness with which the most significant attributes are selected should be weakened (number of alternatives and attributes taken into account).

These theories will now be applied to an estimation of the information needs of consumers of financial services. Based on the differences relating to functions of use, it was decided to omit a description of what takes place in the financial system at large and to focus on specific and sufficiently representative banking business areas. The choice has fallen on the offer of medium-to-long term loans (mortgages) and consumer credit.

11.6 The information needs of consumers of financial services

The following section offers an analysis of the information needs of consumers of financial services. Two cases may be considered:

- mortgages;
- consumer credit loans.

The following sub-paragraph provides an overview of the information needs, in connection with mortgage transactions.

In the following pages, the assumption is made of easy access to the available information.

11.6.1 Mortgages

A mortgage is a medium-to-long-term loan generally arranged to finance the purchase, construction or refurbishment of real estate property.

The size and term of the loan:

- highlight how taking out a mortgage is a choice capable of significantly affecting the borrower's economic and financial situation (high disbursements);
- justify the low frequency with which this service is purchased (low experience).

Both of these observations refer to the significant consumer involvement in the phases required to select the service provider and define the characteristics of the loan: only a strong interest in purchasing this service, in fact, can justify the decision to undertake such a level of indebtedness; they also suggest a high perceived risk.

In consequence of the large amount of red tape associated with these transactions (banks require a large number of documents to be produced and investigations to be made before granting the mortgage and making the funds available, under the law the mortgage deed must be drafted by a public notary, and the borrower is required to provide security to the financial intermediary), potential borrowers are perhaps prepared to wait

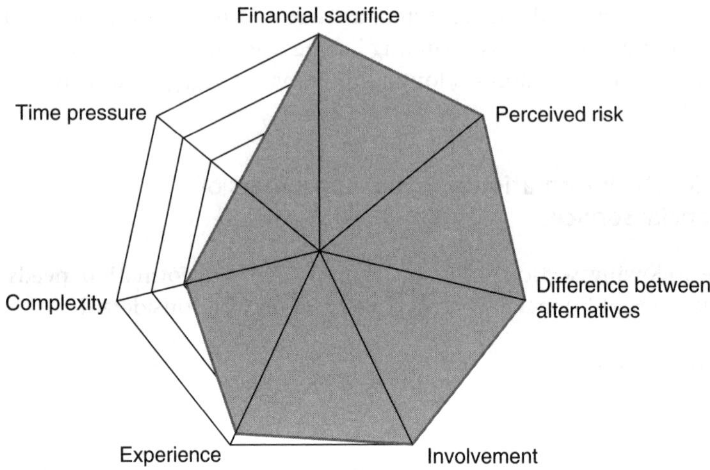

Figure 11.2   Motivation to search for and process information when taking out a mortgage

for a considerable length of time before receiving the money from the lender. Therefore, one may reasonably assume that time pressure is not particularly stringent, even though consumers are obviously concerned to complete the formalities as soon as possible and to be granted the money and the property in the shortest possible time.

A mortgage as such is not a particularly complex service. However, consumers find it hard to compare the numerous alternatives available on the market, all of which differ – more or less considerably – in terms of interest rates, currency, term and amortization schedule.

Figure 11.2 summarizes the contents of this sub-paragraph, with respect to the factors (such as the required financial sacrifice and perceived risk) capable of influencing the type of decision-making process implemented by consumers when taking out a mortgage.

In Figure 11.2, the grey area approximates the intensity of the motivation to search for and process information. The area is rather large, which justifies the assumption that consumers apply an extensive decision-making process.

In the case of extensive processes, one can reasonably expect the use of compensatory decision-making rules. The preference here for compensatory rules means that consumers search for and process a considerable number of alternatives and attributes. The required information typically features a high level of detail.

The inherent difficulty in making an effective comparison between the numerous available options would suggest the adoption of multi-phase decision-making strategies. In an initial, exploratory phase consumers would probably apply particularly selective non-compensatory rules. They would hardly search for detailed information, but would be interested, primarily, in straightening out the purpose of the mortgage and its general characteristics (maximum and minimum mortgage borrowing, mortgage term, related fees and disbursements, repayment amount and frequency, role of the notary public and of the security). Later on, they would try to find out who the principal service providers are. The examination of the various alternatives would obviously involve the most visible market providers (importance of the image and reputation of the intermediary)[5] or those which offer a positive past track record (based on direct or indirect experience). At this stage, consumers appear to be more interested in receiving a synthetic cost indicator, with a view to making an initial comparison of the alternatives. The information collected here is essential for assessing whether to admit or discard each option and, if necessary, to alter one's general objectives, in terms, for example, of the amount of the loan and of the admissible financial sacrifice and time frame of the mortgage.

Once a shortlist of the alternatives has been compiled, consumers probably make a careful comparison of the options, with respect to factors such as the strictly financial aspects, the quality of the service and an estimate of the performance risks. At this stage, the previously collected information should be supplemented with more detailed data.

Having regard to the strictly financial details of the service, the potential borrower would be interested in receiving detailed information on the expense items involved, such as the amount and frequency of the repayments, the mortgage term, the trends of the basic parameters involved, in the case of variable rate mortgage, the applied spreads, the arrangement fees and legal fees, the insurance fees, the other charges and the relevant tax deductions (Ranyard, Hinkley, Williamson and McHugh, 2006). In order to examine the alternatives based on a criterion of efficiency, consumers would also like to receive detailed information as to the documents required in connection with the mortgage application, besides clarifications as to the procedures for registering and cancelling the mortgage, the legal formalities involved and providing additional security.

Having regard to the quality of the service, the potential borrower would probably be interested in receiving information relating to the mortgage amount, the maximum amount under a supplementary mortgage, repayment flexibility, conditional insurance, mortgage term and amortization schedule, the conditions relating to the sale of property concerned (the prohibition on selling before the term of the mortgage expires and the cumulative assumption of the mortgage). Other conditions deserving attention concern the amendment of the mortgage agreement and the early repayment of the loan; which information is useful to assess the flexibility afforded the customer in taking advantage of a possible drop in the interest rates.

Having regard to the estimate of the performance risks, consumers would probably like to receive historical data on the variation of the base parameters, besides information on how moratory interest is calculated, on any conditions allowing unilateral termination of the agreement by the lender and, generally speaking, on the consequences of the delay or failure to repay the loan on their assets and social status. Other information of interest could be the effects on the mortgage agreement of any unfortunate events happening to the borrower (if borrower dies before the loan is paid off, or if he or she becomes temporarily disabled or loses his or her job) or to the property encumbered by the mortgage (earthquake, floods, attacks) (Williamson, Ranyard and Cuthbert, 2000). Consumers would also like to receive information on the causes warranting amendments to the conditions of the mortgage agreement – to the extent the bank is unilaterally entitled to do so, of course.

11.6.2   Consumer credit loans

Consumer credit products consists of loans granted to applicants, who may use the money for any of the following purposes:

- to purchase goods and services for current consumption (food, medical services, clothing, travel);
- to purchase durable consumer goods (household appliances, furniture, consumer electronics, motor vehicles, boats);
- to invest in jewels, collectibles, financial activities or real estate property.

These loans can take the form of vehicle and point-of-sale financing, generic personal lending, revolving credit, with or without a card, and salary-guaranteed loan schemes.

Consumer credit loan agreements can be concluded at either the premises of the bank or the specialist arranging the loan, or of the dealers where the goods/services are being purchased.

The consumer's desire to obtain the goods, or the sum of money to spend, explains his desire for the loan to be approved quickly; it is an urgency which can distract him, in part, from the characteristics of the service (Kamleitner and Kirchler, 2006; Lewis and van Venrooij, 1995). The consumer's moderate interest in defining the characteristics of the service is also justified by other factors, such as the low level of the management fees, the limited customization flexibility (due to fixed interest rates and level-payment amortization schedules, on a monthly basis)[6] and the average frequency of purchase (average experience).

The limited customization flexibility of the service highlights the simplicity of this product and the small differences between the alternatives available on the market. Revolving credit, salary-guaranteed loan schemes and personal loans feature a greater degree of differentiation. However, it is only rarely that the differentiation is such as to entail difficulties for consumers when they compare the alternatives.

The small amount of the loans is such that only a sizable reduction in market rates would be able to have a considerable (and negative) effect upon the performance of the service. Consequently, the key components of the perceived risk are the conditions for contract termination,[7] and, generally speaking, how any delays or the failure to repay the loan can affect the borrower's assets and social status. In the case of point-of-sale financing, the close link that exists between purchasing goods and applying for a loan also means that the customer needs to pay attention to the risks relating to the purchase contract and loan agreement (suffice it to mention, for example, the consumer exercising his right of withdrawal or any disputes arising with the seller). Therefore, it can be assumed that consumers perceive consumer credit loan transactions, overall, as medium- or low-risk operations (Williamson, Ranyard and Cuthbert, 2000).

Figure 11.3 summarizes the arguments outlined above, with respect to the factors (such as the required financial sacrifice and the perceived risk) capable of affecting the type of decision-making process implemented by the consumer, with respect to consumer credit loan transactions.

In the graph, the grey area approximates the intensity of the motivation to search for and process information. The area is rather small, which justifies the assumption that consumers employ a limited decision-making process.

In the case of limited processes, one can reasonably expect the application of a non-compensatory decision-making process. The preference for non-compensatory rules entails that consumers search for and process a

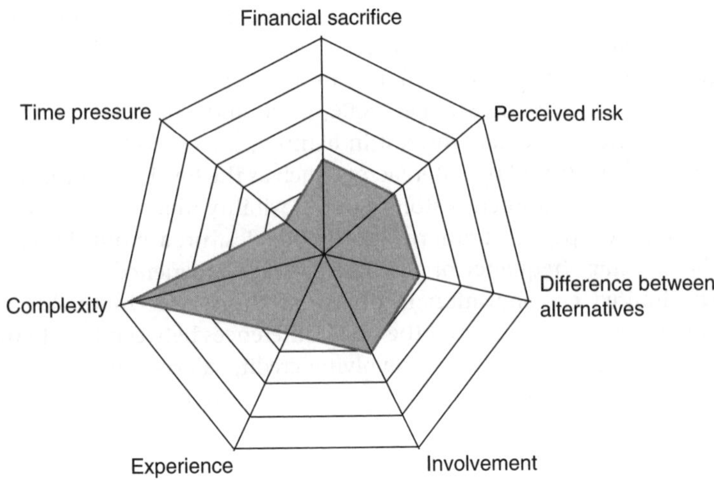

Figure 11.3   Motivation to search for and process information when respect to consumer credit

limited amount of attributes and alternatives. In particular, consumers limit themselves to examining synthetic cost indicators; at the most, they might consider the repayment instalment amount in absolute terms (Raynard, Hinkley, Williamson and McHugh, 2006). The consumers' focus would also seem to be on synthetic service quality indicators. Their desire to purchase the goods or obtain the money to spend would seem to suggest that the loan approval speed is a synthetic quality indicator.

Customers would also seem to be interested in receiving information indicating which documents should be attached to the loan application. The timely availability of this information, in fact, would allow them to comply speedily with the required formalities and obtain either the goods or the money within a reasonable time frame. Reducing the loan approval time, in the customers' eyes, is tantamount to improving the quality of the service.[8]

Consumers also seem to focus on those aspects deemed capable of producing or preventing significant negative effects on their assets or their social status. With respect to this, significant information might include early termination conditions, the reporting requirements of credit bureaus and credit registries, the possibility of unilaterally amending the conditions of the relevant agreement, conditional insurance, and the risks related to the occurrence of catastrophic events.

Only rarely do consumers find it hard to effectively compare the available alternatives. This seems to suggest the adoption of single-phase decision-making strategies.

11.7 Conclusions

Factors such as the spread of complex financial instruments, the broadening of available alternatives, the general interest in making sure that financial activities are conducted efficiently and effectively, and the opening up of markets to international competition, have fostered more decisive public intervention in support of greater transparency between banks and their customers.

The new transparency standards require that the conduct of financial intermediaries should be aimed at rebalancing the information asymmetry typical of relations between banks and their customers, by transferring to the latter information on the characteristics and the general conditions of purchase of the services provided.

The effectiveness of the public intervention measures, of course, depends upon the correctness of the underlying assumption that customers are interested in receiving the information contents transmitted to them; in short, it depends on the actual information needs of consumers.

The aim of this chapter is to assess the extent and characteristics of the information needs, by analysing the decision-making processes: in particular, the greater the commitment and perseverance consumers are ready and willing to invest in the search for and processing of information, the greater appears to be their interest in receiving large amounts of detailed information. This information should concern the costs and quality of the service and an estimate of the relevant performance risks.

Factors such as high financial sacrifice, high perceived risks, considerable differences between the available alternatives, a high degree of involvement, seem to justify an intense search for information and a commitment in processing this information. The precision with which information is searched for and the time dedicated to making a choice would be reduced as an effect of financial experience and knowledge, and perceived excessive complexity of the service and stringent time pressure.

In the case of decision-making processes that require a limited effort and time pressure it can reasonably be assumed that there has been a thorough selection of the available information.

In the development of this chapter, and in connection with the differences emerging in terms of significant information, it was decided to omit a description of what takes place in the financial system at large and to focus instead on specific and sufficiently representative banking business areas. Consequently, we have proceeded to identify the information needs with respect to taking out mortgage and consumer credit loans.

Information needs, however, are not the only factor capable of explaining the efficacy of the standard-setting measures. The capacity of these measures to accomplish their purpose, in fact, depends upon whether or not another two assumptions can be made: (i) that consumers are capable of receiving the contents transmitted to them; and (ii) that they can understand and make effective use of them.

Assumption (i) focuses necessarily on the availability of information and on the delicate choice of the proper information transmission channels, access to which must be both easy and cheap.

Assumption (ii) focuses on the intelligibility of the information as communicated. Clearly, in fact, for any information to be effective, the notices issued by the bank – in accordance with the standards – must be built on the basis of expressive actions for the addressee-consumer – that is, they must be able to understand their meaning and, therefore, interpret it correctly. The addressee-consumers' inability to construe the meaning of the information renders the banks' action useless and, consequently, threatens the efficacy of the public intervention measures.

Based on this interpretational framework, a possible suggestion for future research could concern an investigation into the manner in which the following affect the effectiveness of the public intervention measures:

- consumer preference, with respect to information transmission channels;
- the customers' capability of understanding the communicated information.

Notes

1. Other examples of compensatory rules are: the equal weight rule, the additive difference rule, the majority of confirming dimensions rule, and the number of good and bad features rule. For more information, reference should be made to Bettman J.R., Luce M.F., Payne J.W. (1998, pp. 190–192).
2. The non-compensatory nature of the rule is obvious: the good evaluation of an attribute, in fact, does not trade off against the value – slightly below the limit – of another feature. Further examples of non-compensatory rules are: the

lexicographical rule, the elimination-by-aspects rule. For more information, reference should be made to Bettman J.R., Luce M.F., Payne J.W. (1998, pp. 190–192), Tversky A. (1972).
3. Beach and Mitchell (1978) have claimed that the choice of any one rule is the result of a compromise between the desire to accurately analyse the available alternatives and the desire to minimize the effort related to the application of the rule. For more information see Bettman J.R., Luce M.F., Payne J.W. (1998, p. 192), Johnson E.J., Payne J.W. (1985), Fennema M.G., Kleinmuntz D.N. (1995, pp. 21–24).
4. The risk of undergoing significant restrictions, with respect to access to credit, and the use of certain payment instruments, in connection with reports being made to the credit bureaus and credit registries, should stimulate the customer's interest in the abovementioned contents.
5. For a description of the role played by brand names in financial services, see Munari (1995, p. 550).
6. The desire to facilitate financial planning for buyers justifies the simplicity of the amortization schedules proposed by financial intermediaries. Furthermore, the prevalence of simple repayment schemes exemplifies the scarce attention by demand for complex instalment schemes and for the excessive customization of loan agreements.
7. The failure to make even only one repayment may entitle the lender to terminate the loan agreement unilaterally. On top of this, the customer is also liable to end up in the list of bad payers and to be reported to the credit bureaus and credit registries, which rate the borrower's creditworthiness and which share this information with the entire banking and financial system. At the end of the whole process, the outcome is a bad credit rating and further difficulties in obtaining credit in the future.
8. Consistently with this theory, many financial intermediaries have decided, in recent years and for small loan applications, to cut down considerably on the amount of documents required to be produced by the applicant. In the customer's eyes, this is tantamount to a considerable reduction of the loan approval time.

References

Andersson, P. (2004) 'Does Experience Matter in Lending? A Process-Tracing Study on Experienced Loan Officers' and Novices' Decision Behavior', *Journal of Economic Psychology*, 25: 471–92.

Beach, L.R. and T.R. Mitchell (1978) 'A Contingency Model for the Selection of Decision Strategies', *Academy of Management Review*, 3: 439–49.

Beatty, S.E. and S.M. Smith (1987) 'External Search Effort: an Investigation across Several Product Categories', *Journal of Consumer Research*, 14: 83–95.

Bettman, J.R., E.J. Johnson and J.W. Payne (1991) 'Consumer Decision Making', in T.S. Robertson and H.H. Kassarjian (eds), *Handbook of Consumer Behavior*. Englewood Cliffs, NJ: Prentice Hall.

Bettman, J.R., M.F. Luce and J.W. Payne (1998) 'Constructive Consumer Choice Processes', *Journal of Consumer Research*, 25: 187–217.

Dalli, D. and S. Romani (2000) *Il comportamento del consumatore. Teoria e applicazioni di marketing*, Milan: FrancoAngeli, Milan.

Engel, J.F., R.D. Blackwell and P.W. Miniard, *Consumer Behavior*, Chicago: The Dryden Press.

Fennema, M.G. and D.N. Kleinmuntz (1995) 'Anticipations of Effort and Accuracy in Multiattribute Choice', *Organizational Behavior and Human Decision Processes*, 63: 21–32.

Goldberg, J. and R. Von Nitzsch (2001) *Behavioral Finance*, New York: John Wiley & Sons Ltd.

Gollwitzer, P.M. and H. Heckhausen (1987) *Breadth of Attention and the Counter-plea Heuristic: Further Evidence on the Motivational vs Volitional Mindset Distinction*, Munich: Max Planck Institut für Psychologische Forshung working paper.

Howard, J.A. (1994) *Buyer Behavior in Marketing Strategy*, Englewood Clifs, NJ: Prentice Hall.

Johnson, E.J. and J.W. Payne (1985) 'Effort and Accuracy', *Management Science*, 31: 395–414.

Kahneman, D. and A. Tversky (1979) 'Prospect Theory: an Analysis of Decision Under Risk', *Econometrica*, 47: 263–92.

Kamleitner, B. and E. Kirchler (2006) 'Personal Loan Users' Mental Integration of Payment and Consumption', *Marketing Letters*, 17: 281–94.

Lewis, A. and M. Van Venrooij (1995) 'A Note on the Perceptions of Loan Duration and Repayment', *Journal of Economic Psychology*, 16: 161–8.

Lichtenstein, S., P. Slovic, B. Fischhoff, M. Layman and B. Combs (1978) 'Judged Frequency of Lethal Events', *Journal of Experimental Psychology: Human Learning & Memory*, 4: 551–78.

Maslow, A.H. (1943) 'A Theory of Human Motivation', *Psychological Review*, 50: 370–96.

Maslow, A.H. (1954) *Motivation and Personality*, New York: Harper.

McGuire, W.J. (1974) 'Psychological Motives and Communication Gratification', in J.G. Blumler, and C. Katz (eds), *The Uses of Mass Communication*, Beverly Hills, CA: Sage Publications.

McGuire, W.J. (1976) 'Some Internal Psychological Factors Influencing Consumer Choice', *Journal of Consumer Research*, 2: 302–19.

Munari, L. (1995) 'Il sistema di offerta dei servizi bancari', in W.G.Scott (ed.), *Manuale di marketing bancario*, Turin: UTET.

Murray, H.A. (1938) *Exploration in Personality*, London: Oxford University Press.

Murray, H.A. (1955) 'Types of Human Needs', in D. McLelland (ed.), *Studies in Motivation*, New York: Appleton-Century-Crofts.

Olshavsky, R.W. and W. Wymer (1995) 'The Desire for New Information from External Sources', in S. Mackenzie and R. Stayman (eds), *Proceedings of the Society for Consumer Psychology*, Bloomington: Printmaster.

Punj, G.N. and R. Staelin (1983) 'A Model of Consumer Information Search Behavior for New Automobiles', *Journal of Consumer Research*, 9: 366–80.

Ranyard, R., L. Hinkley, J. Williamson and S. McHugh (2006) 'The Role of Mental Accounting in Consumer Credit Decision Processes', *Journal of Economic Psychology*, 27: 571–88.

Rheinberg, F. (2003) *Psicologia della motivazione*, Bologna: il Mulino.

Rumiati, R. and N. Bonini (1996) *Le decisioni degli esperti*, Bologna: il Mulino.

Rumiati, R. and N. Bonini (2001) *Psicologia della decisione*, Bologna: il Mulino.

Schaninger, M.C. and D. Sciglimpaglia (1981) 'The Influence of Cognitive Personality Traits and Demographics on Consumer Information Acquisition', *Journal of Consumer Research*, 8: 208–16.

Schmidt, J.B. and R.A. Spreng (1996) 'A Proposed Model of External Consumer Information Search', *Journal of Academy of Marketing Science*, 24: 246–56.

Simon, H.A. (1955) 'A Behavioural Model of Rational Choice', *Quarterly Journal of Economics*, 69: 99–118.

Solomon, M.R. (1996) *Consumer Behavior*, Englewood Cliffs, NJ: Prentice Hall.

Srinivasan, N. and B.T. Ratchford (1991) 'An Empirical Test of a Model of External Search for Automobiles', *Journal of Consumer Research*, 18: 233–42.

Tagliavini, G. 'La gestione dei patrimoni familiari: il ruolo della consulenza', *Economia & Management*, 14: 106–18.

Tversky, A. (1972) 'Elimination by Aspects: a Theory of Choice', *Psychological Review*, 79: 281–99.

Wells, W.D. and D. Prensky (1966) *Consumer Behaviour*, New York: John Wiley and Sons.

Williamson, J., R. Ranyard and L. Cuthbert (2000) 'Risk Management in Everyday Insurance Decisions: Evidence from a Process Tracing Study', *Risk, Decision and Policy*, 5: 19–38.

Wyer, R.S. and T.K. Srull (1980) 'The Processing of Social Stimulus Information: a Conceptual Integration', in D.E. Carlston, E.B. Ebbesen, D.L. Hamilton, R. Hastie, T.M. Ostrom and R.S. Wyer (eds), *Person Memory: The Cognitive Basis of Social Perception*, Hillsdale, NJ: Lawrence Erlbaum Associates.

12
Corporate Disclosure Determinants: A Cross-Country Investigation

Vincenzo Farina

12.1 Introduction

The wave of bankruptcies that have followed rapidly in recent years as the consequence of financial scandals (such as the infamous cases of Enron, Worldcom and Parmalat) and the integration among the financial systems of various countries have given rise to a search for mechanisms suitable for protecting investors and regulating growing capital flows.

More and more frequently, scholars are looking upon the disclosure as a very important tool within the context of the said mechanisms. In fact, a high level of disclosure may succeed in increasing both the investors' confidence and the capital markets' efficiency (Caruana, 2003).

Based on this assumption, one needs to consider that the investors' protection against the opportunistic behaviour of corporate managements is the major determinant of financing decisions, financing costs, and the concentration of corporate ownership (La Porta, Lopez-de-Silanes, Shleifer, Vishny, 1998).

In particular, with reference to the latter factor, a negative relation is detected between the level of disclosure and the protection that the regulations afford to shareholders rather than creditors.

When the level of market disclosure is low, the high financing costs translate into a concentration of corporate control in the hands of a few people, giving rise to the greater probability of opportunistic behaviour in relation to other financial backers. In contexts characterized by low disclosure, reputation mechanisms are of great importance for raising financial resources through both the capital market and the financial intermediaries.

From a general viewpoint, the significance attributed in individual countries to disclosure for the development of capital markets (which is based upon the operators' confidence) and credit relations between banks and enterprises is conducive to a more thorough analysis of the actual factors that may affect it.

This analysis starts from the assumption that, at the level of each country, the efforts to get to an international harmonization of the accounting standards – a direct consequence of the introduction of the IAS[1] (International Accounting Standards) – still come against considerable differences in the disclosure levels.

Adhikari and Tondkar (1992) affirm that the accounting standards and the disclosure level of enterprises in any given country reflect the characteristics of the special environment in which they develop. The differences present in such environments determine a variety of ways to conceive and bid compliance with disclosure-related standards.

From a practical viewpoint, it may be interesting to consider disclosure as an intermediate variable that, being directly connected to the efficiency of the judicial procedures and the national culture, is capable of affecting the operation of both the capital markets and the financial intermediaries within the various countries.

Some studies have endeavoured to explain these differences on a national base by referring to factors linked to the efficiency of the judicial procedures (La Porta, Lopez-de-Silanes, Shleifer, Vishny, 1998; Levine, 1998; Kothari, 2000). The central assumption of these studies is that the greater protection of the actors who operate in the financial system afforded by the greater efficiency of the judicial procedures may bring greater pressure to bear on the corporate disclosure.

On the other hand, different studies take culturally related variables into consideration (Gray, 1988; Gray and Vint, 1995; MacArthur, 1996; Zarzeski, 1996, Jaggi and Low, 2000). Even the latter move from the assumption that the culture that characterizes a given nation may affect the behaviour of the people working in the financial system and result in differences in both the application of and the compliance with the accounting standards requirements.

After a more thorough analysis of the determinants of the different levels of disclosure and the mode through which such differences may affect the bank–firm relationship insofar as it concerns the credit policies, the remainder of this chapter will present an empirical verification based on data produced from a sample of 45 countries. This verification strives to show how the efficiency of the judicial procedures and the national culture affect the levels of corporate disclosure.

Hence, the model being introduced is based on a synthesis of the outcome of various studies concerning the determinants of the disclosure and the corporate compliance with the accounting standards. The conclusions will highlight the major results of this verification, debating the practical implications of the application of the model of analysis and indicating its major limitations.

12.2   Determinants of corporate disclosure

12.2.1   Definitions

Corporate disclosure is a precondition for the proper working of the capital markets. It may be viewed as a special protection instrument that investors and creditors (in particular, banks) have at their disposal to protect their interest. For instance, the access to correct information about the issue of securities or the economic and financial situation shown in the financial statements of enterprises is a precondition for a proper evaluation of the risks inherent in the decisions of the individual market operators.

Therefore, corporate disclosure is an extremely critical aspect for ensuring the stability and development of the capital markets and, in addition, is a priority object of supervisory authorities.

The search for the disclosure determinants is quite a complex task as there are many variables that are likely to exert either a direct or an indirect influence. In view of this, one needs to narrow down the field of analysis and research, and to investigate only those variables that are likely to affect the disclosure to a considerable extent.

The relations between disclosure and efficiency of the judicial procedures. A factor that may explain the level of corporate disclosure within a country is the efficiency in the enforcement of judicial procedures. In fact, the first hypothesis to be tested in this study is:

Hypothesis 1: the quality of both disclosures and accounting standards becomes higher as the efficiency in the enforcement of legal regulations increases.

The mere existence of adequate regulations is not enough to ensure the protection of shareholders or creditors in general, if these regulations are not complied with (Kothari, 2000).

If the compliance with a few accounting standards by an enterprise is understood to mean the compliance with a legal regulation, it is hard to imagine a situation where the scarce efficiency of the judicial procedures is matched by a considerable compliance with the provisions of the law. However, in a fully mirror-like manner, it should not be taken for granted that in an extremely efficient judicial system there is a considerable compliance with the provisions of the law (La Porta, Lopez-de-Silanes, Shleifer and Vishny, 1998).

La Porta, Lopez-de-Silanes, Shleifer and Vishny (1998) single out four major families of legal systems that have taken shape as a result of political developments over the last few centuries:

- The common law system, adopted in the United States, Canada, Australia, and New Zealand, as well as in many countries in Africa and in Eastern Asia that are members of the Commonwealth;
- The tradition of the Napoleonic civil code, adopted in France and Spain, and in many of their former colonies, including Latin America as a whole, as well as in a number of countries, including Italy, which were affected by the Napoleonic conquests;
- The tradition of the German civil code, adopted in the German-speaking European countries, as well as in Japan, South Korea and Taiwan;
- The tradition of the Scandinavian civil code, adopted in the Scandinavian countries.

The fundamental argument of their empirical analysis is that an efficient judicial system may compensate for the want of regulations on the disclosure of businesses and, therefore, may make it easier for investors to assert their rights.

In fact, as a result of the classification of these 49 countries into the various legal families, the analysis of the level of protection of the investors (both shareholders and creditors) and of the level of enforcement of the rules shows significant variations depending on the relationship of a country to a given legal family.

In brief, those countries characterized by a common law tradition, together with those whose legal systems are based on the German and Scandinavian tradition, implement the greatest protections for investors, while the countries whose legal systems are based on the French tradition move to the other extreme, with a level of protection that is on the average lower (with the exception of France). Even with respect to the efficiency of the judicial procedures, the authors place those countries with a Scandinavian-type legal system at the highest level, followed by those with common law and German-type systems. On the other hand, the French-type systems are always placed at the lowest levels.

Levine (1998) emphasizes the fact that greater levels of efficiency within the judicial procedures determine the presence of more progressive capital markets, which also entails an increase in the opportunities for businesses to have access to bank credits.

With specific reference to bank loans, Bianco, Jappelli and Pagano (2001) point out that a one-month increase in trial duration, *ceteris paribus*, reduces the availability of credit by half a percentage point. Furthermore, studying the effects of the efficiency of the judicial procedures on the credit market in Brazil, Pinheiro and Cabral (1999) suggest that loans could be increased up to 8.5 per cent of GDP should there be a 17.5 per cent improvement in efficiency.

However, one needs to consider that the risk associated with the mere improvement of the judicial efficiency corresponds to a reduction of the incentive for banks to make a careful screening of borrowers and this would make the allocation of credit worse (Zazzaro, 2003). In fact, in contexts where a high efficiency of the judicial procedures makes it easier to collect financial collaterals and there are high screening costs, the banks are stimulated to offer loans reducing the screening and requesting higher collaterals (Manove, Padilla and Pagano, 2001).

12.2.2   The relations between corporate disclosure and national culture

Another factor that may explain the level of corporate disclosure within a country is its culture. Hofstede (1983) defines culture as the 'collective programming of the mind' that individuals share with the other members of their country, region or group, but not with other members of different countries, regions or groups, and that, therefore, distinguishes the members of one human group from another. It is extremely hard to modify the resulting conditioning since 'within a country or part of a country culture changes only so slowly, as what is in the mind of the individuals crystallizes in the institutions'.

The various empirical studies based on the differences among national cultures have to cope with the difficulties inherent in the quantitative measurement of a variable that may actually only be expressed at a qualitative level. The first attempt to define scales that were likely to measure the various dimensions at the base of the culture of a country was made by Hofstede (1980) who, through a survey of a sample of IBM employees, located in a number of different countries, succeeded in attributing a score to each one of the dimensions he had identified:

- *Individualism vs Collectivism*: it corresponds to the degree to which the people of a country prefer to act as individuals rather than as members of a group (Hofstede, 1994). In case of an individualist culture, individuals act exclusively based on their immediate personal interest or that of their household. Instead, in case of a collectivist culture, what counts is the principle whereby an individual's interest comes after the interest of the group to which the individual belongs.

- *Large vs Small Power Distance*: this corresponds to the degree of inequality considered 'normal' or 'acceptable' in a culture (Hofstede, 1994). It relates to the question of the relation between subordinate positions and dominant positions within society and in the organizations and translates, for instance, in different management styles and in the definition of the degree of centralization of authority and of 'autocracy' of the leadership.
- *Strong vs Weak Uncertainty Avoidance*: it corresponds to the degree to which a culture prefers 'structured' situations, where the rules of behavior are clear, with respect to those that are not (Hofstede, 1994). It depends upon how the persons in the various countries cope with the circumstance whereby future is unknown and, as such, represents a source of risk.
- *Masculinity vs Femininity*: This corresponds to the degree to which 'masculine' values prevail over values associated with the 'feminine' role (Hofstede, 1994). Cultures may be classified based on whether they give greater or lower emphasis on the role division among the sexes. As a rule, such a division results from the fact that different values prevail.

Nonetheless, it should be specified that even though such variables have been used extensively in cross-country studies, there is a date-related problem (prior to the 1970s) with respect to the data on which scores were calculated.

Adopting Hofstede's conclusions in the study of the differences among various accounting environments, Gray (1988) identified the following dimensions:

- *Professionalism*: it reflects a preference for the greater autonomy of judgement by those who carry out the control as opposed to prescriptive legal requirements.
- *Uniformity*: it reflects a preference for the enforcement of a standardized approach to the control of financial statements – that, therefore, does not take into account differences among companies – as opposed to an approach based on a greater flexibility.

Table 12.1   Relation among variables as identified by Gray and Hofstede

	Professionalism	Uniformity	Conservatism	Secrecy
Individualism	HIGH	LOW	LOW	LOW
Power Distance	LOW	HIGH	–	HIGH
Uncertainty Avoidance	LOW	HIGH	HIGH	HIGH
Masculinity	HIGH	–	HIGH	LOW

- *Conservatism*: it reflects a preference for a cautious approach to the draft of financial statements to cope with the uncertainty of future events, in contrast with a more laissez-faire approach.
- *Secrecy*: it reflects a preference for the confidentiality of the accounting information, in contrast to a more transparent approach.

According to Gray (1988), the links with Hofstede's dimensions (Hofstede 1980) may be summarized as follows (Table 12.1):

Most interesting finding from Table 12.1 with regard to dealing with the relations between national culture and disclosure is the considerable link that is assumed to exist between the secrecy dimension and the power distance and uncertainty avoidance dimensions. In fact, in greater detail, Gray (1988) upholds that:

- The countries with the highest scores for individualism but with lower scores for uncertainty avoidance and power distance are more oriented towards the dimension of professionalism.
- The countries with the highest scores for uncertainty avoidance and power distance, but with lower scores for individualism are more oriented towards the dimension of uniformity.
- The countries with the highest scores for uncertainty avoidance, but lower scores for individualism and masculinity are more oriented towards the dimension of conservatism.
- The countries with the highest scores for uncertainty avoidance and power distance, but with lower scores for individualism and masculinity are more oriented towards the dimension of secrecy.

A number of studies have followed one upon the other to get to an empirical validation of Gray's assumptions (Gray, 1988) with respect to the link with Hofstede's dimensions (Hofstede, 1980).

In a survey based on a sample of 27 countries, Gray and Vint (1995) reported significant relations between the dimension of secrecy and

Table 12.2   Relations identified by the various studies

	Individualism	Power distance	Uncertainty avoidance	Masculinity
Gray and Vint (1995)	▲		▲	
MacArthur (1996)	▲	▲		
Zarzeski (1996)		▲		
Jaggi and Low (2000)	▲			▲

the dimensions of uncertainty avoidance and individualism, while the link to the degree of masculinity and of power distance did not prove significant.

In a study of 47 companies located in nine countries, MacArthur (1996) found important links to the dimensions of individualism and power distance, while he pointed to merely partial relations with uncertainty avoidance and masculinity.

Zarzeski (1996) highlighted that a large power distance may be related to the lack of activities promoting the circulation of information and, therefore, is negatively correlated with the degree of disclosure.

Finally, Jaggi and Low (2000) reported a positive relation between disclosure level and individualism and, unlike Gray's proposition (1988), a negative relation with the degree of masculinity.

The links identified as a whole within the context of the various studies (Table 12.2) point to significant relations between Hofstede's national cultural dimensions (1980) and Gray's (1988) secrecy-oriented variable.

With special reference to the cultural variable of individualism, the latter emphasizes the role of individual rights and warrants the adoption of appropriate measures to enhance the protection of those rights.

Furthermore, with reference to collectivistic cultures, Greif (1993) upheld that they are more efficient than individualist cultures insofar as it relates to the regulation of phenomena through in-group arrangements. In fact, this reduces the need to have recourse to the mechanisms of justice which come from outside the organization.

Moreover, the cultural differences in the attainment of a certain interest or right (in favour of the individual or of the group) legitimate different levels in the orientation towards the dimension of disclosure (Etzioni, 1996).

In this sense, it is possible to find higher levels of disclosure in individualistic countries, in which personal interests and rights are more protected than in collectivistic ones. According to this analytical perspective, the further hypothesis to be tested in this study is:

> Hypothesis 2: the countries where 'individualism' scores highest will bring greater pressure to bear on disclosure.

12.3   Empirical analysis

12.3.1   Methodology

This verification is based on a cross-section style analysis, meaning that it entails the observation of data over a given period, and reviews a sample of 45 countries drawn at random from both economically developed and economically developing areas.

Taking into consideration the evidence of the various studies referred to above, this empirical verification assumes the feasibility of explaining the level of disclosure in force in a given country based upon the efficiency of the bankruptcy and debt collection procedures and on the individualist cultural variable.

A further variable being used in the model is the quality of the information provided by the (public and private) credit registers. In fact, with reference to the function carried on by the financial intermediaries within credit processes, they contribute to an increase in the disclosure level existing in a given country insofar as it concerns the relation linking creditors and debtors. Therefore, it may be assumed that the higher quality of credit information they are able to disseminate, the estimate of which is based on a few typical characteristics (analysed in the paragraph below), may contribute to an increase in the corporate disclosure level.

In detail, it may be inferred that the linear regression analysis is based on the following relation:

$$\text{Disclosure} = \alpha \text{Enforcement\_1} + \beta \text{Enforcement\_2} + \gamma \text{Culture}$$
$$+ \delta \text{Cred\_Info} + \varepsilon$$

The model identifies with the Disclosure variable the level of public disclosure of any information concerning a company, whether on a voluntary or on a statutory basis. The Enforcement_1 variable identifies the cost of the procedures to be borne by the company in case of bankruptcy; the Enforcement_2 variable identifies the debt recovery rate in case of insolvency; the Culture variable identifies the level of individualism which characterizes a country; while the Cred_Info variable identifies the quality of the information given by public and private credit registers.

12.3.2   Description of data

Disclosure

Broadly speaking, the term 'disclosure' refers to the fact of disclosing any information concerning a company, whether on a voluntary or a statutory basis.

The measurement of the degree of disclosure for every country takes into account the following elements (World Bank, 2004):

- existence of the obligation to report all the events considered relevant for investors (information on family, indirect ownership, beneficial ownership and voting agreement between shareholders);
- recourse to auditing companies from outside the enterprise;
- level of company-related information available on the market.

The disclosure index values range from 0 (showing low disclosure) to 7 (showing high disclosure).

Cost of the bankruptcy procedures

The cost of the procedures to be borne by the company in case of bankruptcy is an initial measure of the efficiency of the judicial procedures and its calculation is based on estimates made on the strength of questionnaires handed out to legal experts within each country (World Bank, 2004). This cost includes the bankruptcy procedure charges, the fees owing to lawyers, consultants, and any other party involved. The datum is expressed as a percentage of the value of the company at the time of its bankruptcy.

Recovery rate

The recovery rate is considered to be a second measure of the efficiency of the judicial procedures that, in this specific instance, are implemented for debt recovery in the case of insolvency (World Bank, 2004).

Therefore, this variable is expressed as a percentage of the debts recovered in case of insolvency.

Individualism

This index is considered to be a measure of the national culture and takes on the dimension originally identified by Hofstede (1980). The measurement is the same as that proposed by the said author based on the analysis of the answers to the questionnaires of his survey.

Quality of the information disclosed by credit registers

This measure evaluates the quality of the information provided by credit registers based on the following characteristics (World Bank, 2004):

* reporting of both positive and negative information about debtors' behaviour;
* reporting of data relative to both companies and individuals;
* due consideration is given to information disclosed by suppliers and creditors of commercial and financial institutions;
* all reported data are maintained for a period in excess of five years;
* reporting of data that, as a whole, relate to loans amounting to more than 1 per cent of the per capita income of the country;
* all reported persons are entitled to access their data.

The index values range from 0 (minimum) to 6 (maximum).

12.3.3 Results

The regression analysis model confirms the initial assumptions relative to the existence of a relation that links corporate disclosure to the efficiency of the judicial procedures, the culture of the country and the quality of the information disclosed by credit registers. Initial evidence is provided by the classification of the 45 countries within two clusters having the following characteristics (Table 12.3).

An initial review of the two clusters shows that higher disclosure levels are matched by higher-quality levels of the information provided by credit registers, higher recovery rates and a higher level of individualism.

The composition of the clusters tends to be quite balanced insofar as it concerns the number of observations (21 in cluster 1 and 24 in cluster 2). In fact, there is an ideal line that cuts across the sample of countries being surveyed and that groups them within a special category characterized by a greater corporate disclosure.

Starting from this presupposition, one may endeavour to delve into the relations among the variables taken into consideration within the linear regression model referred to above.

In short, even in this case, the results confirm the initial hypothesis, as shown in the table below (Table 12.4).

All of the identified variables show a good significance of the coefficients and signs consistent with the initial hypotheses.

Table 12.3   Results of the cluster analysis

Cluster		
	1	2
Disclosure	5.76	3.54
Enforcement_2	28.86	14.88
Culture	70.67	24.04
Cred_Info	5.05	4.08

Table 12.4   Results of the regression analysis

Coefficients	Unstandardized coefficients	Std. error	Standardized coefficients	t	Sig.
Enforcement_1	6.758E-02	0.023	0.337	2.986	0.005
Enforcement_2	4.671E-03	0.002	0.146	2.173	0.036
Culture	3.280E-02	0.010	0.349	3.428	0.001
Cred_Info	0.230	0.131	0.220	1.750	0.088

Table 12.5   Synthesis of the model

R	R square	Adjusted R square	Std. error of the estimate
0.958	0.919	0.911	1.4796

Table 12.4 shows that the cost of the procedures to be borne by the company in cases of bankruptcy and the debt recovery rate in cases of insolvency are strongly positively associated with corporate disclosure levels – a finding that is consistent both with the prior literature and with Hypothesis 1. Moreover, as predicted, individualism is positively associated with corporate disclosure, thus confirming that culture is another important explanatory factor for disclosure levels, consistent with Hypothesis 2.

Table 12.4 also shows that higher quality levels of the information provided by credit registers contribute to an increase in the disclosure level existing in a given country. Furthermore, the solidity of the model is backed up by the high value reported for R^2, equal to 0.911 (Table 12.5).

Even the ANOVA test, founded on the analysis of the coefficient variations, is passed with a high significance value. In particular, what results is a low variability of the estimated coefficients (Table 12.6).

Table 12.6   ANOVA

	Sum of squares	df	Mean square	F	Sig.
Regression	1014.246	4	253.561	115.828	0.000
Residual	89.754	41	2.189		
Total	1104.000	45			

12.4 Conclusions

This chapter has aimed to show how corporate disclosure is linked directly to the level of efficiency of the judicial procedures and to a few characteristic features of the national culture.

This assumption is made all the more significant by the evidence that the corporate disclosure plays an important role in the development of capital markets and the credit activity of financial intermediaries within the various countries.

Furthermore, the different disclosure levels within each country are at odds with the efforts to establish an international-wide harmonization of the international accounting standards. That having been said, the outcome of the analysis conducted on a sample of 45 countries shows a few important elements.

First, those countries that show greater efficiency in the judicial recovery procedures in the case of insolvency of the counterparty are characterized by greater levels of disclosure. Even the economic aspect connected with the costs to be borne by a company for the recovery procedures leads to a greater disclosure. Hence, the deterring mechanism that results from the efficiency of the judicial procedures would seem to carry considerable weight in the corporate decisions to disclose information to the various categories of investors and creditors.

The second evidence concerns the role of national culture in determining greater levels of corporate disclosure. In particular, the Individualism dimension would seem to be linked to the adoption of greater measures for the protection of individual rights. Therefore, within a given context, it is able to bring greater pressure to bear on the corporate disclosure. The results of the analysis confirm this hypothesis.

The final evidence concerns the role of the quality of the credit information available within the various countries. The presence in (public and private) credit registers of a few characteristics, such as the collection of positive and negative informations on the behaviour of debtors, the possibility for the latter to have access to their individual reports, and the role played by not only the financial but also the commercial institutions in reporting the debtors' behaviours, lead to a greater level of corporate disclosure.

However, one needs to point to a limit that may be incurred by the analysis and that characterizes most empirical studies based on cross-country cultural differences. In particular, the problem relates to the type of representation given to the national culture. Many empirical studies that are based (1980) on Hofstede's evidence take culture to be a static variable and, therefore, quite stable within a given context.

In fact, the major criticism to this approach is founded on the consideration that the culture of a given country may evolve over time and, somehow, turn out to be dynamic. In fact, it may integrate the peculiar features of different cultures simply on account of the integration processes that involve various countries.

Notes

1. The IAS are the accounting standards laid down by the IASC (International Accounting Standards Committee), a private and independent organization set up in 1973 with a view to harmonizing the accounting principles used in their financial statements by enterprises and other organizations throughout the world (www.iasc.org.uk).

References

Adhikari, A. and R.H. Tondkar (1992) 'Environmental Factors Influencing Accounting Disclosure Requirements of Global Stock Exchanges', *Journal of International Financial Management and Accounting*, 4: 75–105.

Bianco, M., T. Jappelli and M. Pagano (2001) 'Courts and Banks: Effects of Judicial Enforcement on Credit Markets', CSEF Working Papers 58, Centre for Studies in Economics and Finance (CSEF), University of Salerno.

Caruana, J. (2003) 'The Importance of Transparency and Market Discipline Approaches in the New Capital Accord', *BIS Review*, November.

Etzioni, A. (1996) *The New Golden Rule: Community and Morality in a Democratic Society*, New York: Basic Books.

Gray, S.J. (1988) 'Towards a Theory of Cultural Influence on the Development of Accounting Systems Internationally', *Abacus*, 24: 1–15.

Gray, S.J. and H.M. Vint (1995) 'The Impact of Culture on Accounting Disclosures: Some International Evidence', *Asia-Pacific Journal of Accounting*, 2: 33–43.

Greif, A. (1993) 'Contract Enforceability and Economic Institutions in Early Trade: the Maghribi Traders' Coalition', *American Economic Review*, 83: 525–48.

Hofstede, G. (1980) *Culture's Consequences: International Differences in Work-Related Values*, Beverley Hills, CA: Sage Publications.

Hofstede, G. (1983) 'The Cultural Relativity of Organizational Practices and Theories', *Journal of International Business Studies* 14: 75–89.

Hofstede, G. (1994) *Culture and Organisations: Software of the Mind*, London: McGraw Hill.

Jaggi, B. and P.Y. Low (2000) 'Impact of Culture, Market Forces, and Legal System on Financial Disclosures', *International Journal of Accounting*, 35: 495–519.

Kothari, S.P. (2000) 'The Role of Financial Reporting in Reducing Financial Risks in the Market', in E.S. Rosengren and J.S. Jordan (eds), *Building an Infrastructure for Financial Stability*, Federal Reserve Bank of Boston Conference Series no. 44.

La Porta, R., F. Lopez-de-Silanes, A. Shleifer and R. W. Vishny (1998) 'Law and Finance', *Journal of Political Economy*, 106: 1113–55.

Levine, R. (1998) 'The Legal Environment, Banks, and Long-run Economic Growth', *Journal of Money, Credit, and Banking*, 30: 596–613.

MacArthur, J.B. (1996) 'An Investigation into the Influence of Cultural Factors in the International Lobbying of the International Accounting Standards Committee: The Case of E32 Comparability of Financial Statements', *International Journal of Accounting*, 31: 213–37.

Manove, M., A.J. Padilla and M. Pagano (2001) 'Collateral vs Project Screening: a Model of Lazy Banks', *RAND Journal of Economics*, 32: 726–44.

Pinheiro, A.C. and C. Cabral (1999) *Credit Markets in Brazil: the Role of Judicial Enforcement and Other Institutions*, Mimeo, Centro de Estudios de Reforma do Estado, Rio de Janeiro.

World Bank (2004) *Doing Business 2004*, Washington, DC: World Bank Group.

Zarzeski, M.T. (1996) 'Spontaneous Harmonisation Effects of Culture and Market Forces on Accounting Disclosure Practices', *Accounting Horizons*, 10: 18–37.

A. Zazzaro, *Should Courts Enforce Credit Contracts Strictly?*, Quaderno di ricerca dell'Università di Ancona no. 181, Ancona (2003).

13
Single European Payment Area: Opportunities for Consumers and Corporates

Lucia Leonelli

13.1 Introduction

Payment systems enable the transfer of funds between economic agents and efficient and reliable cross-border payments services are essential for the smooth functioning of markets. In the European market, large-value payment systems and cash are consolidating. In securities settlement systems, there have been some advances, but little progress has been made in terms of integrating retail payment systems.

Financial integration in Europe needs both consumers and corporate entities to be able to make cashless payments throughout the euro area from a single account under the same basic conditions, regardless of their location.

The European Commission and the European Central Bank (ECB) have expressed their ambition of realizing an integrated market for payment services where there is no distinction between cross-border and national payments. One of the European Commission's main goals was to encourage competition and innovation in the field of European retail payment system while maintaining prudent supervision requirements. This is achieved when the euro area is considered a single retail payment market, all technical, legal and commercial barriers are removed, there are equal conditions to gain access to the market, and market participants have equal treatment.

The European banking industry's first attempt to address the issue of integration needs through the creation of a Single Euro Payment Area (SEPA) which was intended to transform the different euro payments instruments into a single European Payments Area. The European Payments Council (EPC) is the decision-making and coordination body of the European banking industry in relation to payments and its declared purpose is to both support and promote the creation of the SEPA.

This chapter shows that the SEPA project is of great relevance to banks, since it does not only call for operational changes involving the back office information systems of individual intermediaries and a review of interbank procedures. It also manages to exert considerable influence over the strategic choices relating to the offer of payment services. In fact, it succeeds in affecting the decision-making processes relative to the spread of productive processes involved in the offer of individual services, the margins of this business area, the set-up of the service market and the competition among the various operators that offer payment services. The SEPA project also affords a considerable opportunity to innovate the system of payments by making the most of the chances offered by the information technology advances, benefiting from the advantages arising out of the standardization of the processes, and checking the costs linked to the complexity of the management for those who are required to operate with payment systems belonging to various EU member countries.

The chapter is organized as follows: it looks at the current situation of the European payment system which is still composed of national markets with different payment habits (section 13.2). Then it moves on to consider factors influencing innovation and integration in payment sector (section 13.3). In particular, it analyses retail payment market needs in Europe and the role of regulation. It shows how self-regulation is supporting and creating the Single Euro Payment Area (section 13.4). The chapter looks at the impact of SEPA on bank's strategies and investments on developing new processes, products, and services (section 13.5) and then analyses the consequences for competition and innovation and possible modifications of retail payment market (section 13.6).

13.2   The European payments system

To a large extent, Europe is still composed of national markets which are characterized by different payment habits and industry structures. Within the euro area, the payment instruments, the standards and the infrastructures for retail payments are still noticeably diverse (European Central Bank, 2005).

The current regime of 27 national payments markets, with divergent legal conditions and widely differing prices and speed of delivery, denies EU citizens the efficiencies that could be gained through a consolidated payments processing system (Godeffroy, 2005). In the past ten years, the number of systems has remained the same, so it seems that banks did not use the introduction of the euro as an opportunity to consolidate (Tumpell-Gugerell, 2005).

Over the past two decades, the most significant long-run trend in retail payment services to end users has been the relative shift in all countries away from the use of cash for consumer payments and towards IT-based payment methods, in particular towards the use of payment cards, but more generally towards electronic credit and debit transfers (Committee on Payment and Settlement Systems, 2002).

However, cards – both debit and credit – have proven to be very successful in the euro area. Statistics show that in the last five years the use of cards has doubled. Cards are currently one of the three most popular cashless payment instruments.

13.3   Factors influencing innovation and integration

Innovation and integration in the retail payment system are influenced by many factors. Two of these drivers – market needs and regulation – are particularly important in industries with network effects, such as the payment sector (Krueger, 2002).

13.3.1   The needs of retail payments markets in Europe

The demand for payment services points to unsatisfied needs that may be considered from various standpoints. Payment services should be developed to meet the needs of corporates, when transferring funds and the underlying data to counterparties in particular within European countries and across Europe. The retail trade needs a supervision of the payment processing system, in particular with regard to transparency, market forces and the evolution of technology. Consumers need more efficient and secure payment services.

From the point of view of the enterprises, payments themselves are processed efficiently by banks, but payment initiation and reconciliation may require considerable work on the part of both the payer and the payee. The differences in local payments standards and the defects of the legacy interbank infrastructure prevent multi-country enterprises from achieving end-to-end straight-through processing (STP), in particular for cross-border payments. The need to pay and collect in different countries prevents corporates from standardizing their payments processes and managing their liquidity from a single account.

Automated matching of cross-eurozone receivables or payables against payments will reach domestic levels when common standards are available and enriched payment information (such as IBAN) is included throughout the payments processing chain. Typically, receivables are matched against incoming payments at rates no higher than 60–70 per cent, as the result of missing reference information. Automated matching will be facilitated by reengineering of bank back offices and the interbank payments infrastructure (Twist, 2006).

Another point of view concerning the merchant shows how each commercial transaction includes a payment to pay for products and services delivered. A well-designed payment process enables commerce to flow efficiently, both within a country's boundaries and when crossing borders. Merchants complain that a lack of competition between banks limits their choices (particularly for acquiring services) and prevents supply and demand from producing optimal market prices.

For example, in respect of card payments, the merchant sector believes that they are currently funding the consumer sector through interchange. Heated debates are ongoing about the economic need for this funding, with interchange adherents claiming that issuers would not issue cards if there were no interchange mechanism to compensate them for the payment guarantee cost, the free funding cost and the processing costs. Merchants that operate in multiple countries (like large retail stores) would welcome the option to have one provider service all their card acquiring. However, the situation has not improved for cross-border debit card acquiring. Without interoperability, it is too costly for providers to respond to this need.

The commerce sector wants to provide all customers with the largest range of efficient, secure, cheap and reliable means of payments, as long as none of them is so expensive that it results in increasing the prices of goods. In the current systems, there exists a distortion between the pricing and the cost of payment services in all European countries. The resulting cross-subsidization of payments means leads to inefficiencies, which are detrimental for consumers and businesses (Eurocommerce, 2005).

More transparency in bank fees would certainly help consumers and businesses to choose the most efficient means of payment. This kind of transparency would serve as an incentive to the industry to compete on composition and level of fees, while at the same time it would enable consumers to make an informed choice regarding the best method of payment for a particular transaction. In their role as both users and promoters of the payment processing systems, retailers are prepared to pay for the payment services they wish to buy, which is not the case today

(Leonelli, 1999). In the current system, they are too often faced with non-negotiable 'package deals'.

The need to make these services available in a competitive way implies that at present the costs that the banks impose on retailers should become transparent, competitive and negotiated individually; if 'package fees' were to be developed anyway, their components should be known by the retailers and 100 per cent negotiable.

From the point of view of the consumers, cross-border payments account for only between 1 and 2 per cent of total payments. The users very rarely make cross-border transactions in relation to their cost, complexity and inefficiency. Expatriates often transform their cross-border payments into national payments by opening an account in each of the countries in which they have an economic interest. They need to have only one bank account to make credit and debit transfer anywhere in the euro area. They also need more efficient payment cards able to be used for all euro payments. Consumers are interested in value added services like e-invoicing, mobile or internet payment initiation, airline e-tickets. This will reduce the necessity for people to carry cash and consumers will spend less time handling payments (European Central Bank, 2006).

13.3.2 The role of regulation in retail payment markets

The institutional framework is considered one of the most important factors of innovation. Regulation can influence innovative activity in various ways. It can influence market structure, interoperability between different payment services providers, infrastructure integration, adoption of common standards, co-operation between payment networks.

13.3.2.1 The role of oversight in retail payments

Retail payment systems and instruments are significant contributors to the broader effectiveness and stability of the financial system – in particular to consumer confidence and to the functioning of commerce. Moreover, the efficient and safe use of money as a medium of exchange in retail transactions is an essential function of the currency and a foundation of the trust people have in it (Bank of Italy, 1999). For these reasons, the efficiency and safety of retail payments are of interest to central banks (Committee on Payment and Settlement Systems, 2002). Oversight is part of the statutory task assigned to the European System of Central Banks (European Central Bank, 2003).

The European Central Bank (ECB) has developed guidance on SEPA requirements and set the implementation timelines as part of its remit to ensure an efficient and orderly payments market in the euro area.

The Governing Council of the European Central Bank (ECB) has stressed the importance of a single payments market: '... All euro area payments should become domestic and reach a level of safety and efficiency at least on par with the best performing national payment systems today.'

The European Central Bank estimates that creating a single market will lead to a 1 per cent increase in GDP across the eurozone. Even more important, the new market structure will open up the eurozone as a domestic market in which banks can offer their payments services to more than 300 million consumers and more than 15 million corporations.

Regulation is often beneficial to competition as it creates an enviroment in which firms can compete on equal terms (Tumpel-Gugerell, 2006). The industry has to generate the standards that are necessary to ensure compatibility between systems. Only when compatibility is ensured will there be the positive effect on volumes and, subsequently, the economies of scale in an integrated single market (Godeffroy, 2006).

The successful implementation and migration of the SEPA instruments depend heavily on payment-related standardization. The Eurosystem welcomes the development of common technical standards, which enable the smooth connection of systems and transfer of messages between different players.

The Eurosystem addressed the priorities that are considered important for standardization of the different payment instruments, infrastructures and account identifiers. All electronic payments will be impacted as a result and core credit transfers, direct debits and card payments will migrate to interoperable formats and processes.

At the same time, national market features and practices in relation to the core instruments will gradually be phased out.

13.3.2.2 *The Payment Services Directive (PSD)*

In March 2007, European financial ministers agreed on the text of the Directive on payment services. The Directive's ultimate goal is to improve the competitiveness of the EU through integrating national payment markets and providing support for the European payments industry in building the infrastructure necessary for a single payment market (European Commission, 2005).

To achieve this ultimate goal, the Directive has three main objectives, which are:

- to enhance competition by opening markets and creating a level playing field;

- to increase market transparency for providers and users;
- to standardize rights and obligations of providers and users of payment services in the EU, with a strong emphasis on a high level of consumer protection.

The Directive will have two main objectives:

- the Directive will create a new EU-wide licensing regime for 'Payment Institutions' (that is, providers of payment services that are not credit institutions or e-money issuers). There are currently significant differences between the regulatory regimes for payment services in EU Member States. These regimes are not harmonized and 27 sets of different national rules exist.
- the Directive will also introduce conduct of business rules for all payment service providers (including credit institutions and E-money issuers). In doing so, the Directive should harmonize legal and technical requirements relating to the provision of payment services, give Payment Institutions access to other EU markets and facilitate the creation of SEPA.

The Commission proposes the introduction of a new license for non-credit institution payment service providers which do not take deposits or issue e-money ('payment institutions'). This license aims to increase competition in the market by removing any existing barriers and to facilitate entry into the market of new payment service providers such as retailers, money remitters or mobile operators. The compromise formula that member states agreed on allows non-banking institutions to be able to offer credit but only 'within a limited' 12-month period.

The Directive focuses on a harmonized set of rules with regards to transparency conditions of payment services and information requirements provided to the payer/user. It sets out full harmonisation rules on the provision and use of payment services including on execution time, liability of a payment provider in case of non-execution or defective execution, liability of the payment service user in case of misuse of a payment instrument (limited to €150) and the introduction of the full amount principle and conditions for revocability and refunding.

The Directive covers electronic payments made in any currency where either or both the payer's payment service provider and/or the payee's payment service provider are located within the EU. The Directive will not apply to cheque payments or most cash transactions.

The EPC's self-regulatory initiatives and the PSD proposal are seen by the European Commission as complementary, with the PSD creating the legal platform on which market forces can build SEPA.

One key difference is that the PSD will apply to payments in any currency and is not limited to euros, as is the case for the EPC schemes and rulebooks and the EPC Cards Framework.

The Directive provides clarity and certainty with regard to the core rights and obligations of users and providers of payment services. It also provides the necessary legal framework for SEPA, as it will harmonize existing, and differing, national legal requirements.

13.4   Towards self-regulation in SEPA

The issue of banking regulation is at the centre of an important international debate, with respect to its role and the modalities in which the supervisory functions are exercised.

In the last few years the regulation of banks and financial intermediaries has changed radically, becoming increasingly indirect (from structural regulation to prudential and consensual regulation and self-regulation) (Gualandri, 2001; Carretta, Schwizer and Stefanelli, 2003).

The intervention of authorities to promote integrated and competitive retail payments markets does not necessary imply regulation. The authorities can leave sufficient scope for the self-regulation of private players to define market standards, and may only intervene to give deadlines or when the desired outcome is not achieved.

The efficacy of this arrangement depends primarily upon the level of competition in the financial market. In high competition, operators become more sensitive to the judgement of the market, and are therefore encouraged to adopt a 'virtuous' management approach, within a self-regulatory framework (Carretta, Farina and Schwizer, 2005)

There are efficiency gains to be made in the areas of payment processing and payment system infrastructures in the euro area. There is a clear international dimension to any payment system and respective adjustments are clearly needed. While the national payment instruments and infrastructures within the euro area are for the most part very efficient, they have a very strong national identity and, as they stand, cannot cater for pan-European needs.

The European Payment Council (EPC) was established in June 2002 and brings together the European payments industry (European Payment Council, 2007). It now consists of 66 members, composed of banks and banking associations. EPC is the decision-making and coordination body of the European banking industry in relation to payments. Its purpose is to support and promote the creation of a Single Euro Payments Area (SEPA) through industry self-regulation.

The EPC is developing the building blocks upon which the SEPA project is founded. First, EPC is devoted to developing the two new Pan Euro Payment Schemes for electronic credit transfers and for direct debits and to design a Cards Framework defining a single market for cards. Secondly, EPC has worked to create rules and standards for common procedures. The next step will be to develop value-added services which can stimulate a paperless payments area, with end-to-end STP of all SEPA-compliant payments.

The SEPA credit transfer (SCT) scheme is an interbank payment scheme that defines a common set of rules and processes for credit transfers denominated in euros. The scheme defines a common service level and a time frame under which financial institutions participating in the scheme must as a minimum conduct SCTs.

The SEPA direct debit (SDD) scheme is an interbank payment scheme that defines a common set of rules and processes for direct debits denominated in euros. The scheme defines a common service level and a time frame stating when financial institutions participating in the scheme must, as a minimum, be able to act in their role as debtor banks.

SEPA card payments will take place according to a set of high-level principles to which issuers, acquirers, card schemes and operators will have to adapt. These principles have been developed by the EPC and are referred to as the SEPA card framework (SCF).

In the new SEPA environment, the rules and standards are defined in the SEPA schemes, which are generally separated from the processing infrastructures. This separation will allow infrastructure providers to compete and offer their processing services to any bank or card scheme provider.

EPC has defined a framework that clarifies the rules and procedures to be followed by infrastructure providers (that is, ACHs, card scheme processors and other processors that handle, transfer and exchange payment-related information for financial institutions). Traditionally, these infrastructure providers have been responsible for the management of the rules, practices and standards related to payments made within a country, and they also typically offer their processing services to financial institutions. The national infrastructures of Eurozone countries, of EFTA countries and of the countries on the threshold of joining the European Union are still incompatible with each other in respect of business models and technological infrastructure. Effective standardization, to be achieved in a short space of time, needs common formats, messaging and communication standards (Vanetti, 2006).

The EPC has adopted a common approach to the development of standards. Standards are rules that govern technology, behaviour and interaction. Technical standards are necessary to allow interaction and interoperability between IT systems, to foster automation of the payment process and to allow automated (straight-through) processing of all euro-denominated payments.

The EPC has identified the business requirements that describe the data elements to be exchanged between financial intermediaries. He has then translated the business requirements into logical data elements. The International Organization for Standardization (ISO) has translated these logical data elements into universal financial industry (UNIFI) message standards, namely the UNIFI (ISO 20022) XML message standards. These standards will form the basis for building messages in a standardized language. The EPC has developed a set of SEPA implementation guidelines that define the use of the UNIFI message standards.

The EPC has decided that the UNIFI standards will be compulsory in the bank-to-bank domain, and recommended in the customer-to-bank domain.

13.5 The impact of SEPA on banks' strategies

Over the past few decades, payments services have not received much attention. Many banks considered them a commodity and left product management in the hands of technology leaders.

Today banks face significant changes in their European payments business. The retail payments market in Europe offers more business opportunities than payments alone. In Europe at the present time, approximately 52 billion non-cash payments are processed every year. The cost of payments, including cash, represents 3–4 per cent of GDP. Payments services typically account for at least 33 per cent of present-day banking revenues (Capgemini, ABN AMRO and EFMA, 2005).

Demand from both consumer and corporate customers is on the increase. Consumers are exhibiting lower levels of loyalty, and they 'cherry-pick' the best offerings from different banks. Traditional banks may end up with the payments operations, while specialized providers offer the profit-generating products. Corporate clients demand value-added, integrated payments services, and banks face fierce competitive pressure in relation to both payments and cash management services.

Non-bank providers of payments services are beginning to penetrate the European market. US processors, for example, are quickly building a European presence in card processing. It is too early to say if these providers are competitors of banks or potential partners, but banks have to be aware of their power.

Regulatory changes and compliance requirements need investments, and many of these projects are related to payments. European and national legislation have reduced euro cross-border payments revenue, and have put downward pressure on interchange fees and other sources of interbank income.

Banks will also have to manage the significant programme risk of the transition, and operate multiple payment systems during the transition phase. All of this will be in the face of a serious erosion in their payments revenue.

Bank payments revenue will decline as prices converge on the 'best in class' and they may need to compensate by attracting net new payment volumes. Even though SEPA will increase the levels of efficiency, these gains will not match the combined effect of the revenue losses that banks will suffer combined with the investments they will need to make in adopting it. This could raise barriers to the speed and success of SEPA's implementation.

SEPA benefits will accrue mostly to multi-country banks, operating in several countries (with a similar structure to multi-country corporates). They will benefit from the increasing efficiency of European payments operations as STP rates rise to domestic levels, and from economies of scale, platform consolidation, standardization of the process, reducing the costs linked to the complexity. International banks will also be able to leverage the new 'domestic' euro market in order to win market share, develop new pan-European payment products, and enter new markets (Profumo, 2006).

SEPA presents domestic banks with a real challenge. They will have to invest, prices will decline and competition will increase in their home markets. If they do not have the scale to play in the euro market, they will be forced to consider some drastic strategies, including exiting the payments production function altogether.

Banks will attempt to compensate for lost revenue by implementing new pricing strategies. They are likely to introduce differentiated pricing for payments services, stimulating the more efficient instruments (such as payments delivered through Internet banking) and charging for inefficient processes (for instance, cash, paper-based payments and exceptions). Value-added services linked to e-invoicing are a valuable source of profitable business to banks – at relatively minor additional cost in process design. The trend is towards a transparent model of pricing for payments services, where banks will charge their own client directly, instead of using the interchange mechanism.

Product standardization and the consolidation of payment infrastructures will maximize the economies of scale. Most banks intend to reduce costs by increasing STP, searching for economies of scale, and outsourcing and offshoring as many functions as possible. Full back-office rationalization and concentration need standardized and harmonized business rules.

13.6   The impact of SEPA on the retail payments market

The impact of SEPA on retail prices is likely to depend upon the degree of competition in their respective domestic banking markets, with a substantial degree of education required for consumers to reap the benefits of increased choice when making cross-border payments (European Commission, 2007).

In payment systems it can be argued that the risk of collusion is even higher, since cooperation between competitors is needed in order for the system to work. In addition to the lack of competition between incumbent banks and new entrants, there may also be a similar lack of competition between those credit institutions and other players within the payment system.

There are several investigations underway in a number of countries with regard to the fees that processors charge for retail payments. If these charges are found to be excessively high, this can be evidence of collusion on the part of the banks or can lead to a lessening of competition amongst those paying the fees and potentially higher prices for consumers.

SEPA's focus on electronic payment methods – which are cheaper than paper-based and cash payment instruments – may lower barriers to entry to new entrants, which could lead to increased efficiency and lower prices to end users.

Another effect would be that economies of scale and scope will, once realized, lead to at least some consolidation in payment services, as acknowledged by the European Commission in its Incentives Paper (European Commission, 2006).

SEPA leads to increased competition amongst infrastructure providers, provided that the contract for the scheme's payment processing is opened up to regular competitive tendering. The consequences of this competition should allow for increased efficiency and lower end prices to customers.

It was widely recognised that substantial investments would be necessary in order to implement SEPA, which would fall mostly on corporate organizations and banks. This would entail the updating of legacy systems, IT infrastructure investment and would also be likely to mean an increase in consumer prices – at least in the short run.

It was also possible that there could be an asymmetric distribution of costs and benefits during the introduction of SEPA, with the majority of costs ultimately borne by consumers in the form of higher prices, whilst the banking and corporate sectors would be the main beneficiaries through lower transaction costs and cost savings in back-office payment processing.

The ideal of the Commission is to create a single European market in which there is cross-border competition between payment service providers. Customers (both private and business) should be able to switch to a bank in another Member State as easily as they can switch to a bank in their own country. Today this is not possible because there are still considerable legal barriers.

The creation of a consistent European system of bank account numbers would create the possibility of the introduction of 'number portability' on a European level. Of course, the costs of investing in such a system would be huge. This, however, could be more than matched by the long-run economic benefits of increased cross-border mobility and the creation of a level playing field in the European payment systems sector.

A short-run solution could be the harmonization of existing domestic switching facilities, as national best practices have proved effective in increasing customer mobility.

13.7 Conclusion

According to the European Commission (2006),

> the realisation of the Single Euro Payment Area (SEPA) will result in tremendous gains in potential savings for society to bring benefits to all stakeholders. An efficient single market for payment services will increase competition, facilitate new business opportunities, the realisation of economies of scale and foster specialization and innovation.

At present it is still questionable whether or not the SEPA project has a significant impact upon innovation and competition: it depends upon the way in which the system develops new payment services and the value added services that are being requested.

It is quite certain that large corporates might have more buyer power under SEPA, which would enable them to squeeze the margins for retail banks serving this sector and would have a consequent impact on competition. In terms of competition for SME, there would be little impact for firms with mainly domestically-oriented trade, but potentially increased competition for firms which trade regularly with other countries. SEPA would lead to lower barriers for international trade, particularly for business-to-business payments. Firms involved in international trade might have substantial savings.

The banking industry has to consider payment services as a business area, and every single bank has to decide the role it wants to play. Every bank has understand where it lies in the payment services' value chain in order to understand what to do in-house and what to outsource. A breakdown of the processes of operations permits the singling out of sectors – characterized by limited value added and considerable absorption of human resources – that may be outsourced, with consequent savings – particularly when the employing organizations work on a large scale for a variety of users. On the other hand, a few leading functions may be centralized in hubs that work on behalf of various sectors. This calls for a review and, if necessary, a thoroughly new design of the corporate models of operations.

Payment services is not a stand-alone product. In most cases, they are bundled together with other products such as credit. Consequently, the success of a payment provider depends partly on the efficiency with which all credit-related tasks are carried out.

Banks also have to communicate to customers the advantages and opportunities of SEPA, since only if consumers are well informed will they able to appreciate the new value added services.

Finally, the new legal framework has to ensure transparent and nondiscriminatory terms of access for services provided by infrastructures to increase competition and innovation in retail payment market.

References

Bank of Italy (1999) *White Paper on Payment System Oversight Objectives, Methods, Areas of Interest*, Rome, November.

Capgemini, ABN AMRO and EFMA (2005) *World Payment Report*, Internal report.

Carretta, A., V. Farina and P. Schwizer (2005) *Banking Regulation Towards Advisory: the 'Culture Compliance' of Banks and Supervisory Authorities*, paper presented at

European Academy of Management (EURAM) 5rd Annual Conference, Munich, Germany.

Carretta, A., P. Schwizer and V. Stefanelli (2003) 'Oltre la regolamentazione: il sistema dei controlli interni degli intermediari finanziari. Cultura del controllo o controllo della cultura?', in AA.VV., *Ottavo Rapporto Fondazione Rosselli*, Milan: Edibank.

Committee on Payment and Settlement Systems (2002) *Policy Issues for Central Banks in Retail Payments*, Basel, September.

Eurocommerce (2005) *Preparation of an Impact Assessment on a Proposal for a Directive Concerning a New Legal Framework for Payments in the Internal Market*, Brussels.

European Central Bank (2003) *Oversight Standards for Euro Retail Payment Systems*, Frankfurt, June.

European Central Bank (2005) *Blue Book*, Brussels, August.

European Central Bank (2006) *The Single Euro Payment Area*, Frankfurt am Main.

European Commission (2005) *Proposal for a Directive of the European Parliament and of the Council on Payment Services in the Internal Market and Amending Directives 97/7/EC, 2000/12/EC and 2002/65/EC*, Brussels.

European Commission (2006) *SEPA Incentives*, Brussels, February.

European Commission (2007) *Final Report on Competition Retail Banking*, Brussels.

European Payment Council (2007) *Making SEPA a Reality: Implementing the Single Euro Payments Area*, Brussels, January.

Godeffroy, J.M. (2006) *SEPA: an Ambition for Europe*, paper presented at the Symposium of the Belgian Financial Forum, Brussels.

Godeffroy, J.M. (2005) *There will be a SEPA*, Speech presented at the Euro Finance Week, European Central Bank, Brussels, November.

Gualandri, E. (2001) 'Il ruolo della banca centrale e degli altri organismi di controllo: amministratori del sistema e attori nel cambiamento culturale delle banche', in A. Carretta, *Il governo del cambiamento culturale in banca*, Rome: Bancaria Editrice.

Krueger, M. (2002) *Innovation and Regulation – The Case of E-Money Regulation in the EU*, Electronic Payment Systems Observatory – Institute for Prospective Technological Studies Background Paper no. 5, Seville.

Leonelli, L. (1999) *I servizi di pagamento. Mercato, gestione, regolamentazione*, Turin: UTET.

Profumo, A. (2006) 'Gli impatti della SEPA e dell'armonizzazione normativa sulle banche italiane ed europee', *Bancaria*, 9: 62–7.

Tumpel-Gugerell, G. (2005) *Interchange in a Changing Market: Observations from the Euro Area Perspective*, Speech for conference organized by the Federal Reserve Bank of Kansas City at Santa Fé.

Tumpel-Gugerell, G. (2006) *Building the Future – Integrating Europe's Financial Sector*, Finland's EU Presidency Conference, Helsinki.

Tumpel-Gugerell, G. (2006) 'The Drivers of Change: Regulation versus Competition', *Bancaria*, 9: 46–55.

Twist (2006) *Realising SEPA Benefits – Corporate Requirements and Key Elements of the Business Solution*, White Paper, London: Twist.

Vanetti, R. (2006) 'A Shared Path in a Competitive Europe', in AA.VV., *SEPA: Today's Challenge*, Milan: SIA.

14
Coordination and Cooperation in Financial Regulation: Do Regulators Comply with Banking Culture?

Alessandro Carretta, Vincenzo Farina and Paola Schwizer[1]

14.1 Introduction

This chapter identifies cultural gaps as a possible stumbling block in the efficient exchange of information and the sharing of problems and goals among regulators and the industry, with respect to the recent innovations introduced in the financial sector, which are orienting the supervisory authorities towards the adoption of new interaction models with the supervised financial intermediaries.

In greater detail, the chapter describes how financial supervisory models have evolved towards solutions based on increasing cooperation between the regulators and financial intermediaries (section 14.1). This has led to the definition of a new role for the supervisory authorities, which, in parallel, encourages the innovation of the organizational tools employed for communicating and exchanging information with the supervised entities (section 14.2). These tools are classified and analysed, with respect to their field of application and their connections with the supervised fields (section 14.3). Consequently, in order to analyse the sharing of knowledge and cultural models between the supervisory bodies and the supervised entities, it is important that there is an in-depth assessment of the current extent of the cultural gap. The chapter then presents a cultural survey, based on the application of a text-analysis model to a corpus of reference texts produced by three samples, drawn from among the supervisory bodies (the Basel Committee and the Bank of Italy) and the supervised entities (section 14.4). The empirical survey results reveal many fields of cultural differentiation, alongside several important areas in which the orientations of the parties tend to overlap (section 14.5).

14.2 Recent trends in supervisory models

The issue of banking regulation is at the centre of an important international debate, with respect to its role and the ways in which the supervisory functions are exercised. Generally speaking, the supervisory authorities' actions are based on a rather broad and complex system of activities and instruments. The survey by the World Bank on the regulation and supervision of banks in 107 countries comprises 12 separate parts, covering the following aspects of a country's banking system: domestic and foreign bank entry, government ownership of banks, capital adequacy, restrictions on bank activities, supervisory power, independence, resources, loan classification stringency, provisioning standards, diversification guidelines, deposit insurance system, provisioning and risk management requirements, information disclosure requirements, crisis management (Barth, Caprio and Levine, 2001).

In the past few years the regulation of banks and financial intermediaries has changed radically, becoming increasingly indirect (from structural regulation to prudential and consensual regulation and self-regulation) (Gualandri, 2001; Carretta, Schwizer and Stefanelli, 2003).

According to the first empirical assessments, the most effective supervisory policies in ensuring improved conditions of stability and enhanced performance appear to be those aimed at promoting 'private' supervision, by means of transparent and significant accounting and information disclosure requirements, principles of governance and management control, common criteria of sound and prudent management (Barth, Caprio and Levine, 1999, 2001).

In the consensual regulatory approach, which reduces outside intervention in a bank's management, a reduction of the regulatory costs incurred by the intermediary can be discerned (Elliehausen, 1998). This occurs if the supervisory action is effective in promoting and encouraging the adoption of internal control systems. Building a mindful and responsible management, through mechanisms of self-analysis and self-control, enhances the possibility of pursuing 'economies of scale and scope', in terms of the broadness of the benefits descending from regulation, and of the reduction of the time needed to adapt to it.

The efficacy of this arrangement depends primarily upon the level of competition in the financial market. In high competition, operators become more sensitive to the judgement of the market, and are therefore encouraged to adopt a 'virtuous' management approach, within a self-regulatory framework. Moreover, this approach encourages the development of a supervisory culture, which can then become a powerful tool for guiding individual actions towards the achievement of sound and prudent management. The latter is also determined by the supervisory bodies' actual capacity to get to understand and guide the management behaviour of the supervised entities, taking account of the differences existing among them, in terms of shareholding structure, size, and business activities (Carretta, 1998). This is no easy task, which requires a certain reorientation of supervisory activities towards the production and organizational processes of the supervised entities; the use, for this purpose, of all of the available information; and the development, by the supervisory bodies, of a banking culture (which unquestionably differs from the traditional regulatory culture), which can be achieved also by means of further efforts in collecting information and broadening its knowledge base.

In any case, within a more balanced supervisory framework, it is important to achieve improved conditions for a microprudential view – that is, a focus on the behaviour of the individual financial intermediaries – to balance the current trend that focuses on a macroprudential view, which, by itself, might be viewed as too abstract and distant from the actual market behaviour (Carretta, 1998).

In fact, in recent years the supervisory authorities have focused increasingly on how the financial intermediaries organize the production, administration and distribution processes of the respective business areas, and have established principles and rules aimed at promoting suitable corporate organizations (Pisanti, 2002). They interact with the supervised entities, encouraging the improvement of the organizational and internal control processes, according to a certificatory – rather than strictly regulatory – approach. They have become consultants of the financial institutions, thereby helping to spread knowledge of the best practices: supervision and management support are becoming increasingly intertwined, with a view to achieving stability and efficiency, by encouraging sound and prudent management practices. From this point of view, the search for cultural consistency between the supervisory authorities and the financial industry is an important objective for improving supervisory activities.

14.3   Moving towards a new role for supervisory authorities

The implementation of new supervisory arrangements, based on self-regulation and the coordination of external and internal supervision, determines an evolution in the role played by the supervisory authorities, and in the manner in which they interact with the governance bodies of the banks, such as the board of directors, top management and external and internal auditors.

Delegating supervision by the supervisory authorities to the supervised entities entails the capacity, by the former, to define the minimum objective compliance requirements for the internal control systems (Bank of Italy, 1998, 2002), while at the same time encouraging organizational and management decision-making that is compatible with the supervision objectives.

The aim of the regulatory intervention also includes developing the banks' ability to avoid fraudulent behaviour, which is capable of jeopardizing their stability, and that of the system as a whole, encouraging the intermediaries' attitude to adapt their production processes continuously to strategic decisions that are consistent with market evolution, and fine-tuning the corporate governance bodies' ability to take on the various types of risk related to operating and financial innovation.

This new supervisory arrangement requires that compliance with the criterion of sound and prudent management – pursued through the functionality and adequacy of the internal control systems – must become a rule of conduct for intermediaries; that is, an intermediate objective capable of combining the approach of both the supervisory bodies and the supervised entities: for the supervisory authority, the first guarantee of a sound and prudent management resides in a business' capacity of prevention and intervention, by means of an appropriate internal control system. On the other hand, the management itself must reach more or less the same conclusion: greater capacity of governance is required because of the increased exposure of banks to new and old risks, in consequence of the opportunities granted to each business under the new regulatory framework (De Maio and Patalano, 1995).

This overlapping of the objectives of both the supervisors and the supervised, by increasing the degree of consistency between the regulatory principles, on the one hand, and the intermediaries' management criteria, on the other hand, will in all likelihood lessen the weight of the restrictions and the measures introduced by the regulatory authorities (Airoldi, 2002).

Furthermore, the revised Basel Accord on Capital (Basel 2) envisages the possibility for banks to adopt internal procedures for assessing asset requirements, with respect to credit and operational risks, like in the previous Accord of 1996 on market risk. Moreover, the banks opting for an internal approach to credit and operational risk management for supervisory purposes must provide evidence, to the supervisory authority, that they are capable of meeting a set of minimum requirements, on an ongoing basis. These requirements may be identified, inter alia, in the management's attitude to ensure widespread communication of its corporate strategy and risk management policies, aimed at the creation of a risk culture; in the structured interaction between the management itself and the risk control units, with a view to pursuing the implementation of criteria relating to control system efficiency, adequacy of resources, and efficacy of corrective measures, vis-à-vis any shortcomings identified by the control procedures put into place. Therefore, banks are required to systematically map the activities most exposed to the risks in question, and to develop suitable procedures aimed at consistently assess expected losses over a certain period of time. These must be reported in historical data series, subject to appropriate back-testing. Banks are also required to adopt their risk measurement methods in decision making and day-to-day management activities.

The internal risk management models must be approved preventatively by the supervisory authorities. The procedure aims to make sure that they take account of both corporate needs and the minimum requirements laid down by the authority, representing a solution achieved by 'mutual consent', so to speak, resulting from a dialogue between the supervisors and the supervised. In this case the standard-making proposals also feature a supervisory approach based on a bilateral dialogue, founded on the gradual 'delegation' of supervision from the supervisory body to the supervised entity, and on the transition from an approach based on the 'supervision of activities' to one based on the 'supervision of controls'. In encouraging intermediaries to adopt the advanced approaches, due to the possibility of achieving benefits, in terms of the regulatory capital, the regulations promote improved responsibility and awareness, with respect to the actual corporate risk levels. Therefore, the Basel Committee highlights that the prudential control process acknowledges the bank management's responsibility in developing an internal risk assessment process, and in establishing asset objectives commensurate with the bank's risk profile and control structure. The type of control that is gaining ground at supranational level, therefore, fosters general self-regulation mechanisms, which does not mean self-determination of the rules, but the independent management of the rules established externally and inspired by the best practises within the industry.

To approve the internal control procedures proposed by the banks, it is not possible to build an automatic process, but it is necessary to put into place a set of competencies and benchmarks capable of ascertaining the supervisor's professional skills, independence and objectivity in the assessment of these models.

Aware of this need, the Basel 2 Accord (Basel Committee, 2004) has specified in a number of occasions that the supervisory authorities must employ the suitable resources and competencies suited to, (i) the assessment of the adequacy of the internal control systems adopted, and (ii) the approval of the internal methods for determining the asset requirements related to credit and operational risks.

This outlines a new role for the supervisory authority, that of a 'certifying body', with respect to the consistency of the practices and models adopted by the banks, on the one hand, and the principle of sound and prudent management – and, specifically, the independent risk assessment requirements – on the other hand.

The role of certifying body carries with it new operational duties and relationship models, between the supervisory authorities and the supervised entities, which imply an 'active' and 'driving' function by the former, in respect of regulatory compliance by the latter. This development corresponds to the growing need, by banks and financial intermediaries, of assistance in the implementation of the risk assessment and risk management processes.

The importance of the supervisory authorities' advisory role also emerges with regard to the control procedures put into place by the banks and, in particular, to the complex system of relations between the various internal and external auditing bodies. Regarding the operating mechanisms and information instruments on which the control functions are based, the Basel Committee assigns a guiding role to the supervisory authorities, which are called on to encourage the internal auditors – and, indeed, the structure as a whole – to adopt the necessary measures to ensure the effectiveness of the internal control system.

The capacity to perform advisory functions adequately entails the existence of: (1) consistent objectives by both the supervisory authorities and the supervised entities, which is one of the basic principles of the consensual regulatory approach, in order to overcome the traditional division between the parties; (2) consistent knowledge, which allows both parties to clearly understand the business activities; and (3) consistent cultural models, especially as regards the basic values and means of communication.

14.4 The organizational solutions for developing a common knowledge base, shared by banks and supervisory authorities

Financial intermediaries and supervisory authorities may develop a common knowledge base by implementing coordination procedures that are capable of encouraging the exchange of information and mutual interaction in problem analysis and solving (Mintzberg, 1985).

These tools, which must be suited to the specific organization of the banks, as well as to the specific coordination procedures, fall into four distinct categories:

- economic incentives;
- organizational structures;
- integration mechanisms;
- information and communication flows.

Similar considerations, taking account of the specificity of the problem and, therefore, the nature of the proposed tools, have been formulated with reference to the issue of coordination between the supervisory bodies and the banks' internal and external auditors (Schwizer, 2005).

14.4.1   Economic mechanisms: incentives for supervisory compliance

The parallel analysis of the Basel 2 proposals and the domestic regulations on internal control systems (Bank of Italy, 1998, 2002) highlights a significant interdependence between the two sets of regulations, whereby the latter is the necessary and indispensable premise of the former. What emerges, in fact, is a potential competitive edge for the banks that adopt a 'compliant' control system, thus finding that, in this manner, they already possess most of the organizational requirements needed for the approval of the internal methods for determining capital requirements for credit and operational risks. According to the current supervisory arrangements, banks are encouraged to adopt a suitable and functional internal control system enabling them both to comply with the regulations set forth by the Bank of Italy, and to achieve savings in terms of regulatory capital.

14.4.2   The organization of the internal control body: from functions to projects

The adoption of an internal control system obliges banks to address the need to adopt process-based organizational models, integrated with the basic functional or divisional structure, in order to identify the various risk-entailing micro-activities and the monitoring responsibilities.

This requires the overhauling of the organizational structures and roles, by means of the introduction of communication flows and information collection systems across the structure, consistently with the types of risks for each business area. The result is a 'quasi-matrix' structure, in which the business responsibilities (formulating strategies and defining operating plans, and the related decision sustainability assessments, with respect to both the risks taken on and the available control systems) interact with those managing the various types of risks.

Such an arrangement also affects the procedures for collecting and processing the risk-related information, and the consequent production of knowledge by the banks and other financial intermediaries. The functional activity-based logic is replaced gradually by a process- or problem-based approach.

In order to ensure the effective performance of its supervisory activities by the supervisory authorities, according to an advisory approach (capable of assuring a basic understanding of the problems of the supervised entities), besides a shared viewpoint of the problems, it is also expedient to establish a symmetry between the abovementioned organizational structures (organizational units and responsibilities) and the supervisory structures.

This means, on the one hand, enhancing the uniformity of the problems and risks related to the various business areas, rather than the similarity of organizational structures; and, on the other hand, scrapping the principle of function or activity-based supervision and moving towards a problem-based approach, which can be implemented by introducing 'working by projects', which can enable the supervisory authorities: (i) to extensively monitor each type of risks – across the supervised entities' structures and activities – developing the appropriate professional skills with respect to each issue, and (ii) to propose cutting-edge and innovatory proposals for solving new problems related to each business.

What ensues is a large-scale requirement of organizational flexibility within the supervisory authority, which can be met by introducing appropriate tools, not just of a technological nature – which, indeed, are necessary for collecting, transferring and processing the information, in support of the decision-making and supervisory processes – but also consisting of cross-company coordination bodies (as product, process and business area managers), associated with objective-based management systems and horizontal communications systems, aimed at promoting the sharing of information and goals and determining the accelerated creation of specialist skills.

These tools must be strengthened through the dissemination of cultural models inspired by the principles of cooperation and teamwork. There must also be an enhancement of the staff's entrepreneurial spirit and participation in the development of services with the aim of achieving maximum professional growth. This will underpin both the effectiveness of the control activities, and also the quality of the advisory services provided to its counterparts.

As W.J. McDonough, president of the Federal Bank of New York, stated some time ago, at the presentation of the new organizational structure of his control unit: 'we've organized ourselves better, in order to share with you (the supervised entities) our point of view and our competencies, with respect to the best practices used by all financial institutions' (McDonough, 2003).

14.4.3 Integration mechanisms: towards more efficient coordination

In order to enhance mutual adjustment, flexibility and systematicity of relations and, therefore, the efficiency of decision-making and problem-solving processes inside the supervisory system (which comprises the supervisory authorities, the supervised entities, the authorities supervising over connected industries, and the authorities of other countries), integration mechanisms (Mintzberg, 1985) can be put into place. These mechanisms may comprise: committees, task forces, integration managers (program or project managers).

The Basel Committee adopts this solution explicitly, within the framework of the 'Basel 2' (Basel Committee, 2004). With a view to supporting the implementation of the Accord, the Committee has set up two integration bodies, respectively called the AIG (Accord Implementation Group) and CTF (Capital Task Force). The former is a committee composed of the representatives of the regulatory bodies of the various Accord-member countries, and is a forum where they can exchange information on the practical problems encountered in the application of the new arrangement, and on the relevant problem-solving strategies. The latter is a working group of the Basel Committee, responsible for examining significant amendments to and interpretations of the New Accord. The Committee views these two bodies as key long-term tools, especially once the banks have started implementing the prescribed provisions. In particular, the CTF has the responsibility of analysing new banking products, and the implications that the developments in the risk management processes may have on the new arrangement, also after its entry into force.

14.4.4   Information exchange and communications systems: knowledge management and supervision

The indispensable tool for creating knowledge is the permanent and systematic exchange of information, at various levels:

- between bank management and the banking supervisors;
- between external auditors and the supervisors;
- between the supervisors, with respect to different financial sectors, and between the authorities of different countries.

With regard to the first bullet point above, it is necessary to point out that the implementation of the internal control systems – in accordance with the requirements laid down in the Supervisory Instructions at national level – has encouraged the intense exchange of information and documents (organizational regulations, strategic plans, audit plans, and so on), between the Bank of Italy and the banks.

The Basel Committee too has underlined, on a number of occasions, that the frequent exchange of information between the banks and the supervisors is fundamental for the effective implementation of the 'Basel 2' Accord. In this sense, Himino (2004) argues that 'Basel 2' framework provides a common language that improves communication among banks, supervisors and investors.

With regard to the second bullet point above, the specific provisions by the Basel Committee oblige the supervisors to cooperate and exchange information with the external and internal auditors, and to advise the banks on how the bodies can cooperate. This cooperation is particularly important with a view to ensuring the efficiency and functionality of the overall system of internal control.

The Committee points out that there is a complementary interest between the supervisors and the external auditors (Basel Committee, 2002), with special reference to the internal control system and information disclosure systems, which must justify a constant flow of information between the bodies, and cooperation in monitoring the risks taken on by the banks.

With regard to item three, the exchange of information between the supervisors of different countries concerns primarily the cross-supervision of complex international banking groups, but also supervisory activities of different financial sectors, for the purpose of monitoring the risks in the banking groups and multi-business financial risks.

The coordination process could also be functional for the improved allocation of resources and competencies for supervisory purposes: a more closer collaboration, in fact, would make it possible to support the supervisors in countries that lack the means to collect the necessary information for the effective implementation of the New Accord. With regard to this issue, principles have been developed aimed at encouraging closer practical cooperation and the exchange of information among the authorities (Basel Committee, 2003b).

Therefore, the strategic importance of learning is also asserted with regard to regulatory issues, which must be pursued through the integration of explicit and tacit knowledge, promoting the creation of 'communities of practice' (Gherardi, 1999) and 'communities of knowing' (Boland and Tenkasi, 1995), and enhancing the social dimension of knowledge. These perspectives are at the basis of the notion of the 'learning organization', which aims to encourage organizational learning and the creation of knowledge as key intangible assets and core competencies of a company.

In order to improve knowledge management within the system and, in particular, in the extended community that includes the supervisors, it is necessary to accept and, therefore, strengthen the role of information, communication and knowledge as management and control tools. This means, first of all, accumulating and making available – within the network of organizational relations – the knowledge on corporate experience, by means of an extensive use of information technology. Secondly, it is necessary to maximize consistency between the subject of the knowledge base and the manner of diffusion. The quality of knowledge management, in this case, can be recognized primarily in connection with the expected likelihood of the effective and efficient re-utilization of a certain 'packaged' knowledge, i.e. in the fact that – once the knowledge transfer process has been activated – it may prove successful, translating into effective and efficient management behaviour. Thirdly, it is necessary to enhance access to and the transfer of knowledge. Knowledge can be transferred only if the following conditions are ensured: there must be trust between the parties; the parties concerned must be able to meet; they must, preferably, share the same language, or have a mutually accessible language; all the parties concerned must be motivated to exchange the information. All these prerequisites may be more easily achieved if the system features a stable and strong culture (i.e. with a strong sense of identity), characterized by rules and systems of mutual relation, capable of consolidating the sense of belonging and sound principles of reciprocity.

14.5   The culture of banks and supervisory authorities: a measurement analysis model, within the framework of a 'culture compliance'

In the attempt to measure certain profiles of the current level of consistency of the knowledge base and cultural models, between supervisors and supervised entities, this chapter focuses on the cultural gap between the parties, which is investigated by means of a text-analysis approach.

Corporate culture is perceived as the set of values and decisions that represent the manner in which individuals can perform their activities within the organization, and defines which behaviours may be considered appropriate (Schein, 1985).

The study of corporate culture through language is a relatively new approach in economic literature. It is based on cultural anthropology – that is the methodologies for studying cultures based on the interpretation of their symbols and artifacts. The meaning ascribed to these aspects is subject to change, both in time, following evolutionary processes, and in respect of the cultural context taken into consideration. In this perspective, language may be considered a peculiar symbol and artifact of culture and, in consideration of the linguistic-textual differences when examining diverse cultural contexts, is a useful tool for understanding them.

In terms of the issues of concern in this chapter, the issue has been only partially tackled in the literature, and never with regard to financial institutions.

Geertz (1973) speaks of culture in 'semiotic' terms, when he maintains that his study 'is not an experimental science in search of laws, but an interpretational science in search of meanings'. In a nutshell, he asserts the possibility of analysing social phenomena and organizational processes and behaviours by considering them as the symbols and artifacts typical of a cultural system. Schein (1985) identifies language as an artifact of the corporate culture and claims that it is possible to analyse the different cultures through the vocabularies they are capable of expressing. Wuthnow (1989) claims that the linguistic categories and lexical expressions typical of a certain context allow the analysis of different corporate cultures, because their definition is closely related to the vocabulary developed within them. Lastly, DiMaggio (1997 and 2002) considers language the result of both social interaction and individual cognition. He maintains that, through the empirical analysis of written texts it is possible to determine the cultural aspects of language. This means that when the members of an organization use a term drawn from the vocabulary of their organization, what they're really doing is making reference to an individual cognitive representation transformed into organizational behaviours shared by and common to the organization to which they belong (Rosa and Porac, 2002). As regards the role of vocabularies (Berger and Luckmann, 1967), of linguistic categories, it is further specified that – although in certain contexts it is (theoretically) possible to develop cultural categories even without a language – vocabularies play a very important role in their development and sharing (Levinson, 2003).

All of this implies that the analysis of culture is closely connected to the analysis of the type of vocabulary used by the members of an organization, as reflected in all forms of internal communication – both oral and written – produced by that organization. The distinctive characteristics of every organization, therefore, are reflected in the documents it produces, and the language used may represent a key for their interpretation. In other words, if the organization leaves traces of its peculiar characteristics in the documents it produces, then it is possible to use text analysis to observe and 'measure' these traces and determine their cultural implications.

Based on this assumption, various surveys have been carried out in literature with the aim of gaining an understanding of a series of issues concerning corporate culture, including research on the leadership characteristics within organizations (D'Aveni and MacMillan, 1990), the determinants of corporate reputation (Fombrun and Shanley, 1990), the measurement of the intensity of orientation to 'corporate social responsibility' (Wolfe, 1991), and the classification of the types of organization based on the existence and intensity of certain cultural values (Kabanoff, Holt, 1996). These studies have two objectives in common:

- to provide representations of the content of the corpus of texts;
- to extract information, that is, several properties, from the corpus of texts through quantity-based measurements.

Compared to the previous studies, this chapter focuses on an evolutionary aspect of text analysis, concerning standardization in the treatment of data, combined with the use of standard vocabularies. This allows a greater comparability of the output of the various studies, enabling us to further refine the analysis methodology.

The analysis model includes the definition of several key concepts, at the base of the development of banking culture and that represent basic goals of the prudential regulation (Carretta, 2001). These must represent

Table 14.1 Key concepts for the culture of both intermediaries and supervisory bodies

Change
Customer
Disclosure
Innovation
Risk

key management aspects, with respect to the banks concerned, and the attention by the supervisors (Table 14.1). This ensures that the same concepts are treated with high intensity and frequency in the examined documents.

The model also includes categories that reflect Osgood's semantic differential findings regarding language (Osgood, Suci and Tannenbaum, 1957) and other categories drawn from the Harvard IV Psychosocial Dictionary (Zuell, Weber and Mohler, 1989) and the Lasswell Value Dictionary (Lasswell and Namenwirth, 1969), both used as a gauge for the abovementioned key concepts. The different intensity of these categories, expressed in terms of 'orientations', characterizes each concept and allows us to compare the corporate culture against the various benchmark contests. Here we present the results of four orientations (Carretta 2001; Carretta, Farina and Schwizer, 2005), among those surveyed, which are particularly significant for the parties in question (Table 14.2):

- *Semantic orientation*, which relates to the meaning of the key concepts. According to Osgood, Suci and Tannenbaum (1957), most of the judgements referring the meaning of a particular concept could be classified as one of three types: (i) an overall evaluation (positive–negative); (ii) an assessment of potency (strong–weak); and (iii) a commentary on the degree of activity (active–passive). However, these factors or dimensions structuring the meaning are not considered to be exhaustive: 'the representational state indexed by the semantic differential is not the only determinant operating in lexical encoding. It is a necessary but not a sufficient condition'.
- *Cognitive orientation*, relating to the decision-making process that depends to a significant degree upon the cognitive style of people. Generally, in fact, when formulating a decision referring to a certain problem it is necessary to analyse, to evaluate and to individuate the ways to solve it. In this sense, some cognitive attitudes, such as

Table 14.2   The main categories for measuring cultural orientations

---

Semantic orientation
Positive–Negative
Strong–Weak
Active–Passive

Cognitive orientation
Understanding
Evaluation
Problem solving

Disciplinary orientation
Academic
Business

Power orientation
Authority
Cooperation

---

understanding or information treatment, evaluation and problem-solving abilities, and different levels of these could characterize the process in the case of different phenomena taken in consideration.

- *Disciplinary orientation*, relating to the ways with which a certain phenomenon is described and comprises a (more theoretical) academic profile, and a business profile, which implies a more management-based approach.
- Power orientation, relating the ways in which an organization is oriented, in terms of the propensity to share and cooperate, or in terms of authority and of the importance of the hierarchy (Table 14.2).

14.6   Survey methodology and main results

The empirical assessment has been carried out as follows:

- definition of the sample of banks to be analysed;
- selection of the corpus to be analysed, for the institutions under investigation (that is, the Basel Committee, the Bank of Italy and Italian banks);
- analysis of the 'concordances', in respect of the key concepts for the culture of above mentioned institutions (this analysis allows the extrapolation of all the words contained in a text, listing them in alphabetical order accompanied by a context that makes it possible

to grasp their meaning, and by a series of indications allowing the retrieval and location of a passage within the structure of a text);

- analysis of the context 'occurrences', in respect of the key concepts of the culture of Basel Committee, Bank of Italy and Italian banks (this analysis allows the obtaining of lists of words making up a text, accompanied by the number of times in which they occur, besides the percentage compared to the total number of words);
- comparison of the context occurrences and the language categories extracted from the Harvard IV Psycho-Social Dictionary and the Lasswell Value Dictionary;
- determination of the predominant cultural orientation and of the relevant intensity.

The survey was carried out on a uniform and representative sample (86.3 per cent, based on total assets) of the top 15 banking groups in Italy.

Consistent with the other text analysis applications, the selection of the corpuses concerned public documents (Bowman, 1984; D'Aveni, MacMillan, 1990; Kabanoff, Waldersee, Cohen, 1995), such as financial reports, presentations and speeches by the top management of each institution. The study of the cultural differences was conducted for two years (1999 and 2004), according to a dynamic view of culture (Herskovits, 1955). For the text analysis proper, we used the Wordsmith 4 software developed by Oxford University (Scott, 1999).

The analysis of concordance was carried out for each of the key concepts, so that the cultural analysis can be referred only to the terms that are actually associated with the key concepts.

The final stage of the analysis concerned the comparison of the context occurrences of the key concepts and the vocabulary terms. The following formula was used to measure the intensity of the cultural orientation (Carretta, Farina and Schwizer, 2005):

$$\text{Cultural Intensity Index} = \frac{(Cx - Cy)}{(Cx + Cy)}$$

We assume that:
If the Cultural Intensity Index > 0: the cultural orientation tends to the category X;
If the Cultural Intensity Index < 0: the cultural orientation tends to the category Y;
If the Cultural Intensity Index $= 0$ and Cx or Cy are different from 0: the cultural orientation is neutral.

The formula allows us to obtain an index value standardized for all categories and comprised between $+1$ and -1. In fact, an index values of $+1$ or -1 means that the text is entirely culturally oriented, as regards the analysed category.

With regard to the survey results, the methodology highlights proof of the differentiation between the culture of the Basel Committee, the culture of the Bank of Italy and that of Italian banks, but it also emphasizes some significant examples of reduction of the cultural gap over the period of the survey. The values of the surveyed items are given in Table 14.3.

Regarding semantic orientation, the gap concerning the meaning of the key concepts is not relevant for the parties (Italian banks, the Bank of Italy and the Basel Committee). However, in the period under consideration, it is possible to observe a gradual reduction of the gap between Italian banks and, respectively, the Bank of Italy and the Basel Committee.

In the first case (Italian banks and the Bank of Italy), gap reduction is particularly significative for the concepts of 'change' and 'disclosure' (Figure 14.1).

In the second case (Italian banks and the Basel Committee), gap reduction is relevant for all key concepts considered in the analysis and it is particularly significative for the concept of 'customer' (Figure 14.2).

Regarding the cognitive orientation (Figure 14.3), the significance of the various components (understanding, evaluation and problem solving) that guide the decision-making processes is constant over the survey period. The samples differ, albeit slightly, in the evaluation component, which appears larger for banks, and the component relating to understanding of the phenomena, which decisively characterizes the orientation of supervisors.

Regarding disciplinary orientation (Figure 14.4), the business approach prevails in Basel Committee and in banks, while in the case of Bank of Italy the textual analysis indicates a greater theoretical severity in representing the phenomena, typical of an academic approach.

Regarding power orientation (Figure 14.5), the cooperative approach prevails in Bank of Italy and in Italian banks, while in the case of Basel Committee the the textual analysis indicates an authoritative approach.

Moving on to examine each one of the key concepts for the banking business for the three samples, a distinction can be made between the situations explainable in terms of role-related necessity, and situations in which the reasons for the gap are less straightforward.

Table 14.3 Final results on disclosure, customer, innovation, change, risk measured on banks, on Basel II and on the Bank of Italy

Key concept	Year	Institution	(A)	(B)	(C)	(D)	(E)	(F)	(G)	(H)
Change	1999	BANKS	1.00	1.00	0.31	0.40	0.20	0.40	−1.00	−1.00
Customer	1999	BANKS	0.48	0.62	0.52	0.44	0.25	0.31	−0.25	−0.50
Disclosure	1999	BANKS	1.00	0.67	0.60	0.00	0.50	0.50	−0.50	0.00
Innovation	1999	BANKS	0.74	0.93	0.61	0.00	0.00	1.00	−1.00	−1.00
Risk	1999	BANKS	0.71	0.81	0.70	0.39	0.25	0.36	−0.04	0.00
Average score	1999	BANKS	0.79	0.81	0.55	0.25	0.24	0.51	−0.56	−0.50
Change	2004	BANKS	0.60	0.87	0.41	0.29	0.43	0.29	−0.11	−1.00
Customer	2004	BANKS	0.66	0.58	0.35	0.43	0.25	0.32	−0.24	−0.45
Disclosure	2004	BANKS	0.86	0.86	0.67	0.00	1.00	0.00	−0.14	−1.00
Innovation	2004	BANKS	0.68	0.86	0.65	0.50	0.50	0.00	−0.09	−1.00
Risk	2004	BANKS	0.65	0.74	0.55	0.36	0.28	0.36	−0.26	0.00
Average score	2004	BANKS	0.69	0.78	0.52	0.32	0.49	0.19	−0.17	−0.69
Change	1999	Basel Committee	0.67	0.63	0.40	0.50	0.50	0.00	1.00	0.00
Customer	1999	Basel Committee	1.00	0.78	0.00	0.67	0.00	0.33	0.00	0.00
Disclosure	1999	Basel Committee	0.81	0.79	0.40	0.60	0.20	0.20	−1.00	0.00
Innovation	1999	Basel Committee	0.33	0.67	0.69	0.00	0.00	1.00	0.00	1.00
Risk	1999	Basel Committee	0.90	0.96	0.42	0.38	0.33	0.29	0.00	0.33
Average score	1999	Basel Committee	0.74	0.76	0.38	0.43	0.21	0.36	0.00	0.27
Change	2004	Basel Committee	0.54	0.60	0.59	1.00	0.00	0.00	0.00	0.00
Customer	2004	Basel Committee	0.43	0.87	0.67	0.29	0.29	0.43	−0.71	1.00
Disclosure	2004	Basel Committee	0.63	0.85	0.71	0.50	0.25	0.25	−1.00	1.00
Innovation	2004	Basel Committee	1.00	1.00	0.50	0.00	0.00	0.00	0.00	0.00
Risk	2004	Basel Committee	0.65	0.55	0.41	0.32	0.32	0.36	0.11	0.20
Average score	2004	Basel Committee	0.65	0.77	0.57	0.42	0.17	0.21	−0.32	0.44
Change	1999	Bank of Italy	0.54	0.89	0.77	0.60	0.20	0.20	−0.20	−1.00
Customer	1999	Bank of Italy	0.66	0.84	0.53	0.43	0.14	0.43	−0.25	0.00
Disclosure	1999	Bank of Italy	0.43	0.94	0.63	0.20	0.40	0.40	1.00	1.00
Innovation	1999	Bank of Italy	0.89	1.00	0.68	0.67	0.00	0.33	1.00	1.00
Risk	1999	Bank of Italy	0.61	0.84	0.57	0.47	0.20	0.33	0.09	−0.50
Average score	1999	Bank of Italy	0.63	0.90	0.63	0.47	0.19	0.34	0.33	0.10
Change	2004	Bank of Italy	0.71	1.00	0.69	1.00	0.00	0.00	0.00	0.00
Customer	2004	Bank of Italy	0.33	0.75	0.58	0.43	0.00	0.57	0.00	−0.33

(Continued)

Table 14.3   (Continued)

Key concept	Year	Institution	(A)	(B)	(C)	(D)	(E)	(F)	(G)	(H)
Disclosure	2004	Bank of Italy	0.60	0.87	0.76	0.43	0.14	0.43	0.50	0.50
Innovation	2004	Bank of Italy	0.68	0.85	0.74	0.57	0.14	0.29	0.33	0.00
Risk	2004	Bank of Italy	0.51	0.81	0.46	0.44	0.20	0.36	0.00	−0.60
Average score	2004	Bank of Italy	0.57	0.86	0.65	0.57	0.10	0.33	0.17	−0.09

(A) Semantic orientation – Positive (X) vs. Negative (Y)
(B) Semantic orientation – Strong (X) vs. Weak (Y)
(C) Semantic orientation – Active (X) vs. Passive (Y)
(D) Cognitive orientation – Underst
(E) Cognitive orientation – Eval
(F) Cognitive orientation – Solve
(G) Disciplinary orientation – Academic (X) vs. Business (Y)
(H) Power orientation – Authority (X) vs. Cooperation (Y)

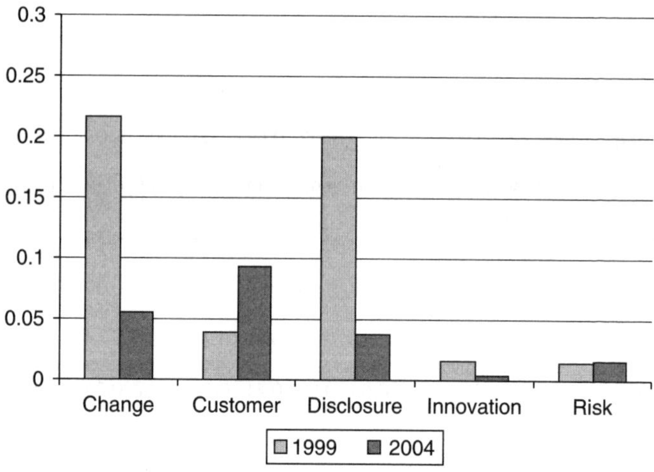

Figure 14.1   Semantic orientation gap: Italian banks – Bank of Italy

The first category includes the concepts of change, customer and innovation. In this case, differences between the Basel Committee, the Bank
of Italy and Italian banks may be explained by the different roles played.
On the one hand, the Basel Committee and the Bank of Italy have played
a decisive role in promoting innovation within the system and encouraging the adoption of new types of businesses, new management models
and new systems of objectives. On the other hand, financial intermediaries can be considered to be the effective player of these change and
innovatory processes.

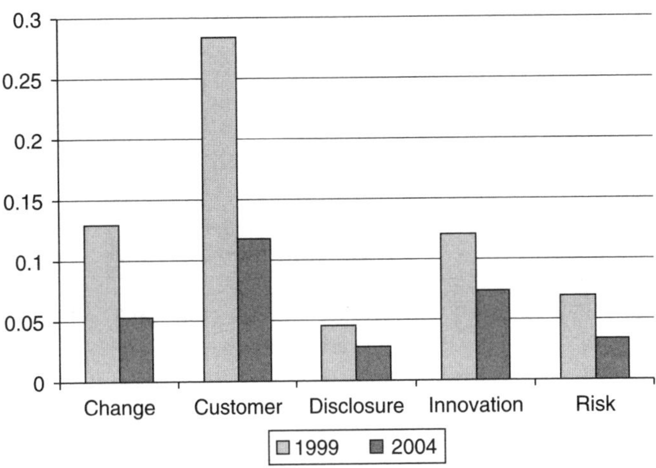

Figure 14.2 Semantic orientation gap: Italian banks – Basel Committee

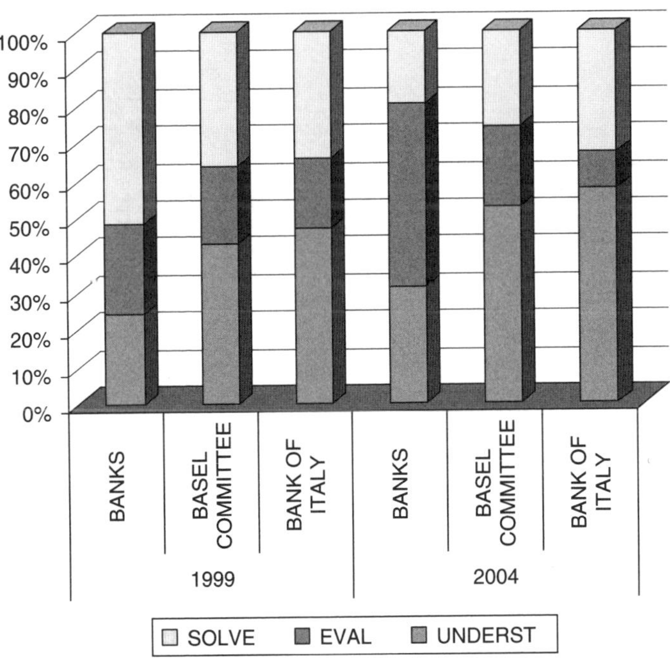

Figure 14.3 Cognitive orientation

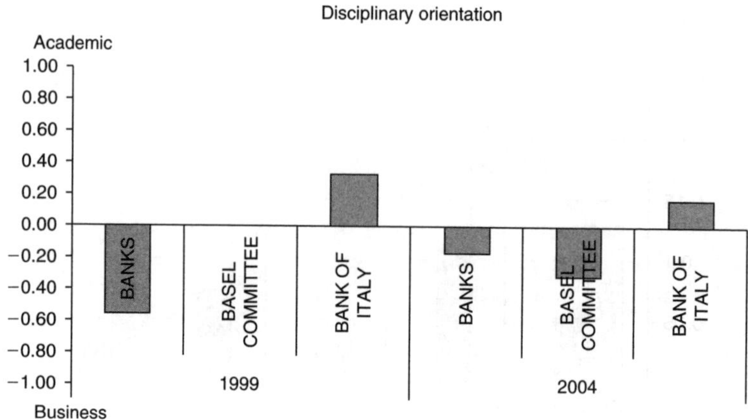

Figure 14.4   Disciplinary orientation

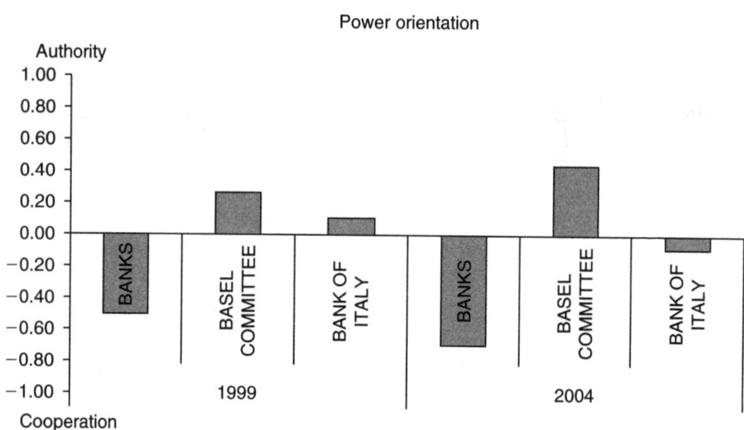

Figure 14.5   Power orientation

Cultural gaps are less easy to explain concerning the concepts of risk and disclosure. In this case, significant differences highlight a problem of divergent judgements and also determines the need to reduce the surveyed gap. Effectively, with regard to risk, gap features a constant and gradual downward trend but differences are still substantial, although there is a growing attention, in connection with the major financial scandals, with regard to disclosure.

14.7　Conclusions

Bank regulation models and supervisory approaches have changed significantlyin recent decades. The new relationship models between the supervisory authorities and the banks must be supported by organizational tools capable of fostering the sharing of information and promoting the advisory function of the supervisors. The new role of the supervisory bodies requires a significant degree of consistency between the knowledge bases and cultural models with the supervised entities.

This chapter represents a first attempt made to measure the cultural gap between the three groups of stakeholders, through a text analysis model. This approach does not exhaust the perspective of cultural analysis, but it does open up a broad field of survey and suggests further investigation, also by means of ethnographical tools. In the terms of the chapter, the issue has been only partially explored in literature and never with respect to financial institutions.

The contribution of this chapter concerns three aspects – two relating to content and one to method. First, what we observe is an overall convergence of meanings (in terms of semantic orientation) concerning all key concepts in the surveyed period.

However, the results expressed by other categories highlight several significant cultural gaps, relating to important issues for the development of the system and the activities of banks, such as risk, disclosure, change and innovation. The different focus on these concepts in the examined texts highlight the opportunities for identifying new opportunities of comparison between the parties and promoting the exchange of information and knowledge, as the basis for the improved sharing of objectives and guidelines.

Secondly, there has been a gradual convergence of certain orientations and this means a virtuous trend towards a common cultural development. This trend can be fostered by banks through the full implementation of the internal control systems.

Thirdly, from a methodological point of view, the significance of the cultural analysis in the reference industry can be highlighted. Therefore, it is expedient to develop this line of study, which can be done by applying the model in question to increasingly 'internal' corpuses of texts and firm-specific documents, such as circular letters and internal service orders, organizational regulations and other materials reflecting the day-to-day performance of the corporate activities, for the purpose of bringing closer the survey method to the characteristics typical of ethnographical studies of culture.

Note

1. This chapter is the result of a close cooperation between the authors. However, Alessandro Carretta and Paola Schwizer have contributed to sections 14.1 and 14.6 and the other sections can be attributed to Vincenzo Farina.

References

Airoldi, G. (2002) 'Le responsabilità delle imprese e i sistemi di controllo interno ed esterno', Lettera ISVI, 2.

Bank of Italy (1998) 'Sistema dei controlli interni, compiti del Collegio Sindacale', *Istruzioni di Vigilanza per le Banche*, October.

Bank of Italy (2002) *'Istruzioni di Vigilanza per gli Intermediari Finanziari iscritti nell' Elenco Speciale*, October.

Barth, G.R., G. Caprio Jr. and R. Levine (1999) *Financial Regulation and Performance*, World Bank Policy Research Working Paper, Washington DC: World Bank.

Barth, G.R., G. Caprio Jr. and R. Levine (2001) *The Regulation and Supervision of Banks Around the World*, World Bank Policy Research Working Paper, Washington DC: World Bank.

Basel Committee on Banking Supervision (1998) *Framework for Internal Control Systems in Banking Organisations*, Basel, September.

Basel Committee on Banking Supervision (2002) *The Relationship between Banking Supervisors and Banks' External Auditors*, Basel, January.

Basel Committee on Banking Supervision (2003a) *High-level Principles for the Cross-border Implementation of the New Accord*, Basel, August.

Basel Committee on Banking Supervision (2003b) *Consolidated KYC Risk Management*, Basel, August.

Basel Committee on Banking Supervision (2004) *Basel II: International Convergence of Capital Measurement and Capital Standards: a Revised Framework*, Basel, June.

Berger, P.L. and T. Luckmann (1967) *The Social Construction of Reality: a Treatise in the Sociology of Knowledge*, New York: Anchor Books.

Boland, R. and R. Tenkasi (1995) 'Perspective Making and Perspective Taking in Communities of Knowing', *Organization Science*, 6: 350–72.

Bowman, E.H. (1984) 'Content Analysis of Annual Reports for Corporate Strategy and Risk', *Interfaces*, 14: 61–71.

Carretta, A. (1998) *Banche e intermediari non bancari: concorrenza e regolamentazione*, Rome: Bancaria Editrice.

Carretta, A. (2001) *Il governo del cambiamento culturale in banca. Modelli di analisi, strumenti operativi, valori individuali*, Rome: Bancaria Editrice.

Carretta, A., V. Farina and P. Schwizer (2005) *Banking Regulation Towards Advisory: the 'Culture Compliance' of Banks and Supervisory Authorities*, paper presented at the 5rd Annual Conference of European Academy of Management, Munich.

Carretta, A., P. Schwizer and V. Stefanelli (2003) 'Oltre la regolamentazione: il sistema dei controlli interni degli intermediari finanziari. Cultura del controllo o controllo della cultura?', in AA.VV., *Ottavo rapporto della fondazione Rosselli*, Milan: Edibank.

D'Aveni, R. and I.C. MacMillan (1990) 'Crisis and the Content of Managerial Communication: a Study at the Focus of Attention of Top Managers in Surviving and Failing Firms', *Administrative Science Quarterly*, 35: 634–57.

De Maio, A. and C. Catalano (1995) *Modelli organizzativi e di controllo nel sistema bancario*, Milan: Edibank.

DiMaggio, P. (1997) 'Culture and Cognition', *Annual Review of Sociology*, 23: 263–88.

DiMaggio, P. (2002) 'Why Cognitive (and Cultural) Sociology Needs Cognitive Psychology', in K.A. Cerulo (ed.), *Culture in Mind: Toward a Sociology of Culture and Cognition*, NewYork: Routledge.

Elliehausen, G. (1998) *The Cost of Banking Regulation: a Review of Evidence*, Federal Reserve Bulletin, April: 171–206.

Fombrun, C. and M. Shanley (1990) 'What's in a Name? Reputation Building and Corporate Strategy', *Academy of Management Journal*, 33: 233–58.

Geertz, C. (1973) *The Interpretation of Cultures*, New York: Basic Books.

Gherardi, S. (1999) 'Learning as Problem-driven or Learning in the Face of Mystery?', *Organization Studies*, 20: 101–24.

Gualandri, E. (2001) 'Il ruolo della banca centrale e degli altri organismi di controllo: amministratori del sistema e attori nel cambiamento culturale delle banche', in A. Carretta, *Il governo del cambiamento culturale in banca*, Rome: Bancaria Editrice.

Herskovits, M.J. (1955) *Cultural Anthropology*, New York: Knopf.

Himino, R. (2004) 'Basel II – Towards a New Common Language', *BIS Quarterly Review*, September: 41–9.

Kabanoff, B. and J. Holt (1996) 'Changes in the Espoused Values of Australian Organizations 1986–1990', *Journal of Organizational Behavior*, 17: 201–19.

Kabanoff, B., R. Waldersee and M. Cohen (1995) 'Espoused Values and Organizational Change Themes', *Academy of Management Journal*, 38: 1075–104.

Lasswell, H.D. and J.Z. Namenwirth (1969) *The Lasswell Value Dictionary*, New Haven: Yale University Press.

Levinson, S. (2003) 'Language and Mind: Let's Get the Issues Straight!', in G. Dedre and S. Goldin-Meadow (eds), *Language in Mind*, Cambridge, MA: MIT Press.

McDonough, W. (2003) 'Risk Management, Supervision and the New Basel Accord', *BIS Review*, 5: 1–5.

Mintzberg, H. (1985) *La progettazione dell'organizzazione aziendale*, Bologna: Il Mulino.

Osgood, C., G. Suci and P. Tannenbaum (1957) *The Measurement of Meaning*, Chicago: University of Illinois Press.

Pisanti, C. (2002) *I controlli interni degli intermediari finanziari dell'art. 107: stato dell'arte e prospettive regolamentari*, paper presented at the conference 'I controlli interni degli intermediari finanziari specializzati – attualità e prospettive', Milan, January.

Rosa, J.A. and J.F. Porac (2002) 'Categorization Bases and Their Influence on Product Category Knowledge Structures', *Psychology & Marketing*, 19: 503–32.

Schein, E.H. (1985) *Organizational Culture and Leadership*, San Francisco: Jossey-Bass.

Schwizer, P. (2005) 'I rapporti fra collegio sindacale e internal auditing nella banche', in M. Baravelli and A. Vigano (eds), *Il collegio sindacale nelle banche*, Rome: Bancaria Editrice.

Scott, M. (1999) *WordSmith Tools*, Oxford: Oxford University Press.

Wolfe, R.A. (1991) 'The Use of Content Analysis to Assess Corporate Social Responsibility', in J. Post (ed.), *Research in Corporate Social Performance and Policy*, Greenwich: JAI Press.

Wuthnow, R. (1989) *Communities of Discourse*, Cambridge, MA: Harvard University Press.

Zull, C., R. Weber and P. Mohler (1989) *Computer Aided Text Classification for the Social Sciences: The General Enquirer III*, Mannheim: Zentrum für Methoden und Analysen.

Names Index

Subject Index